SHAKESPEARE
The Theatrical Dimension

AMS Studies in the Renaissance: No. 3

Other Titles in This Series:

SHAKESPEARE
The Theatrical Dimension

edited by

Philip C. McGuire

and

David A. Samuelson

AMS Press, Inc.

FIRST AMS PRESS EDITION: 1979

Library of Congress Cataloging in Publication Data
Main entry under title:

Shakespeare, the theatrical dimension.

(AMS studies in the Renaissance; 3)
1. Shakespeare, William 1564-1616—Dramatic-
production—Addresses, essays, lectures. I. McGuire,
Philip C., 1940-   II. Samuelson, David A.
III. Series.
PR3091.S37   822.3'3   77-78320
ISBN   0-404-16002-6

Table of Contents

Preface

I

The reason this anthology begins with both an introduction and a preface has to do with the logistics of the mind. This book slowly developed in letters and long distance telephone talks between East Lansing, Michigan, and Rochester, New York; and no matter how Philip McGuire and I tried in the wrapping-up stages to draw our minds together to the important task of providing a coherent introduction, we simply could not drive our thoughts along quite the same track. Parallel, mutually supportive, within waving distance, yes, but still two minds, two voices, two slightly different objectives. So we gave up on the common introduction, and decided to make a virtue of this vice of thinking along different tracks. Sensibly, we divided the chore: Philip would do the formal introduction, aimed largely at the serious student of Shakespeare who might invest in this book to develop his private library; I would get the easier chore, the more casual preface, which I decided to aim at the general browser, that rare creature who would flip through a preface before deciding whether to risk his funds.

The reason for prefacing this preface with remarks on its genesis is that these practical arrangements unfolded for me what has been the theme of this whole enterprise. This theme is the meeting of minds over long distance.

Let me set up the theme with the literal story of the book's genesis. Philip and I were reading papers at a meeting of the 1975 North Central Conference of the Renaissance Society of America at the University of Buffalo. The topic of our session was "Shakespeare and Performance." We met, heard each other's papers, and afterwards, over drinks, admitted how nice it was we had met. We suddenly felt less alone, less strange than we felt when going about our normal academic business at Michigan State and the University of Rochester. We met of course on an idea, the idea that Shakespeare built his wondrous creations as plays and poems, simultaneous and one. Professors are always meeting other professors on ideas. In fact, that is what professional conferences are for: so the solitary work of thinking up answers to timeless and hitherto unsolved puzzles can have a cheery boost forward in such person to person meetings. When it happens, as it should, it always feels serendipitous.

Actually, such was our enthusiasm, that after a few drinks we felt in a mood to topple temples, ready for a good crusade in criticism. "Why don't we have a body of criticism that is based on the premise that Shakespeare built whole things, not poems for English classes and plays for theater students?" At one of these enthusiastic heights, this book was born: Waldo McNeir leaned forward and said something like, "You guys should get together and collect some of the work that is there." And he was serious, which took us aback and jolted our arrogance. It is one thing to topple temples in one's martini giddiness. It is quite another thing to think about building your own edifice. But, think we did, in a long and frustrating exchange of letters and manuscripts.

The edifice created by this long distance collaboration is for you to appraise, enjoy, ignore—what you will. For us it represents a discovered community of interests.

There is nothing incestuous about this community; it was genuinely discovered, by necessity as it turned out, since from our heady toast to the "crusade," our experience has been that of learning how much fine work was out in the world, waiting to be gathered.

Yet, we also learned of a peculiar discrepancy between the status of performance criticism and the prevailing notions about its place. The place, by and large, was in the past; it had all been done, usually way back, by the illustrious and the unknown alike. Nothing new here! The peculiar thing about this notion was the little evidence supporting it. Yes, even before Granville-Barker, people had been speaking about performance and using stage realities to unfold the literary complexities of Shakespeare's plays. But there was, in fact, a great dearth of publications based on the first principle of performance. Moreover, the work we could find did not seem quite the same: stage history, readings with illustrative stage interpretations, and iconographical studies. The difference is that the studies like those in this collection seem to be moving toward a fundamentally new concept about performance, namely, that it was a part of the bedrock of Shakespeare's creations.

II.

What does this mean—performance as the "bedrock"? Basically, I think it means that it is next to useless to speak about Shakespeare's poetry without grounding our remarks in some kind of possible enactment, presentational or representational, historical or imagined, but an enactment, with human voices shaping the metaphors, articulating the images, sounding the cadences.

To push this idea somewhat, I have distilled the ideas one can infer from this collection of essays and arranged them under topic headings below. I hope you will find these ideas sensible and sane, and yet just a little unsettling.

Shakespeare's Creative Moments

There is little in literature or life to suggest that Shakespeare composed mere "poems on paper" that somehow managed "to work," almost by surprise, on stage. So we assume that as he wrote, Shakespeare heard voices, saw flashes of movement, imagined and felt the stage rhythms. We assume, in short, that Shakespeare created the whole blessed thing—poem and play—as his mind moved his pen across paper.

Shakespeare's Realizations

The average performance in his day probably did as much justice to Shakespeare's imaginings as the average performance does today. Some were doubtless dreadful, some superb. Most of them sufficed. True, the Elizabethan performance had the advantage of an audience whose actors could voice the lines to their full range of effects, and to an audience whose ears were not numbed by the amnesia induced by print-dependence and whose minds were not so saturated by visual images that they needed books on visual literacy to freshen up their perspectives a little. True, too, that today's performance has a considerable edge in terms of elaborate and professional preparation for a performance. Today's productions are better planned and executed with more detailed finesse.

But, on balance, the historical advantages balance each other out. Then and now, the crucial question is quality, the quality of individual performances. The point is that today's performers (and critics) have a decent shot at coming close to Shakespeare's ultimate performance. Certainly, his ultimate performance was but a glimmer in the brain, an incomplete dream. And it would be quite mad to presume that a performance or interpretation could realize Shakespeare's dreaming. Nonetheless, the rueful truth is that there is no other worthwhile goal than to try to come as close as one can. It is virtually an obligation.

The Critical Stance

Since omniscience is impossible (as every teacher duly respectful of Shakespeare's genius knows well from his pre-class panic), why should we mount a platform to try to speak everything, for all time? Better to dive into the play, give in to its depths, feel the currents moving us forward, and try our best to record intelligently this experience.

"Stance" is a misleading term for this experience, and the swimmer analogy is also a bit misleading—too physical a comparison. The principle is immersion, an alert and active experience in the play's motions. We ought to dive in more frequently, if only because the view from the platform is also misleading. From the height of our insecure stance of omniscience, the play is all surface—placid, quiet little ripples, still. And, even though we at times forget the power of the play, we always know better.

The Critical Act

Once we accept the risk of immersion, we become responsible to make our experience coherent. Impressionistic fragments will not do. Nor will an analytic cataloging—riskless dissecting of each moment, piece by piece, tossing each into a labeled jar on a shelf crowded with sundry parts of the play. Our experience should have been much too alive for the spirit of an autopsy. Instead, the critical act should be creative—putting the experience into a whole that others can recognize as something a little bit alive. In sum, the critical act should be lively re-creation.

The Critical Importance of Time

Usually, we tend to read Shakespeare's plays backwards. Beginning with a rather full knowledge from fifth act eventualities, we read all forward motion in terms of how well it marches us to our snug Act Five certainties. This backwardness is not a little perverse, for it distorts the actual experience offered by the play. Consider, for example, "foreshadowing," one of our few "time devices" and a poor one at that; few of us mention it without embarrassment. We feel we have to say a word or two about it, because we were told somewhere in our education that foreshadowing was somehow important. So, for a pattern of linked images, each anticipating a later image or event, we point to the pattern as sign of what? Artistic integrity? Aesthetic inevitability? B "foreshadows" G, and G points to L and W. There! But the way we experience the play is the reverse. W is meaningful because we recall, the way the characters sometimes do, L, then G, all the way back to B. Cordelia's silence in the fifth act, for example, is haunted by our memories of her first act reticence. The process is not the reverse. In effect, we experience the play forward, and "foreshadowing" actually works upon us as "past shadowing," the way waking dreams capture our torments from the week past or the day before more often than they spell our luncheon fortunes five hours later.

Hence, to see what is happening, we should do a better job reading the play forward, the way it was written. It is a riskier direction, yet it forces us to participate in a way we can't if we perch on a notion that the play is done before we begin.

The Critical Importance of Pleasure

The essays in this collection generally read as if their authors enjoyed the writing. Perhaps they did; in writing about performance, our authors worked closely with the play's true objective—to please. This objective is widely ignored in the run of typical Shakespearean criticism, perhaps because of the inadvertent but common confusion of serious thinking with solemn writing. The unfortunate thing about solemnity, in thinking or writing, is that it tends to dull critical perceptiveness. Though it is true that perception always enhances pleasure, pleasure in turn is often the medium of perception. The key is receptivity; we can only see and learn what we are prepared to receive. The solemn state of mind tends to make us remarkably unreceptive. But if we look for our pleasures in the play, which is easiest to do with the performance model, we tend to enter into the play and allow it to enter us. Zen Shakespearean criticism? No, just some critical common sense.

III

One is not supposed to boast in blurbs about the essays in one's collection. But in individual commentary, description tends to slide into appreciation. Moreover, what is boast now was appreciation when each essay was read, enjoyed, admired, and entered into the "accepted" folder that became this book. The editorial test remains delight and instruction. I learned something from each essay and enjoyed them all.

These brief descriptions are meant as a guide for browsers.

"Re-presenting Shakespeare" (Edward Partridge)

Though primarily concerned with responsibilities in teaching Shakespeare, Professor Partridge's essay also offers a sophisticated guide for thinking out the ideal performance for responsible directors.

"Performing the Poem" (David Samuelson)

I enjoyed two things in writing this piece: trying to tighten the conjunction between "stage" and "page," and seeing the play through the eyes of a "literate" director.

"In Search of the Performance Present" (Barbara Hodgdon)

This essay makes wonderful use of the insights of semiotics: it applies the insights to the felt shape of a dramatic moment; it invites us to see "signals" in the seams of the forward motion; and all the while the discussion remains eminently engaging and understandable.

"Poetry of the Theater" (Marvin Rosenberg)

You will not read a more beautifully intelligent evocation of *King Lear's* scenic poetry; the treatment of the "seeing" pattern offers a particularly good instance of the inseparability of verbal and acting images.

"Choreography and Language in *Richard II*" (Philip McGuire)

Philip's analysis of the stage movement is an irrefutable demonstration of visual patterning and, incidentally, illustrates well the dramatic edge in the play's elegant pageantry.

"*Richard II* at Stratford: Role Playing as Metaphor" (Miriam Gilbert)

So sane, shrewd, and evocative is Professor Gilbert's essay, it invites one to imagine a new (and much needed) kind of formal criticism—"production criticism." The McGuire–Gilbert readings complement each other well.

"Speculations on Doubling in Shakespeare's Plays" (Stephen Booth)

Unlike most discussions of doubling, which subtract something from the dimensionality of the play, Professor Booth's "speculations" add theatrical meanings literary critics will savor.

"Changeable Taffeta: Shakespeare's Characters in Performance" (J.L. Styan)

In this witty dissection of the excesses of "character criticism," Professor Styan places something very real between the extremes of poor player and novelistic personage—he gives us satisfyingly solid and moving presences who haunt our brain with their theatrical motion.

"Shakespeare's Visual Stagecraft: the Seduction of Cressida" (Douglas Sprigg)

Professor Sprigg's articulation of the patterning of dramatic sight lines gives the novice "performance critic" an excellent lesson in point of view in an ensemble stage picture.

"*Henry IV:* 'A World of Figures Here'" (James Black)

I love the gusto of this commentary. By some trick (acute perceptiveness, no doubt), Professor Black portrays "the body" of lan-

guage as it materializes into palpable stage doings. Visions become figures, and the thesis of this collection is effectively
documented.

"Some Dramatic Techniques in *King Lear*" (William Matchett)

This essay is the perfect argument for the critical powers of calculated innocence; it gave me a pleasurable and new experience—
reading the play forward, with risk.

"Directions for *Twelfth Night*" (John Russell Brown)

It is impressive how Professor Brown arrays a staggering set of
sane production possibilities, yet calms the panic from this prolif-
eration by insisting on the measure of the "authentic."

"Past the Size of Dreaming" (Bernard Beckerman)

Through a judicious analysis of "theatrical" evidence (how the
play is designed to work), Professor Beckerman may force us to
reverse a favorite article of "literary" belief—that *Antony and
Cleopatra* is concerned with the epic scale.

"Hamlet and Our Problems" (Michael Goldman)

Seemingly without effort, Professor Goldman manages to meld
presentational theater facts (the physical presence of an actor, for
example) with the energy and questioning of the representational
story of *Hamlet*.

IV

Perhaps the most practical use I can think of for *Shakespeare:
The Theatrical Dimension* concerns another kind of mental logistics. Again, I rely upon my experience as having some kinship to
your experiences, for I need to illustrate with a story about my
mind, and what happened to it in stumbling upon the theatrical
approach to reading Shakespeare. It is the infirmities of my mind
in this exemplary tale that matter. Discovering the works of
Brown, Beckerman, and Styan was good for my most particular
infirmity—the Hamlet syndrome, excessive analysis that left my
head in fragments and was helpless before every paradox and
inconsistency. This infirmity was not just intellectual democ-
racy, the openness to all points of view; it was an excessive love
for analysis, of any point, no matter how alien from my deepest
convictions or best perceptions. My "readings," consequently,
were typically centrifugal.

But thinking about the play as alive in Shakespeare's head the way it is on stage forced me to ask more impolite questions of my favorite view of a passage: Can this be played? Can I see this point in a performance? When I said things about Act Five, was I sure it followed from my views of Three and Four? Was I working toward the whole play? Could my readings come together on any imagined stage? If not, and with all due allowance for extremely sophisticated performances, then no, I could not keep this point. Thus, through thinking about performance, I was freed from unending analysis and given a chance at patching together a reading, which, if not beautiful, at least had its life, was coherent, and probably was playable. I now had a model to hang my ideas on and to test them. And, it was much more fun. I even began to develop a theory that in the very center of any scene, its most fun, its sharpest sorrow, resided precisely the meaning Shakespeare was after, and that we could state this meaning as intellectually as we liked, for it was not that Shakespeare liked "*dramatic* meanings" as much as he found the meanings worth his attention eminently and powerfully dramatic. But this is the subject of the next book. The point is, if your infirmities resemble my pre-theatrical analytic illness, you just might find out that the theatrical approach can organize your mental logistics, as it did mine.

DAVID SAMUELSON

Introduction

The fourteen essays gathered in this anthology (nine of them previously unpublished) are rooted in the principle that criticism of Shakespeare's drama must arise from and remain in touch with what happens both on the stage and within us as we experience his plays in the theater. This is not, then, an anthology of literary criticism in the customary sense of that term—not an effort to clarify or evaluate a printed text or to illuminate the engagement of reader with text. The overwhelming bulk of Shakespearean criticism applies to the plays' assumptions, expectations, and techniques of inquiry appropriate to the study of literature rather than drama, but to regard the printed text of a Shakespearean play (more accurately, its script) as the primary focus and final end of one's inquiry is to overlook, if not distort, the processes by which drama moves and enlightens its proper audience—those who gather to see it performed. The essays we offer here are contributions to and manifestations of a movement, increasingly prominent in recent years, that seeks ways of perceiving, responding to, and discussing Shakespeare's plays which, without renouncing the undeniable insights afforded by literary inquiry, will prove more compatible with the plays' character as dramas.

Since they provide diverse examples of Shakespearean criticism which is more than "literary" in its thrust, our contributors do not ignore Shakespeare's language. They look upon the text (script) of the play as the verbal dimension of a work of art which, in its fullness, is also significantly, indeed essentially, extra-verbal. For our contributors the words of a Shakespearean play require and repay careful study because they are the indispensable starting points and guidelines for considering what lies beyond the printed page and comes into being on the stage: the visual, aural, spatial, temporal, bodily aspects of drama—its theatrical dimension.

Shakespeare's plays repeatedly call attention to their nature as works cast in an artistic medium uniting verbal and extra-verbal components. Consider, as one example, the implications of having a dumb show precede the play-within-the-play in *Hamlet*. A non-verbal medium which denies words to its audience—the characters assembled onstage as well as us in the theater—the dumb show does not splinter Claudius' composure. What provokes him to actions revealing his guilt is the play which follows, addressing not just the eyes but also the ears of its audience. The side-by-side positioning of dumb show and play in *Hamlet* affirms drama's capacity to clarify and touch the world beyond it and locates that power in drama's simultaneous and complementary use of the theater audience's aural and visual modes of perception.

The interplay between verbal and non-verbal avenues of perception to which Shakespearean drama frequently refers can be linked to a process, profound in its implications and conse-quences, that was at work during the sixteenth and seventeenth centuries in England and Western Europe. Shakespearean Eng-land was a culture undergoing a radical and extensive seachange as long-established, deeply-engrained modes of perceiving, thinking and expressing which were predominantly oral and aural came to be crossed with and increasingly subordinated to intensely visual modes fostered by the development and prolif-eration of printed books. As a medium which engages its audi-ence in hearing words spoken and seeing actions performed, drama stood astride that change, better endowed than any other art form both to illuminate and be enriched by that colossal shift in sensibilities. No dramatist more fully exploited the oppor-tunities offered by that extraordinary convergence of historical processes with the resources of an artistic medium than did Shakespeare.

However, the fragile and productive balance which Shakes-peare exploited between the older aural—oral modes of percep-tion and the newer visual modes gave way within decades to the dominance of the latter. Succeeding centuries have intensified that dominance as the experience of print—the organization of thought into linearly arranged, visually rendered, repeatable

verbal units perceived (read) by individuals in isolation—
became the shaping configuration of Western thought. Literature, particularly the novel, subsequently emerged as the artistic
medium judged best able to render existence in a typograph-
ically perceived universe. One consequence of that development
was the appearance of literary study as we know it today, and the
primacy of literature has meant that literature and the study of it
have become the dominant models for pondering and valuing
works in all artistic media, including those, like drama, which
have an extra-verbal dimension.

"Thou art a Moniment, without a tombe," Shakespeare's
contemporary and rival Ben Jonson wrote of him,

> And art alive still, while thy Booke doth live,
> And we have wits to read, and praise to give.

An irony of our history as a culture is that the principle means by
which, as Jonson presciently noted, Shakespeare is kept "alive
still" for us today—the printed book and reading—are those
which, almost irresistibly, have led us to devalue the plays as
works of drama. T.S. Eliot's explanation in *Elizabethan Essays* of
why he disliked seeing Shakespearean plays performed offers a
particularly revealing example of our hitherto nearly unshakable
addiction to prizing Shakespeare's creations as literature at the
expense of their character as drama:

> I know that I rebel against most performances of Shakespeare's
> plays because I want a direct relationship between the work of art
> and myself, and I want the performance to be such as will not
> interrupt or alter this relationship any more than it is an alteration
> or interruption for me to superimpose a second inspection of a
> picture or a building upon the first.

For Eliot—as for too many of us—the "work of art" to be
prized is not the play as it exists most completely realized in
performance but the text of the play, its script. The "direct relationship" that Eliot considers violated by a performance of the
play is that private, personal relationship linking reader to
printed text. Fixed in print, that text is static on the page, available like a picture or a building for "inspection" (reading) again
and again. But in the theater a play does not hold still for "a

second inspection," and drama calls upon us to open ourselves to an experience that is public and communal in ways that the experience of reading is not. Drama incorporates the individual spectators into that community we call the audience and requires by its very nature that actors come between us and the script that Eliot prizes as literature. The actors' presence asserts itself most forcefully in the matter of characterization. In the theater we do not encounter characters as they are rendered in decorporealized fashion through printed words but as they are embodied in and through actors.

A play is stable only when fixed, in embryo as it were, on the page. Brought into full being through performance, the play is fluid, shifting, evanescent. It is alive, composed of the actions of living people as they move and speak before us. A play is not an artifact but a process, unique with each performance, of making physically present (of *realizing*) possibilities of perception and feeling that lie attenuated and frozen in the script. The essays collected in this anthology attend to that process of making real, for it is by, through and during that process that drama moves us to feel and to know. In so doing, our contributors alert us to and celebrate the elusive richness of Shakespeare's plays as they exist most fully—in their theatrical dimension.

PHILIP C. McGUIRE

SHAKESPEARE
The Theatrical Dimension

Re-Presenting Shakespeare

EDWARD PARTRIDGE

We should never forget that a play is a play. Even now, with so many opportunities to see plays and after so many helpful books on theatrical production by Harley Granville-Barker, E.K. Chambers, G.E. Bentley, Walter Hodges, Alois Nagler, Eric Bentley, J.L. Styan, and John Russell Brown (to name only a few), some of our best Shakespearean critics forget to remember about plays and many of our most earnest students have too little to remember. I cite Professor L.C. Knights' famous essay of 1933 (reprinted in 1964), "How Many Children Had Lady Macbeth?" In the process of justly taking Bradley and nineteenth-century critics to task for impoverishing the total experience of the play by their habit of regarding Shakespeare's characters as friends or actual persons, Knights claims that a "Shakespeare play is a dramatic poem. It uses action, gesture, formal grouping and symbols, and it relies upon the general conventions governing Elizabethan plays. But, we cannot too often remind ourselves, its end is to communicate a rich and controlled experience by means of words—words used in a way to which, without some training, we are no longer accustomed to respond. To stress in the conventional way character or plot or any of the other abstractions that can be made is to impoverish the total response." But describing dramatic response in this way seems an impoverishment too.

This article was originally published in *Shakespeare Quarterly*, 25 (1974), 201—208. Reprinted with permission. [The article as originally written contained prefatory material not germane to the topic of this article and which has been omitted. Speech heads have been spelled out and placed on separate lines for uniform presentation.—*Ed.*]

Though he acknowledges action and gesture, he clearly thinks of words as the play's primary, if not sole, means of arousing a response. Later he goes so far as to say that "the only profitable approach to Shakespeare is a consideration of his plays as dramatic poems, of his use of language to obtain a total complex emotional response."[1] He has apparently never changed his mind about such an approach and—to show how not even dubious principles can ruin an intelligent critic—has continued to produce excellent books on Shakespeare. Or John Holloway: after saying that he agrees with Knights' statement—"the total response to a play can only be obtained by...an exact and sensitive study of Shakespeare's language"—he asks himself: "Would this kind of approach, studying the language, exclude *anything* from our consideration of a play; or would it even tell us that some things were unimportant, others specially important? Certainly not: there is nothing whatever in a play—not plot, not characterization, not the Girlhood of Shakespeare's Heroines, even, which we could conceivably study in any way save by a study of the language of the play. There is nothing else to study. Whatever aspect of a play we study—relevant or irrelevant to true criticism—where we have to study it is in the language. If we study the language loosely and vaguely, our results are loose and vague; an exact and sensitive study gives exact and sensitive results. So this general principal gives no guide at all as to what things will be important in a play. It leaves every question completely open. In fact, it is a truism."[2] A truism? I can only say that, though believing this principle may have allowed Holloway to write a good book on the tragedies of Shakespeare, the principle itself is neither a truism nor true in dramatic criticism. It is simply not true that in a play "there is nothing else to study" except language. There are—to refer only to obvious things—the expressive movements and the quite as expressive motionless presence of actors, the *mise en scène* and the costumes—in short, the whole visual aspect of the production. There are silences that can be as powerful as any speech, as an investigation of a Stanislavsky promptbook or any performance of a play by Harold Pinter can demonstrate. And beyond these separate elements is that synthesis of things said and done, that whole aesthetic experience of which words constitute a part, but only a part, and a part which has meaning only in terms of the whole synthesis.

Jerzy Grotowski argues that, if one defines the theater as "what takes place between spectator and actor," then the theater can exist without a text.[3] I think it can, though not for one moment would I recommend that, because the theater can do without a text, we should get rid of Shakespeare's words (as sometimes has happened for whole scenes in recent productions). I am only trying to counter Holloway's assumption that there is nothing else to study except language.

Fastidious literary critics may find all this emphasis on the visual and the nonverbal so vulgar that, like Aristotle (or Aristotle in an unguarded moment) they may consider theatrical production the least important of all the elements of a play. Aristotle, apparently nicknamed the "Reader" inside Plato's Academy, may have believed the heresy that reading a play is as good as seeing it. And more than one writer might agree with Thomas Mann that the theater is too "sensual" to attract him. Still, any art that has attracted great writers for twenty-five hundred years must be something more than merely vulgar and sensual. Perhaps the impure combination of the inescapable sensuousness of theater, of actors there in space, their living voices arguing, cursing, pleading, questioning, and the whole movement and urgency of a plot pregnant with its own future, as Susanne Langer says, and embodying its life here and now, is precisely what attracts an artist interested in dominating so powerful a form of art. We must simply accept this impurity and remember that to *read* a play is a contradiction in terms, except as one speaks of reading a score in preparation for playing or listening to music. Plays are to be seen and heard and responded to as one responds to a rite or a spectacle. They can not be simply read as one reads a novel. Words are, first and last, signals from writer to director, actors, scene designers, costumers, and technicians. In a wider sense a play belongs to literature because it uses words as one means of representing its world. Sometimes, as in Greek and Shakespearean drama, words constitute a primary means; other times, as in some of Molière's plays and much of Lope de Vega's, words are subordinate to other means, such as physical action or scenic effect.

A consequence of this impurity is that two kinds of study are severely limited: the merely literary, because words are only part of the dramatic effect; and the merely theatrical, because words *are* part of the dramatic effect and must be subjected to the same kind of linguistic and semantic criticism that is given to any aesthetic use of words. The obvious answer is to fuse the literary and the theatrical, but that is easier said than done. The real reason for this difficulty is not, I think, the one usually given: that those who know literary analysis do not know the theater, and those who know the theater can not analyze words very well. The real reason is that the drama is a unique art which requires a unique kind of imagination. Something quite different—and more difficult—than merely adding literary analysis to theatrical experience is needed. A play uniquely fuses a number of arts and calls for a kind of imagination different from that required for enjoying ballet or oratory or painting or sculpture or architecture or music or poetry, though it draws, in some fundamental sense, on all these arts.

To respond fully to a play, we must understand these four aspects of it:

1. *The play as speech:* the verbal action of the play must be given the same kind of phonetic, syntactic, rhetorical, and semantic analysis that we give to any use of words.

2. *The plot:* the speech belongs to a series of organically related actions whose conflicts are finally resolved. This plot embodies various meanings; and its agents, being images of men and women, possess ethos. The ethos of the characters and the meanings which their actions embody require moral judgment and mature reasoning.

3. *Mimetic action:* the play moves not merely verbally but physically. The play is a mimesis by body as well as by voice.

4. *Mise en scène:* and all is represented as taking place in a certain (not always definite) space and at a certain (sometimes vague) time. Setting, color, lighting, and costume constitute another and valuable language.[4]

In short, we need to interrelate the auditory, the semantic, the architectonic, the choreographic, and the scenic elements of a play. Since every play is written for a particular theater for production in a particular style by a group of actors, a study of it would involve the analysis of the original stage and the original mode of production. Since every play has itself had a history, the analysis could—and, in certain cases, should—involve a selective history of productions from the first one. Such analysis, at once antiquarian yet fully in historical perspective, might seem only to render more complex, because it recognizes historical change, a subject complex enough at any time. But we must see the stage as an instrumentality and the drama as a form which has gradually gained and, once gained, never lost ritual, spectacular, artistic, and social significance, all of which must be attended to.

Now the question is: how are we and our students going to preserve the most intense linguistic analysis and, at the same time, gain some sense of the visual aspect of the play without actually seeing it and some sense of the auditory aspect without actually hearing it? The answer is that we must try to re-create by explication, analysis, and interpretation the play which we cannot actually or often see and hear. John Russell Brown talks about imagining it in the "theater of the mind,"[5] but I am not too happy with this phrase, remembering what Gilbert Ryle has to say about "in the mind"; still, it may not be too dangerous a catch phrase so long as we don't make too much of it and so long as we remember that our minds are in front of our eyes, not in back of them—that is, in the objects we attend to or the situations we are involved in, and not in some close corner of our brains.[6] Brown's theater edition of *Othello* is a fine example of the "re-presenting" or "re-creation" I am calling for. I do not mean anything occult or even particularly unusual by this "re-creation." I only mean that we should systematically draw on whatever actors have told us about the roles they have created, directors about the plays they have directed, critics about the plays they have studied or the productions they have seen, scholars about the stages, the acting companies, the theatrical conditions, and the historical and literary sources of the plays they have learned about; and, then using whatever is significant, we should try to bring alive by our analysis and interpretation the play that is latently there in the text that has come down to us and in the theatrical history we have been able to recover. Good teachers, especially of history and literature, have been re-creating the past or some aspect of "reality" in this way for thousands of years.

Such verbal re-creation of a play is quite different from an actual performance of it. Even in our most imaginative moments we can never "see" the whole play being performed, or "hear" all its lines being spoken, or respond in class or on paper or in our study to the play we re-create as we would respond to the play as performed. What we can do to re-create the play is to draw on all that we can learn from history and previous literature, all that we can remember of our own feelings of pain and joy and hope and love and sorrow, and, fusing our learning and our memories, to call on our imagination for some significant response to the play. In one sense, no imaginative re-creation will be so good as even a bad performance of the play; in another sense, not even the best of performances quite embodies those ideal re-creations of the play we have seen in our inner theater where we recurrently enact our favorite plays. All of which means that we must keep on seeing and talking about plays the rest of our lives. The two feed on each other, the seeing keeps the talk aware of the concrete and sensuous life of a theatrical performance, the talk prepares us to see better next time and revives in words the past that may otherwise slip away.

I want to make clear that I am not suggesting that our students work out elaborate promptbooks or act out scenes in class or make lighting plots or scene and costume designs or write analyses of characters as though they were preparing to act them. All of these are valuable exercises which could lead to greater understanding and enjoyment of the play, but they eat up an enormous amount of the time that both teacher and student ought to spend on other plays. Besides, some of the work, such as the costume and scene designs, are fun to do, but of dubious value unless one is actually preparing for a production. But I do not object to such exercises so much because they take a great deal of time nor even because some of them return relatively little aesthetic good unless they lead to actual production. I object to even the best of them (such as Morris Eaves' excellent example of the workshop method of teaching Shakespeare) mostly because they misconceive the roles of teacher and student in courses of drama.[7] Our business is not to copy the work done in courses in acting, directing, scene design, and play production, though I'd be the first to grant that such courses or, better, some professional experience in the theater can lead to greater understanding of what a play is and how one should respond to it. Our business is finally critical and scholarly and analytic, not technical or professional. We have to recover conceptually, in words, not actions, the experience of a play which we may have seen and heard, so we in part remember it, but which we may never have seen or even heard, so we must produce it in our imaginations. We recover it through long hours of critical analysis and long years of living with it as an object of contemplation until we see it in its total design and possess it—never finally, never completely—but possess it joyfully in so far as we are then able to.

Some brief examples. What should a teacher do with the last act of *Hamlet*? For one thing, he could begin his discussion of the play there and work both forward to the end of the play and backward to the scenes which prepare for this resolution. Whether he begins his discussion there or not, he will want to ask or answer such questions as these: Why does the comment on Ophelia's suicide come first from the gravediggers? Where have Horatio and Hamlet come from? What does Horatio's comment on "custom" echo? Why the allusion to Cain? What is Hamlet's attitude toward the skulls? Why is a special point made of Hamlet's being born on the very day that the elder Hamlet defeated the elder Fortinbras? What is Hamlet's attitude toward Laertes in the graveyard? Why is it important that we learn now what happened to Hamlet on the ship to England? What is Horatio's function in this scene? What is Hamlet's attitude toward "providence"? And so on. The questions are nearly endless. The answers offered will show that the last act is dominated by two powerful scenes, each of which draws together images, ideas, and emotional states rendered in previous scenes. One is the scene in the graveyard, the other the duel in Court. The grave being dug for Ophelia concretely represents all those other graves in this death-ridden play, one of which had yawned to release a ghost early, another the grave into which Polonius had been cast "hugger-mugger," and those other graves to which Hamlet, Claudius, Gertrude, Laertes, Rosencrantz and Guildenstern are taken as the tragedy closes. We see and hear two gravediggers laughing and singing at their grim work and Hamlet standing on the edge of the grave, now capable of joking about the omnipresent leveler he has been haunted by. Then, the duel—the perfect resolution for a play which had been one long duel. It is apparently a courtly contest, but one rapier is deadly, and the wine is poisoned. The King, who had poisoned a brother, tries to poison his nephew, but succeeds only in killing his beloved wife. Laertes poisons the rapier which ends by killing him. Justice comes to Claudius by means of an inexorable and, to us, deeply satisfying ironic reversal: the poisoned rapier and the poisoned wine are used by the poisoned Hamlet to kill him. So Hamlet, the disinterested dueler, ironically achieves his revenge by means of a justice he does not try to bring about. Not even Shakespeare, fertile as he was in creating theatrical images, created more evocative images than the scenes of the grave and the duel, where word is wedded to action, and open grave and grinning skull, poisoned wine and poisoned rapier sum up the "bloody and unnatural acts," the innocent lives doomed, and the "purposes mistook/ Fall'n on the inventors' heads."

Recreating a play imaginatively is, of course, more than a matter of recovering the big scenes, such as Hermione, whose heart has turned to stone, gradually changing from a statue to a woman or Othello giving himself, with both his heroic egotism and his greatness of heart, a court-martial, acting as defendant, prosecuting attorney, judge, jury, and executioner, all in eighteen lines.[8] It is very hard for even the most obtuse teacher to ruin these scenes. Sometimes what needs to be imagined is a passage that might not register at all unless it is fully realized. For example:

> *Fool.*
> Give me an egg, Nuncle, and I'll give thee two crowns.
> *Lear.*
> What two crowns shall they be?
> *Fool.*
> Why, after I have cut the egg i' the middle and eat up the meat, the two crowns of the egg. When thou clovest thy crown i' the middle, and gav'st away both parts, thou bor'st thine ass on thy back o'er the dirt. Thou hadst little wit in thy bald crown when thou gav'st thy golden one away.

> (I. iv. 170–178)

On the surface this expresses a clear, straightforward analogy. Lear's kingdom is like an egg. Dividing the kingdom between Goneril and Regan is like cutting an egg in half. Even the only partly expressed parallels among the three kinds of crown is evident enough because "crown" was then a common term for the two halves of an eggshell, as well as an obvious term for head and king's crown. But at least three implications arise out of the passage because of its total theatrical context. First, an egg is the genetic bond between parent and child, carried by the female. To cut an egg in half is to destory the possibility of the egg's being fertilized. In disowning Cordelia and cursing his other two daughters with sterility, Lear has ensured, in his own mind, at least, that he would not have the grandchildren any man wants. Second, "eating the meat of the egg" becomes an act emblematic of Lear's whole self-destructive egotism. "The acting of eating," Freud reminds us, "is a destruction of the object with the final aim of incorporating it."[9] Lear denies his daughters, banishes Kent, and drives himself mad. Facing the nothingness of death, he obsessively moves toward it, destroying kingdom, family, sanity, and self. To the Fool he appears a "shealed peascod" (shelled peapod). Finally, "little wit in thy bald crown" is a clear anticipation of the madness which soon comes to him. The whole passage then gains a sharp visual point when the Fool introduces Goneril with "Thou hast pared thy wit o' both sides and left nothing i' the middle. Here comes one o' the parings" (ll. 204-206).

If I am right in thinking that a Shakespearean play, like any play, must be "re-enacted" by investing its several aspects— auditory, scenic, choreographic, and semantic—with whatever power our learning and our imagination can bring to this re-enactment, then our duty as teachers is painfully clear. What do we need to know? Everything: everything about the play—what our total dramatic experience of it may be; where its text came from; what editions are most useful; on what stages has it been produced and by whom and for what audiences; what have actors and critics and scholars discovered about it in the last three hundred years. What can we safely ignore? Nothing. Even wrong interpretations or idiosyncratic performances or apparently peripheral historical accounts may give us valuable insights. Is there no rest? No.

Notes

1. *Explorations: Essays in Criticism* (New York: New York University Press, 1964), pp. 18-29, 20.
2. *The Charted Mirror: Literary and Critical Essays* (London: Routledge & Kegan Paul, 1960), pp. 220-221.
3. *Towards a Poor Theatre*, ed. Eugenio Barba (London: Methuen, 1969), p. 32.

4. See J.L. Styan, *The Dramatic Experience* (Cambridge: Cambridge University Press, 1966).

5. J.R. Brown, "The Theatrical Element of Shakespeare Criticism," *Reinterpretations of Elizabethan Drama*, ed. Norman Rabkin (New York: Columbia University Press, 1969), pp. 177-195.

6. See Ryle, *The Concept of Mind* (New York: Barnes & Noble, 1949), esp. pp. 35-51. Also the whole chapter on Imagination (pp. 245-279) is the kind of de-mythologizing that English teachers often badly need.

7. "The Real Thing: a Plan for Producing Shakespeare in the Classroom," *College English*, XXXI (1970), 463-472.

8. For a brilliant chapter on teaching *Othello* by Ephim Fogel, see *Teaching Shakespeare*, ed. Arthur Mizener (New York: New American Library, 1969).

9. *Complete Psychological Works of Sigmund Freud*, trans. James Strachey (London: Hogarth Press, 1964), XXIII, p.147.

Performing the Poem

DAVID A. SAMUELSON

It may seem like an unassuming idea that Shakespeare imagined his plays as he wrote them, but in critical practice, it is an idea seldom allowed. Usually, the literary critic gives us a Shakespeare who thought up or released his plays as passages and poems on paper. Usually, too, the theater critic proposes a Shakespeare who was so concerned with "what works" that the virtue of his lines has to have been accidental. The considerable distance between this poet and this playwright actually can be closed quite a lot if we simply imagine Shakespeare imagining a whole reality as he wrote—speeches, color, gesture, pace, exits, and climax. The purpose of this essay is to promote the idea of the "whole reality" in Shakespeare's head as he wrote. Of course we can argue this idea only on the basis of the result of that imagining—what we have to work with on a page of text or script, and the possibilities our disciplined intelligence can imagine on that page. The term I use to point to what Shakespeare created is an awkward one—"play/poem." The lack of a better term argues that we do have a problem with our "unassuming idea"—we have no agreed-on term for a performance created out of intricate and interdependent structures creating a whole. So—this essay will begin on that slash between "play" and "poem," and offer an argument for what just may seem obvious. To the theatrical reader, the argument must offer evidence of verbal control over performance—that not just anything goes on stage and Shakespeare shaped acting and directoral choices along certain directions. To the literary critic, also, the argument must demonstrate pattern. To either, evidence of pattern is

paramount, for the play as conceived and performed in enor-
mously fluid and intricate: it is "sights and sounds, stillness and
motion, noise and silence, relationships and responses."[1]

This richness of Shakespeare's realized performance makes
it difficult to pin down controlling patterns. Let us consider, for
example, the difficulties of pattern in *Measure for Measure*. The
literary analysis gives us certain verbal motifs we know are
critical to Shakespeare's conceptual design, simply because
these motifs resonate with meaning, on stage or page. So—if we
approach the play with words like "Grace/grace," "power,"
"sleep," "touch," and "made," we have something fairly useful
in verbal patterns for composing our own reactions. By contrast,
eveyone's experience with staged interpretations argues an almost wide-open directorial relativism. In speaking of the stage
interpretations of just Duke Vincentio's role, Jane Williamson
reports this kind of variety: "The royal prince of the 1950s and the
Godlike Duke of the 1960s had given way [in the 1970s] to a genial
bumbler."[2]

Such variety is impossible to outwit with visions of the
authoritive interpretation, but we can begin to look at a play like
Measure to see how poem and play meet and give us patterning
that will resist frivolous critical rendering. Marvin Rosenberg
has a fit phrase for this convergence into pattern—he calls a play
"the poem of Shakespeare's gestures."[3] Like Beckerman, Brown,
Charney, Styan, and all the other recent theatrical critics,[4]
Rosenberg refuses to discuss the poem apart from the play, and
shows us how nicely the full richness of the page is expressed in
plausible performances.

This reading of *Measure* will try to illustrate how the richness
of the page comes to life in the patterns of performance to give us
a poem of significant gesture. We will start with that puzzling,
maddeningly drawn-out ceremony of justice in Act Five. Here
we see one very solid pattern of stage imagery in the three
unmaskings: Lucio saucily pulls off the friar's cowl behind which
Duke Vincentio has been maneuvering the plot as ghostly
Lodowick: Marianna just before lifts off her veil to expose
Angelo's treachery; and a little later the Provost unmuffles his
prisoner to reveal Claudio, saved by the Duke to preserve the
comic denouement. The imagery is clear, and the recurrence of
literal unmaskings fits the comedy's main concern, which one

might partially describe as the cloaking of one's humanity with the robes of official and legalistic conduct. The two chief victims of the literal unmasking, Angelo and Isabella, had cloistered their human identity behind abstractions, behind safe and inhuman codes. That delicious moment when Lucio plucks off the Duke's hood brings the pattern of stage imagery into line with the pattern of verbal imagery. First, Lucio's gesture, to reach out and touch Lodowick/Vincentio, neatly invokes prior verbal patterns and stage business; two instances: Lucio urges Isabella to make contact with the man behind Angelo's role as Deputy to move him to save her brother: "Ay, touch him; there's the vein." (II. ii. 70): the Duke's friar describes illicit sex to Pompey as "beastly touches" (II. ii. 22).[5]

"To touch" in *Measure* means to move, quicken, and warm, to become more human; but for the Duke, Angelo, and Isabella, human touching is virtually synonymous with "soiling." Hence the comedy here—the rogue who has been staining the Duke's good name with the ironic slander of the "dark corners," who sticks to him like a burr, now places his hand upon the Duke's person. William Hutt's Vincentio in the 1975 Stratford, Ontario, production slapped Lucio's hand away—and the Duke dramatically unmasked himself. But this decision seems out of temper with the Duke's line following his unveiling; surrounded by surprised onlookers, the unmasked Vincentio wryly thanks Lucio: "Thou art the first knave that e'er mad'st a Duke." The point is stressed again when Lucio reminds the Duke of his words: "I made you a Duke," to elude the punishment of "making [him] a cuckold." "Made" here is linked to the act of exposure, and Lucio suggests to us (and perhaps to Vincentio, who remits the whipping and hanging after Lucio's reminder) how much he, too, like Angelo and Isabella, has been the cloistered virgin, living at a remove from the responsibilities of his ducal office and from simple human desires. Now, exercising his power before the citizenry he once shied from, and now a lover too, bent on that surprising marriage, the Duke perhaps has been "made" both more man and more Duke than before. "Make/made" throughout the play carries double meanings: creation and coercion. "Made" is thus a good term for this comedy Vincentio manufactures by guile, luck, and force. Together, "touch" and "made" expand the meaning of the unmasking gestures, and Shakespeare seems to want us to see those enforced marriages as both coerced and generative, to see the humanity of our three virgins bared so they can be wed to life itself.

I have tried to illustrate in *Measure* a pattern of visually enacted verbal imagery, and to show how this pattern is thematically grounded. It is true, of course, that the patterns in the poem of Shakespeare's gestures are much more difficult to locate and track than purely verbal motifs, and that we can point out far fewer instances of performance patterns. Yet I suggest that by attending to these visual patterns the way we typically observe verbal patterning, we may locate far more than we had expected. For the rest of this essay I will try to demonstrate the critical usefulness of patterns that are simultaneously verbal and visual. I use "critical" in its two basic meanings: "crucial" and "interpretive." The theory runs thus: the play is *necessary* to the poem; and the poetic structures *shape* the staging. To illustrate this interdependence and how the full play/poem effects are both necessary and cognitive, I have chosen two scenes for analysis. The first illustrates the "crucial" effects of the model in technical terms; the second focuses on the "interpretive" function.

The case for the crucial presence of the play in the poem has been presented most often and emphatically by those who discuss pictoral composition within the dramatic action—Kernodle and Merchant, Berry, and Rose, to cite a few.[6] At its most polemical, the case for pictoral presentation stands on two assumptions: 1) that a picture must have a received definition apart from its meaning in the play (if a stage composition seems to be drawn from a familiar emblem or iconographic figure from extradramatic sources, the staged image will mean that much more); 2) the picture "means" by its separation from language: action and dialogue halt, a tableau is formed, it "speaks" silently, and then action, gesture and speech resume. It is as if that dazzling, semi-miraculous moment of awe when Hermione is unveiled as statue is held up as model for the power of staged pictures in general—a still, emblematic segment separable from the motion of drama. These two premises, by disassociating the function of language and spectacle, tend to dissolve the play/poem construct at its very point of alleged juncture.

Let us examine this disconnecting model of language and

picture in practical terms. A good illustration lies in that well-known section of the fifth act of *1 Henry IV* (81-128) where Prince Hal stands in poignant triumph over the two bodies of Hotspur and Falstaff. Hotspur, dead and bleeding, and Falstaff, feigning a death that saved him from the sword of Douglas, lie closely together to frame Hal in a single triangular picture. What we see is our young Prince, heir to crown and legend, ascendant over the two defeated models of un-princely conduct. The possible implications of this famous picture seem limitless. Indeed, its formulaic rigidity invites us to bathe in a stream of emblem book abstractions. Hal is obviously Magnificence, the bodies base Vices. Or, now safely inert, Hotspur can be reduced to Choler, or the unprincipled Warrior ideal. Falstaff usually lies on his back to display his "huge hill of flesh" as an ample image for the World of the Moralities. If the actor lets us in on the fact that Falstaff is faking, the very proneness of all that bulk also spells out Coward-ice. The verbal text of the play further invites us to see in these two bodies the plastic definition of their running anatomical epithets: Hotspur is always "heart" and Falstaff, "belly" or "guts." So rich and potent is the opportunity to allegorize this still moment in the action that we are sure Shakespeare wanted us to see the picture as an irresistible interpretation of some kind. Sherman Hawkins has described the tableau as an illustra-tion of the Aristotelian mean (Hal as true courage), a picture with antecedents in the *Psychomachia* of Prudentius.[7] Such readings are plausible enough, but they rely upon the play to halt its action and present this silent, glowing emblem in flesh and blood. But, does the play halt and "mean" in its stillness? More realistic is the model of action Mark Rose offers us: "the presentation of character in Shakespeare is perhaps less like a modern film in which figures are in constant motion than an album of snapshot stills to be contemplated in sequence," like "a series of speaking pictures;"[8] that is, a stage picture may be formed, but it "means" in sequence and dramatic motion.

What happens then to the still tableau if we register the motion of reaction? Let us assume a fifteen-second freeze right after Hotspur falls; unaware of Falstaff, Hal gazes down on Hotspur, completes his "and food for—" with "for worms, brave Percy," and then stands there and arranges the rest of the words he will shortly pronounce over his rival's corpse. This is our silent tableau. But when Hal begins to speak, what happens to the emblem book picture? I think Hal's words destroy it: "Fare thee well, great heart" (a tribute)/ "Ill-weaved ambition; how much art thou shrunk" (an insult). This little elegy imposes an ambivalent view upon the body of Hotspur, in contrast to the allegorical abstractions that invite us to simplify, shrink, and flatten Hotspur. And are we to see more simply than Hal? Clearly not; if anything, we see more complexly. To complicate the elegy further and to heighten the note of loss, we next see a significant gesture, the picture in motion: Hal performs that highly visible rite of "tenderness" during his speech, honoring the corpse of this "stout gentlemen" with his favors. Had Hotspur been successfully translated into flat symbol, even for a moment, he now becomes so much more here re-viewed through Hal's dramatic language and gesture. Perhaps the point of the tableau is its destruction.

The drama of the scene also resists a like flattening out of Falstaff, the more obvious Vice, for to this cartoon-like rotundity Hal continues the frame of ambivalence: "Poor Jack, farewell!/ I could have better spared a better man." We savor both Hal's valedictory jests and the tension between loss and dismissal. The net effect of language and moving action is to work against the neat allegorical picture. The sequence in the scene is enough to caution us against confusing abstraction with the sensuous actuality of theater, simple perceptions with complex apprehension—a book of homilies with Shakespearean drama. The continuing motion of the action, moreover, spells out more eloquent pictures of Falstaff's being. Hal exists, leaving just the two inert bodies. For a second we see in Falstaff a shadow of the sod revealed sleeping behind the arras in the tavern. Now he rises—and if we were *not* let in on his playacting, if the ideal rhetoric of the play is to have Falstaff stage a death convincing enough for Douglas, it at least half convinces us (a rare but not implausible staging), then his rising becomes what is for those who love him the Falstaffian principle itself: revival, resiliency, irrepressibility, vitality. This is the Falstaff of Richard Wilbur's appreciative poem "Up Jack"—"nature's kindest earthly sun," though "yellow pulp within."[9] For Wilbur and for an audience in on Falstaff's pretense of death, it is not a still tableau that speaks, but the dramatic action-motion, the rising movement. Falling and rising is exactly the visual shape of Falstaff's ability to elude capture by any man's wit—even the Hal who thought to win the Gadshill romp: "Mark how a plain tale shall put you *down*" (my emphasis). Falstaff is always only temporarily "down." For Falstaffians, his ever bouyant rising here becomes "the World" in the largest terms, much larger than the one-dimensional world in a morality like *Mundus et Infans*.

The significant motion of the scene continues and takes another complicating turn. Not to be captured by a tableau, the Falstaff of the theater as he rises jests on honor to deflate the honored Hotspur into mere decaying corpse: grisly, ironic "honor." Briefly, he converts us into fellow skeptics. But then Falstaff performs that quick unitalicized gesture which gives Falstaffians fits. He sinks his knife into Hotspur's venerated body—"Therefore, sirrah...." With this sudden gesture without emblem book analogue, Falstaff swiftly defines what is most wrong with him. From his soaring seconds before, Falstaff now plummets well past the downward motion of his blade. Hal immediately returns onstage, speaking to John, and in his words he retrospectively casts an ironic verbal frame on the stabbing: "Full bravely hast thou fleshed/ Thy maiden sword," he says, language we can not help apply to the unmanly and unmanning wounding seconds earlier of Hotspur's "thigh." Such is the drama in the motion of this brief section. By the time Hal gives Falstaff credit for slaying Hotspur, we have experienced a series of wildly opposing perceptions. The aggressiveness of the stage rhetoric (action *and* language) following the hypothetical tableau reminds us that we can no more isolate a still picture from dramatic speech or the motion of the action, than we can isolate a long philosophical or poetic passage and expect it to stand for the full communication of the whole play. It is not my point that extra-dramatically derived stills inserted into the play tend to dismiss the complicated life of such gloriously Shakespearean creations like Falstaff and Hotspur (though they do), for in Falstaff's non-emblematic motion with his knife there is much greater cause to reject his claims upon us. The point is that non-emblematic pictures in sequence seem to carry the typically Shakespearean meanings, and that this kind of spectacle and accompanying language are "crucially" linked to one another. The play so conjoined to the poem is a fuller, more active, and therefore more complete communication. It is more "Shakespeare" to ask the most of our reaction in his play/poem imagining.

In displaying the "crucial" linkages between play and poem in *1 Henry IV*, I have tried to suppress an interpretive bias for the sake of clarifying the exacting rhetoric of Shakespeare's theatrical technique. But in the illustration of the "interpretive" function of the play/poem model, we must become directly involved in thematics. The illustration comes from *King Lear*, a play for which everyone has a well-developed and firmly held opinion. My reason for choosing *Lear*, however, is technical; its ending perfectly embodies the play/poem model. Here we have that allegedly unstageable long lyric poem, saturated with a complex but coherent pattern of verbal motifs that work upon our brain like a tortuous dialectical essay. Yet at its climactic moments, the tragedy heavily depends upon the staged linkage between spectacle and verbal glossing, picture and responsive language. The play/poem model in *Lear* ferociously assaults our minds. A series of grim pictures is presented, to us and, more intimately, to the survivors of the tragic action. The survivors then react to the spectacle with words seeking the appropriate response. The audience understands what is happening and what it means by attending to how the tragic actors observe and struggle for the words to respond to these pictures. In short, the action itself at the end of *King Lear* focuses on the act of interpreting.

There are basically three units within this rhythm of spectacle and verbal response, from line 238 to the end. The first spectacle is set up when Albany orders the bodies of the murdered Regan and his suicide-wife to be carried out into view. Albany rivets our minds on this spectacle by forcing Kent to behold the bodies: "Seest thou this object, Kent?" It is a grisly picture of justice, and the power of the spectacle moves Edmund to voice a kind of remorse: he urges his fellow onlookers to rush to save Lear and Cordelia from his writ of execution. Too late his change of heart, as Lear makes that awesome entrance, carrying the body of his third daughter, and howls his desolation, commanding all eyes to fix upon his misery. This spectacle is one of gross injustice. Lear has no words adequate to his grief, and so he "howls" and turns on the stunned beholders, rebuking them for their silence: "O, you are men of stones. Had I your tongues

and eyes, I'd use them so/ That heaven's vault should crack."
"Tongues and eyes" is precisely the rationale of the scenic structure, but the problem becomes the obvious inability to find
speech to match what is seen. So, anything but men of stones,
Kent and Edgar grope clumsily, tersely, for words: "Is this the
promised end?" Kent asks numbly, the thought completed by a
dazed Edgar, "or *image* of that horror" (emphasis mine). "Fall
and cease," murmurs Albany, for the pain is unbearable, and
they would have an end. Yet Shakespeare denies a quick end to
this pathos, stretching out the agony for sixty-two more lines, as
Michael Goldman observes, to push our responses to ex-
tremities.[10]

The third and major unit is the most intricate. It is a spatially
designed sequence of witnessing. We, as audience, behold Edgar, Kent, Albany, and sundry gentlemen gazing helplessly on
the old crazed King as he himself kneels, holds Cordelia in his
arms, and tries to find the words for what he sees, indeed to alter
what he sees with these words. First, he holds the feather to
Cordelia's mouth, imagining briefly he sees it stirring from her
breath, "a chance which does redeem all sorrows." Kent moves
forward, determined, despite the incredible inappropriateness
of the moment, to have his long sought recognition from the
King he served so steadfastly as Caius, and "to bid [his] King and
master aye good night." Lear uncomprehendingly rebuffs Kent,
"Prithee away," an echo of Kent's I. i. banishment ("Away."
178), and turns his eyes back to Cordelia's face, now imagining
he hears her voice: "Ha,/ What is't thou say'st?" Perhaps Lear
rises to mime briefly the motion he had just performed on the
executioner with his "good biting falchion." Then he turns to the
ensemble of onlookers, trying to recognize them. "Who are you?/
Mine eyes are not o' th' best," he admits and then somehow
through the shock and dislocation, despite his "dull sight," he
manages to recognize Kent. Pathetically, he refuses Kent his full
glory by failing to absorb the fact that Kent was his loyal Caius:
"He's dead and rotten." "No, my good lord," urges Kent, "I am
the very man." "I'll see that straight," Lear says in distraction,
and in effect ironically repeats his first scene command to Kent,
"Out of my sight!" (158) Kent has good reason to describe the
moment as "cheerless, dark, and deadly," especially since his
long sought reconciliation and reward for service has been de-

nied. Lear, trying to see what is not there, cannot see what is there. Thus it is Albany concludes: "He knows not what he says; and vain is it/ That we present us to him."

It is time to end the comedic agony; and as Lear returns to holding Cordelia, Albany tries to gather up the moment in the words of an affirmative epilogue. He speaks of comfort, his own retirement, rewards, and justice, and he implies a post-catastrophe future. To this world after tragic experience, he seeks to draw all eyes and ears. But his language too is inadequate, for the spectacle of the still-grieving King is too much, the moment too gripping; so Albany interrupts himself, erases momentarily future concerns and points at Lear and Cordelia: "O, see, see!" Now we are back where this third spectacle began, mourners circled around the focal center that is again Lear gazing intently on Cordelia's face. This time it is Lear himself who defines the implications of the image he is creating: "Thou'lt come no more,/ Never, never, never, never, never." The five "nevers" offer the most harrowing recognition in all tragic literature. The "nevers" were not necessary; but Shakespeare seems to insist that we, the audience, not avert our gaze or our minds from the tragic and linear finality of this image. It is as if we were all testing Edgar's aphorism and had dared to think of Cordelia's death, surely "this is the worst." The five "nevers" declare otherwise, as they point to irretrievable extinction in an empty and nihilistic cosmos. Now the stage is darker and deadlier than moments before. The bottom seems to drop out of the bottom.

Up to this point the rhythm of spectacle and verbal response has been one of a desolate scene provoking fumbling verbal gestures toward consolation. The bodies of Goneril and Regan form a grisly picture, but out of that sight comes Edmund's last minute goodness; and our hopes soar briefly. The King and Cordelia's lifeless body appear to dash these hopes. The idea of an end to this tragic scene, the movement of a feather, Cordelia's voice itself, perhaps the tearful reunion of Kent and King, and then thoughts of the future, all try to lift us out of this gloom, but the "nevers" serve to intensify it. Now, the pattern reverses itself, for after the "nevers" the bleakness lightens for a second or two. Lear asks his button be loosened, and suddenly returns our eyes back to Cordelia's face. In answer to the five "nevers," he commands everyone to share his startled gaze; five times he asks:

"Do you see this? Look on her! Look her lips,/ Look there, look there—". The repeated commands create a zoom-lens effect, for suddenly the vivid center of the stage is that tiny distance, two feet at most, between Lear's eyes and Cordelia's lips. Lear then dies holding Cordelia, and our eyes inevitably retreat to take in the whole stage picture. We are looking at the ensemble image the helpless survivors make, and we begin to absorb the implications of the tragic action just concluded. But quite noticeably, no one on stage comments on the last image—Lear thinking he sees signs of life on Cordelia's lips. Instead, the survivors underscore their speechlessness. Edgar musters up the words to end this moment and the play: "We that are young," he says; and with the note of "youth," we have every reason to expect a theme of continuance and affirmation. But Edgar reverses this hope, precisely in the rhythm of spectacle and explication governing the whole scene: "We that are young/ Shall never see so much, nor live so long." Here is no affirmation for the catastrophe.[11]

Few characters in Shakespeare's tragic denouements achieve consolation, and no words of these survivors are meant to suffice. The largest dimensions of Shakespeare's tragic vision are always unspeakable and go unspoken. Iago deliberately preserves his riddle: "What you know, you know./ From this time forth I never will speak word." and so creates the mystery of *Othello*. Hamlet gives Horatio full instructions to repair his public image, and Horatio promises Fortinbras a host of sensational stories, but Hamlet, implying much that could be said ("Had I but time...O I could tell you...") underlines all that he does not and can not explain, with "The rest is silence." Edgar, too, while summing up implies there is no summing up. His silence is eloquent. Instead of trying for suitably official language, Edgar pointedly stresses the spectacle, the "so much" we have just seen; and so he invokes the very rationale of this catastrophic scene: "sight" itself.

But what have we seen? In theory, an acting company can compose the spectacle in any number of arrangements. In pratice, however, the choices are guided by the patterns in the language. Let us consider for example two possible "good ideas" for the staging. We know the very focal center of the third unit in the catastrophe is the old King, kneeling or sitting, holding lifeless Cordelia: a parent cradling a slain child. We decide this image bears a stong likeness to the classic iconographic figure of the *pietà*, suffering Mary embracing her sacrificed son. One can certainly imagine Shakespeare's conceiving of this visual variation of the *pietà* as an ironic version of the type; and the image was common enough in his day for Shakespeare to have counted on his audience to recognize the model. Actors can easily shape their bodily configuration to create this sacred figure. To see this spectacle would mean we would see more, something like a halo effect superimposed over this particular image of grief, an aura of the universal type, a typal image that absorbs the individual instance and mitigates the horror. It is precisely this kind of interpretive effect we often encounter in discussions of Shakespeare's use of tableaux borrowed from pictoral art: received pictures tend to be optimistic, dramatic pictures often devastate. This particular spectacle, however attractive, is rendered implausible by the language "dramatically" controlling our vision, those five "nevers" which at the very least make this staged emblem cruelly sardonic. Again, what we see should be shaped from the force of the language.

More problematic is the picture we see when Lear thinks he sees the final signs of life on Cordelia's breath. The moment is notorious in criticism for a line of post-Bradleyan optimists who would share Lear's need to alter what it is he sees. In the 1974–1975 New York Public Theatre production of the play, for instance, we were all invited to see hopeful invisibilities. Specifically, when James Earl Jones as Lear bid us to look on Cordelia five times, the ensemble intently fastened their attention upon that tiny focal point. A nearly palpable presence thus was created in the intimate space between the faces of father and daughter. Then, as Edgar said "Look up, my lord," the ensemble slowly gazed upward and traced the ascent of some invisible entity— Lear's ghost, it would seem, from Kent's line "Vex not his ghost." This is an attractive staging, for it gives us that elusive note of affirmation. But the language also denies credibility to this spectacle. An unforced look at the text shows that Edgar seems to be saying "look up" to Lear, not Kent; and Kent seems to be telling Edgar to desist and not urge the suffering King to live one second longer. Perhaps in *Lear* most stage tableaux and improvised images have been devised, understandably, in the spirit of Tate's revision—to soften the very forcefulness of the horror Shakespeare added to the tale he inherited and to elude the battering Shakespeare compels us to undergo in the structure of the catastrophe.

In criticizing these two doubtful stage pictures I do not mean to say that what we do see in the catastrophe of *Lear* must be a bleak, nihilistic wasteland. The theatrical actuality of these moments does not submit to the simplicity of choosing interpretive sides—the consolation of Bradley, Granville-Barker, Chambers, and Battenhouse versus readings stressing shock and loss. Rather, I again propose that any staged picture must depend upon the language within the scene, and should be governed by the patterns of language and sequence of tableaux running throughout the whole play. The principle offered here is simply this: it is *crucial* to compose *interpretations* (staged or discursive) on the conjunction of play and poem. As it turns out, the staged pictures suggested by the play/poem (sight/language) construct here happen to be less than bleak or nihilistic.

The stage picture at the climactic moment in the catastrophe resists thematic reductiveness because it is complex. The image here is looking, beholding, seeing. This is the most appropriate stage spectacle for a tragedy whose basic verbal pattern is the famous, oft-explicated motif of sight, which, with blindness, provides perhaps the basic image for tragic vision[12] (*Oedipus Rex, The Wild Duck, Endgame*). The gathered ensemble creates a circle of silhouettes focusing on the weary King, who creates that intimate outline of the caring as he gazes intently on Cordelia's lips. We see, however, not simply the double configuration of "looking." In the intervals between the survivors and Lear and between Lear and Cordelia's face, we have empty space charged with a signifying visibility. The effect of staging is often to make us see things that are not literally there on stage—James Earl Jones's Lear, we recall, made us see the ascent of Lear's soul. As a negative inverts a finished print, here the visual structure of the beholders forces us to see two distinct areas of empty space. The most acute empty space lies in that distance of two feet or so between Lear's eyes and Cordelia's lips. In this same space the tragic action was begun, only then it was a matter of yards, hurt, and painful misunderstanding:

Nothing, my lord.
　　　　　Nothing?
Nothing.
　　　　　Nothing will come of nothing. Speak again.

Here the eyes of the guests beholding this ceremony shift back and forth from Lear's face to the lips of Cordelia issuing these startling refusals to provide the formal language of love Lear insists upon. Now, at the end, the distance has collapsed to this most intimate space; and we watch, pained, as Cordelia again says "nothing" with her silence. Much depends upon the silence in this miniature empty space, and Lear defines it for us with a flash of bitter perception: no breath, no movement, never. The ironic verbal motif made of all those kinds of "nothing," two dozen instances by the end of Act Three,[13] moves to its structural climax here as Lear can not see signs of life on Cordelia's lips. It is the cumulative force of the sequence of verbal "nothings" that enlarges this tiny empty space into a dramatic and visual emblem of a cruelly sardonic universe that would gratuitously take Cordelia without allowing her any words of farewell. When, momentarily, Lear imagines he sees her lips move, he intensifies this space with pathetic illusion. Then he dissolves the empty space by collapsing over her body into his death.

All that space between royal corpses and the circumference of onlookers continues for a few moments, kept alive and charged by the frustrated witnessing until the play's last lines: "We that are young/ Shall never see so much nor live so long." This space, however, does not bespeak a bleak vision. True, Edgar refuses to gild the suffering with high sentence, and no persona steps forth to speak briskly of pushing the human community forward. But our ensemble of helpless onlookers offers us a more heartening image than the post-tragic gestures of Malcolm, Octavius, or Fortinbras provide with their resolute notions of continuance. I suggest what we see here in the configuration of our circle of survivors is the very image of society and the human "bonds" that give society its coherence and meaning. Edmund was, after all, as incorrect in his estimate of human nature as Lear was in his view of Cordelia. We are shown so quite clearly by the way our survivors refuse deflecting commentary and refuse to look away. Instead, they gaze with unspeakable care toward that vanished image of nothingness, and in doing so they evince a human image of "heart," the radical force Cordelia herself represents andwhich underlies the "bonds" in this play. The survivors evince heart in both of its traditional meanings— emotional courage and profound sympathy. Their line of vision marks the empty space as an image of heartening reality. Thus *King Lear* closes with a dignified image of human nature surviving as a community.

King Lear is full of such thematically complex stage pictures, and the more a scene seems to attempt gestures of "meaning," the more acute the ambivalence. Consider the scenes on the heath, especially the moment when Lear looks at naked and filthy Tom and begins to sermonize on how vulnerable and frail is poor unaccommodated man, cast into the indifference of nature. To be sure, this is depressing, and we are tempted to agree with Lear, for the evidence of the moment is bleak—our outcasts are quite alone and vulnerable. But to so agree is to miss the obvious power of this scene, and to be blind to the obvious— which is the vivid picture of all these fellows accommodating the other fellows. Nature may be indifferent, but human beings, these humans at least, are decidedly not indifferent.

The stage picture can not be reduced to a prose paraphrase, for its structure is ambivalent, the way meanings tend to be. And at the end, we see a like ambivalence in those two areas of empty space in the final composed picture of the denouement. The verbal definition supplied by the five "nevers" yields a sense of the void close to the idea of "unaccommodation," and one can almost see it in that silent space between father and daughter. This is dreadfully empty space. But, in the larger space created by the ensemble, we have an atmosphere of "heart," the true trait of the living. The final mix of substance and emptiness, reason for hope and cues for deflation, might be summed up the way Professor Stampfer has in his classic essay:[14] the nature of nature is indifference; the nature of man is really that of heart.[15]

In pointing out the thematic complexity of the final vision *King Lear* offers us, I am most concerned with how we come to perceive this complexity—which is by the inseparable rhythm of language and gesture, words and pictures, poetry embedded in the performance. It is next to impossible to describe this rhythm or the moments when what we call "verbal patterns" take shape

and assume a presence on stage. But, we all know how powerfully the dominant patterns like "sight-blindness," "nothing"
and "nature" do get enacted in this five-act experience.

If these patterns in *King Lear* do not persuade one that
Shakespeare's mind conceived of the play/poem whole, then
there is nothing else in Shakespeare's canon that will.

Notes

1. J.L. Styan's handy description, from *Drama, Stage and Audience*
   (Cambridge: Cambridge University Press, 1975), pp. vii and 24.
2. "The Duke and Isabella on the Modern Stage," in *The Triple Bond*, ed.
   Joseph G. Price (University Park: Penn State University Press, 1975).
3. *The Masks of King Lear* (Berkeley: University of California Press,
   1972), p. 337.
4. Bernard Beckerman's *Shakespeare at the Globe: 1599–1609* (New York:
   Macmillan, 1962) and J.L. Styan's *Shakespeare's Stagecraft* (Cambridge: Cambridge University Press, 1967), foremost among the
   recent studies of Shakespeare's stage, invite us to entertain the
   critical dimensions of production. Their focus very sensibly falls
   upon how we can infer from the text the nature of the fluid, significant and plastic spectacle that is the design of enactment. John
   Russell Brown's collection of essays, *Shakespeare in Performance* (Baltimore: Penguin, 1966) covers a spectrum of interpretive problems
   in performance, and his more recent work, *Shakespeare's Dramatic
   Style* (London: Heinemann, 1970) reconsiders the nature of the
   poetry in dramatic language. Styan's *Drama, Stage and Audience*
   (Cambridge: Cambridge University Press, 1975) and Beckerman's
   Dynamics of Drama: Theory and Method of Analysis (New York: Knopf,
   1970) very sanely and with provocative imagination reexamine
   some old notions about performance, auditing, and how a play
   communicates; in revivifying the act of analyzing drama, they have
   much that is fresh and penetrating to say about reading Shakespeare's drama. Maurice Charney has long been treating the visual
   aspects of Shakespeare's art, and in *Shakespeare's Roman Plays: The
   Function of Imagery in the Drama* (Cambridge, Mass.: Harvard University Press, 1961) and *Style in Hamlet* (Princeton, Princeton University
   Press, 1969) he offers us countless gems about visual imagery while
   discussing history, structure, and verbal matters. Charney's more
   recent *How to Read Shakespeare* (New York: McGraw-Hill, 1971) takes
   up some of the enactment issues more frontally. The theatrical
   approach is earning more and more respect; *Studies in English Literature*, committed primarily to the literary values of the Shakespearean play/poem, published a reading of *Romeo and Juliet* that asserts
   that the cognitive power of stage spectacle in the last act surpasses

(and contradicts) the poetry and language: see James Black, "The Visual Artistry of *Romeo and Juliet*," SEL, 15 (1975), pp. 245-256.

5. Lines and citations are from *William Shakespeare: The Complete Works,* gen. ed. Alfred Harbage (Baltimore: Penguin, 1969).

6. George R. Kernodle's *From Art to Theatre: Form and Convention in the Renaissance* (Chicago: University of Chicago Press, 1943) and W. Moelwyn Merchant's *Shakespeare and the Artist* (London: Oxford University Press, 1959). A stimulating treatment can be found in Mark Rose's *Shakespearean Design* (Cambridge, Mass.: Belknap/ Harvard University Press, 1972). For an interesting critical variation of the tableau approach, see Francis Berry, *The Shakespearean Inset* (New York: Theatre Arts, 1965). John Doebler's *Shakespeare's Speaking Pictures* offers a supple argument for the literal use of iconic imagery (Albuquerque: University of New Mexico Press, 1974).

7. "Virtue and Kingship in Shakespeare's *1 Henry IV*," *E L R*, 5 (1975), 327.

8. Rose, p. 9.

9. In *The Poems of Richard Wilbur* (New York: Harcourt Brace Jovanovich, 1974), p. 188.

10. In "The Worst of *King Lear*," Michael Goldman describes the rhetoric of the last act as a version of Gloucester's trip to the brink— in *Shakespeare and the Energies of Drama* (Princeton: Princeton University Press, 1972), p. 94ff.

11. Fine commentary on Edgar's enigmatic last lines can be found in Peter Brook's *The Empty Space* (New York: Avon, 1968), pp. 84–86. See also Inga-Stina Ewbank's essay, "More Pregnantly Than Words: Some Uses and Limitations of Visual Symbolism," *Shakespeare Survey 24*, ed. Kenneth Muir, (Cambridge: Cambridge University Press, 1971). How right the F1 assignment of this speech to Edgar. Unlike Albany who seems so sure about what ought to be said, Edgar seems dazed by the events after his reporting his father's death. His speech leading up to the closing reaction consists largely of befuddled one-liners: "What kind of help?" "What means this bloody knife?" "Here comes Kent." "Very bootless." "He is gone indeed."

12. Robert Heilman's treatment of the sight motif remains the most penetrating and comprehensive—in *This Great Stage* (Baton Rouge: Louisiana State University Press, 1948).

13. The most extensive and suggestive treatment of the "nothing" motif is Sigurd Burckhardt's "King Lear: The Quality of Nothing," in *Shakespearean Meanings* (Princeton: Princeton University Press, 1968), pp. 237–259.

14. J. Stampfer, "The Catharsis of *King Lear*," *Shakespeare: Modern Essays in Criticism*, edited by Leonard F. Dean (New York: Oxford University Press, 1967). Two further commentaries on this scene take a similar position: S.L. Goldberg, *An Essay on King Lear* (Cambridge: Cambridge University Press, 1974) and Maynard Mack, *King Lear in Our Time* (Berkeley: University of California Press, 1965).

15. Cordelia's symbolic role defies Edmund's skepticism and cuts against that long pessimistic tradition in Western thinking (Hobbes, Darwin, Freud, and contemporary popular novels). This tradition has recently been challenged by humanist anthropologists who argue that something very much like Shakespeare's "bonds" determines the behavior of *homo socius*. They invite us to think that Cordelia ("heart") represents something real. See, for example, Ernest Becker's incorporation of contemporary humanist anthropology in *The Birth and Death of Meaning* (New York: The Free Press, 1962). Visually, what Cordelia symbolizes is best defined when she kisses her sleeping father in IV. vii.: "...restoration hang/ Thy medicine on my lips, and let this kiss/ Repair those violent harms that my two sisters/ Have in thy reverence made."

In Search of the Performance Present

BARBARA HODGDON

"When I look at a play, I read one third of what is there, one third of what I would like to be there, and one third I miss altogether."[1] Terry Hands, currently directing for the Royal Shakespeare Company, is speaking about the difficulty of approaching a Shakespearean text with a view toward staging it. Hands's dilemma is not new: it is shared by first-time readers or playgoers, and by the most knowledgeable critics, commentators and spectators. Although we have abundant historical, scholarly, critical, interpretative, and practical evidence upon which to base conclusions, we still find it difficult to define and describe the specific and comprehensive effects of a Shakespearean play, and to talk about how a play embodies meanings and signifies those meanings to an audience. What we seem to be looking for is an extended metaphor which will not only identify and summarize the kinds of signals present in the texts and in performances but which will also attempt to register the infinite variety of ways in which these signals shift and manipulate our perceptions and responses.[2] What follows explores past readings and performances in order to affirm certain kinds of stage realities present in the text and to imagine ways of realizing Shakespeare's effects in the theater.

In performance, each moment of a Shakespearean play provides us with signals, both verbal and nonverbal, which we, as spectators, "read"; the presence of one or several dramatic signs orders our perceptions toward meaning. In the final moments of *Hamlet*, for example, after speech is over,

Hamlet's body is raised upon a litter; he is borne off the stage. We read death from his immobility; at the same time we may be aware of the reactions of others—reactions read from their physical attitudes and their facial expressions. We will probably notice Horatio and Fortinbras in particular, since the language has recently drawn our attention to both figures. Yet if we attempt a more specific description of the signals available within the moment, we must also account for (among other things): the probable contrasts of costume and color (Hamlet's dueling shirt, the armor of the soldiers), the accentuating effects of stage lighting, the fact of three other bodies— Gertrude, Laertes, and Claudius—on the stage, the possibility that Hamlet's body is taken off toward the battlements where the play began (thus one spatial dimension of the play will seem to have come full circle), and the effect of the sight and sound of marching men and the sudden absence of speech after the various sounds and movements of the duel and of the excited speeches which accompany and follow it, giving us the sense of a gradual formalization of both language and movement. And when we widen our perception beyond whatever highlights we notice within the performance moment, we may sense a patterning in the composition of the stage picture which also contributes to meaning, further affecting and directing our responses.

Regardless of which signal or combination of signals focuses our attention in these impressions surrounding the final denouement, each seems to fall into place. Yet each also bears a weight of meaning resulting from an accumulation and gradual drawing together of all the previous signals which have, since its opening moments, directed and controlled our perceptions of the play. And although we may not recall exactly how each signal—whether a phrase, a speech, a prop, a gesture, a movement—carried meaning at the time we experienced it, we are aware that each represents a deliberate choice, a momentary emphasis; and that each contributes value to our sense of an appropriate ending. If "collecting" signals represents a part, at least, of our response to the play, is there a process of selection that orders these signals toward meaning—within a particular moment, a scene, or a play?

The question implies that the performed play operates

systematically. Yet even the briefest experience of both the printed text and the "two hours' traffic" of the stage shows us otherwise. Those signals we give special attention to in the study—what Banquo's murderers say to each other and the possible identity of the third murderer, for example—may be partially lost in the rush of anticipation and horror we feel when we see Banquo and Fleance set upon in the theater. The moment is not rigidly directed by the text; and we cannot say that sight is more important than sound, but simply that the scene "works" through a collection of signals that trigger various kinds of energies—energies which travel through the scene and which both actors and spectators feel, understand, and respond to in various ways.[3] I should like to explore some of the signals responsible for directing these energies, considering (1) expectations, (2) various types of scenes and sequences and their presentational meanings, (3) the shifting levels of focus within a moment, (4) the handling of stage space, and (5) repetitive or echoing moments or images.

However we approach a play, either through reading the text or attending a performance, we bring a potential current of expectations with us—a current that may be completed, suspended, altered, and redirected by the events we are about to experience. Expectations are present even before the play begins: the naïve playreader or playgoer wonders what will happen; the knowledgeable spectator asks, "How will they (the actors, the director) handle this scene?" However aroused, this energy of expectation initiates meaning: it catalyzes and activates performance, whether its signal is a closed book, a closed curtain, or a momentarily empty, waiting stage. Obviously, specific performances can channel this initial energy by directing the spectator's perception even before the play begins. Peter Brook's white "squash court" box for *A Midsummer Night's Dream* (Royal Shakespeare Company, 1971), with its huge, suspended red feather "couch"; and Buzz Goodbody's shimmering golden drapes hung between two poles and placed center stage for her *Lear* (RSC, 1974) are two examples of sets which both arouse and settle audience expectations. The first signals difference, non-Elizabethan-ness, non-tradition; the second gives the sparest indication of a localized "royal" space. Both provide significant keys to the ways in which the literal presentational imagery of the plays will take shape.

As we, and the actors, go beyond such opening signals, the developing language and actions of the play arouse one set of expectations for those on the stage, another for those in the audience. The difference between the two, as Bertrand Evans has shown for the comedies,[4] creates tensions which control a part of our response to the play. As our attention shifts from scene to scene, we carry both our own expectational energies and those of the characters; sometimes it may be difficult to differentiate the two, particularly if our identification with one character is strong. For example, Hamlet expects to take action as soon as he has proven the truth of the Ghost's story; and we expect that action from him. A significant dimension of the play's experience, both for Hamlet and for us, revolves about the continual denial (the soliloquies), frustration (Claudius' praying), or undercutting (Polonius' murder) and the final fulfillment (exaggerated beyond what we, or Hamlet, have imagined) of that single expectation. At the opposite pole, consider Richard III, who both over-arouses our expectations—by telling us that he will kill Clarence, that he will woo and win Lady Anne, that he will become King—and over-fulfills them. His own expectations gradually narrow to survival; ours are, at least to some extent, historically determined: both meet in the final moments of the play. But although Richmond tells us that "the bloody dog is dead," and although we may see Richard's body on the stage, these facts are qualified by our extended identification with Richard's own current of expectations, an effect contributing to an uneasy sense of disappointment in this kind of resolution of all the excitement Richard has generated.

Although these examples suggest that a structure of rising, falling, and leveling energies of expectation binds both actors and spectators to the play, directing the broad overall rhythms of the stage action as well as governing audience responses, we need to isolate, within moments, the precise signals which may either prompt or deny expectation, which carry the internal rhythms of each scene toward meaning, and which bridge the movement from scene to scene. Do these signals exist in language, in silence, in action or lack of it, in a single gesture, a property, a costume—or, at times, in combinations of all of these? Perhaps it would be most useful, here, to look at a link-ing structure of signals within *Henry V*, and to refer to Terry Hands's excellent 1975 production (RSC) for particulars.

In Shakespeare's text, the opening of the play rests only upon language: the Chorus speaks of failure, of the necessity for the spectator to stretch his imagination beyond language, beyond what can be shown on the stage. Thus any expecta-tions of seeing "the vasty fields of France" or the "proud hoofs" of horses are immediately leveled; but at the same time, Shakespeare's overt challenge to our imaginations suggests other options. The words of the Chorus invite us to create one dimension of the play's experience ourselves; yet they also shift our attention away from setting, and from expecting to see many men, hinting that significant meaning rests elsewhere. Taking his cue from Shakespeare's apology for fail-ure, Hands extends the ideas of incompleteness and process into the stage picture, giving the opening moments of his pro-duction an added measure of contrast: we watch actors in re-hearsal clothes casually assemble on a completely bare stage; they talk among themselves, do warm-up exercises, and finally recline, waiting, on the stage. Like us, they seem to be expect-ing something to happen, so that when the Chorus refers to the "flat unraised spirits," both actors and spectators share a similar, quite literally undercut, perspective on the play's pos-sibilities. But the actor/spectator equation is not sustained, for as the Chorus' speech concludes, the actors begin to "play." Now our expectations of future action, aroused first by the dialogue between Ely and Canterbury, and modulated by Henry's questioning and apparent indecision and by the urg-ings of Canterbury, Exeter, and Westmoreland, rest solely upon the developing sense of what is being said; tones of voice remain flat, matter-of-fact; and the stage is relatively still until Henry calls for the messengers from the Dauphin. Momentarily, our expectation follows the call and travels offstage, but then quickly returns, as the "tun of treasure" is brought in by the Ambassador, who is in costume. The shock of contrast between this single elegant costume and the warm-up clothes of the other actors both energizes and settles our expectations: the play now seems to be moving forward, meeting our anticipations of theatricality as we join with those onstage, awaiting the opening of the casket. All attention rests urgently upon the single property; upon Exeter's face as he opens it, revealing the tennis balls; and then upon Henry's response, which, in Alan Howard's delivery, reveals a suddenly awakened sense of humor, pointed by a downstage smile as he shares his reaction with the audience, and a steadily freshening tone, ringing with purpose. The current of expectational energy, redirected by his language, now points firmly toward the eventual outcome of these moments. As the stage clears, the Chorus returns to report offstage preparations for war. He signals; trumpets call; and a colorful heraldic canopy billows out over the stage (literalizing the line, "For now sits expectation in the air"); a giant cannon rolls onto the upstage area; and actors gather about it, costuming themselves, arming for the war. The sense of presentational failure generated by our first visual and auditory impressions disappears completely, replaced by these brilliantly theatricalizing extensions of imaginative anticipation—exaggerations of expectation which command much of their effect because they have arisen from an original spareness.

Within this beginning sequence, the signals shaping our expectations vary in quality, shifting from language (the Chorus; the opening duologue; the following ensemble moments) to a physical action (the Ambassador's entrance) and then to a property (the casket) before being redirected once again by Henry's changed tone and his speech of resolution and by the formalizing report of the Chorus, which, in Hands's production, evokes visual spectacle. To summarize, Shakespeare's language functions, here, as a signal that "floats" a current of expectation which is then highlighted and further asserted by a sequence of visual emphases, accents either rigidly directed by the text or supplied by the specific aims of theatrical decisions.

On the page, we tend to think of Shakespeare's language as the most explicit directive of that particularly resonant patterning of expectations we call foreshadowing. We watch for those moments initiating future events, either by speeches of intent—"I shall do..."; "Early tomorrow we will rise, and hence"; "At the Duke's oak we meet"—or by statements such as Plantagenet's "...I dare say/ This quarrel will drink blood another day" (1 *Henry VI*, II. iv. 132-133) or the witches' more specific prophecies in *Macbeth*.[5] Yet in the theater, single gestures, properties, and costumes often isolate and direct expectation more effectively than language. In *The Merchant of Venice*, for example, the three caskets of gold, silver, and lead, because we have seen them before (perhaps in I. ii.; certainly in II. vii. and II. ix.), will take on an added urgency as Bassanio finally confronts them in III. ii. Similarly, Macbeth's or Antony's donning of armor presents signals which clearly presage the closeness of battle; and Cleopatra's command for her robe and crown and the sight of these (which, if he is careful, a director will keep from us until now) prepare for, qualify, and exaggerate our expectations, already aroused by her language, of her self-consciousness, and so set up our final impressions of her artifice. Any disguising, regardless of whether it is as simple as the maskings at the ball in *Much Ado About Nothing*, as playful as Rosalind's "change" to Ganymede in *As You Like It*, or as deeply suggestive as Kent's and Edgar's "persona changes" in *King Lear*, heightens our awareness for what may follow.

All of these signals do, of course, register meanings beyond those associated with directing or redirecting the channels of expectational energies within the play. And each meaning, as it is caught up and redefined within the choreography of individual scenes, becomes part of a continually expanding process of signification. Any one signal, in other words, has a particular liveliness in and of itself; yet it may also refer us backwards and forwards to compare or contrast other perceptions, forcing us to assess and reassess what we see—now drawing us toward a heightened involvement, now keeping us at a distance.

Shakespeare controls these shifting levels of involvement, both for actors and spectators, by juxtaposing one kind of scene against another within a play. Roughly, he directs four general types of scenes: ensemble scenes, duologues, soliloquies, and "free access" scenes—that is, those characterized by an open, informal structuring, often determined by location, and by the ability of characters to enter and leave freely. This last kind of scene may turn into a duologue or a soliloquy; it may also gather, through a series of entrances, toward an ensemble scene. In general, the "big" scenes spread and generalize the attention of both actors and audience, while duologues and soliloquies tighten energy exchange, intensifying perceptions.[6] Thus, again in very general terms, our impression of *1 Henry VI*, a play with a large proportion of ensemble scenes, differs from our impression of *Macbeth*, which gives us an immediate, continuing, and close look at its hero. But whatever the text may reveal about the relative proportion of each scenic type within individual plays, the configuration of performance depends, in the final analysis, upon Shakespeare's scoring of various kinds of moments within a scene, and upon how those scenes build into a larger sequence which may function as a whole rhythmic unit of meaning.

What are the possibilities for meaning in, for example, the final, long-awaited battle sequence (V. iv.–V. ix.) in *Troilus and Cressida?* Which events are played down; which are emphasized? Is the emphasis rigidly directed? Is there a choice of emphasis? Or are we asked to see all events in exactly the same way? Can the meanings of the sequence change? The entire action of the play, thus far, has repeatedly denied a battle-meeting between the Greeks and Trojans. And even as "excursions" commence in V. iv., we are at first aware only of Thersites' anticipations of seeing Troilus and Diomed "clapper-clawing one another"; and then we hear him derogate the "policy" of the Greeks. Appropriately, within this very talky play, a shadowy pass over the stage gives way to language which, although it directs us to watch for battle, delays that action temporarily. Briefly now, Troilus and Diomed fight; Hector rejects fighting with Thersites since he is no match for him in "blood and honor"; and Thersites leaves, looking for "the wenching rogues." The Troilus-Diomed fight, which interests us because it seems serious, is undercut by the Hector-Thersites encounter—we may even laugh at Hector's sizing-up of Thersites as one unworthy, and at Thersites' relief at being spared. Then, at Thersites' exit, Diomed re-enters, directing a servant to present Troilus' horse to Cressid. Very quickly, Shakespeare seems to release us from further involvement with a Troilus-Diomed conflict, freeing our attention for other possibilities of action. Yet what follows—three particularly formal, thumping reports by Agamemnon, Nestor, and Ulysses—represents a pausing movement which again delays and detracts from the forceful presentation of war. Then, suddenly, the stage explodes with entrances and exits: Ajax looking for Troilus;

Achilles looking for Hector; Ajax again; Diomed and then Troilus—renewing their earlier struggle. Individual speeches are full of questions: not only do the warriors have difficulty finding and recognizing each other, but they query the progress of the battle as well. These verbal uncertainties receive support from the bustling stage activity, demanding more and more abrupt shifts of vision. Then Hector and Achilles begin to fight—a combat that could decide the course of the action—but apparently Achilles drops or loses his sword or shield, and Hector allows a pause, which Achilles refuses, and exits. Troilus enters and quickly leaves; Hector pursues a Greek for his handsome armor. Now Achilles gathers his Myrmidons about him; and the next potentially significant confrontation—that between Paris and Menelaus—occurs within a brief pass over the stage, fighting, as Thersites comments: "The cuckold and the cuckold-maker are at it." The moment comes next to the last in the series of swift, almost emblematic encounters which precedes Hector's slaughter by Achilles and the Myrmidons, forming part of a building rhythm which pushes toward Hector's death and which is released almost immediately into the confusion of aftermath.

Shakespeare deliberately holds off the moment of Hector's death by managing a sequence of action punctuated by pauses or refusals to act: the whole rhythm is interruptive, and suggests imbalance, questioning, and the hesitancy and futility of this particular war. Although the text quite rigidly patterns and reinforces these notions, through both language and actual or implied stage directions, interpretative opportunities do exist which may further qualify areas of meaning. For instance, if the sequence is played on a darkened stage, the questioning and non-recognition will seem plausible; but if the stage is brightly lit (as I believe it should be), the warriors' uncertain encounterings will receive a different—and ironic—emphasis. Thus a choice of the overall visual emphasis central to the management of the scene can signal a rather drastic shift in meaning. Other possibilities—extending pauses, both for the rhetoric of the three "elder statesmen" and during the first Achilles-Hector meeting; taking or refusing opportunities for laughter—will alter meanings only slightly.

This short study of the *Troilus and Cressida* "battle" easily shows how Shakespeare manages some dimensions of this rhythm, or "movement,"[7] of the play. But going beyond simply determining whether a moment initiates, is in the middle of, or completes a sequence, and then of discovering verbal or nonverbal signals for pace, contrast, and emphasis within that sequence, we must also look at a sequence of performance in terms of how it conserves or releases energy. As a whole, does a sequence tend to hold in energy, or does it act as a vehicle for letting go whatever tensions have been built within the play? Specific moments of performance—one from film, two from stage productions—illustrate how certain signals activate energy conservation or release.

In Grigori Kozintsev's film of *King Lear* (1970), the opening ensemble scene receives a strictly formalized treatment: as the court assembles, the camera movements alternate between fairly full shots which frame the entire occasion and close-up or mid-close-up views of the various participants. Short cuts and forward camera movements balance the exaggerated framing of the close-ups, building a tensed rhythm which invites us to watch closely. But once Lear and Cordelia confront each other, the film builds to a steady, rhythmic series of punching close-up shots of their faces, allowing us to perceive, in minute detail, their reactions to each other. These views are widened slightly toward the end of the scene, but with little freeing of tension. Then, as Lear leaves the court and passes by men, horses, falcons, and dogs, choosing his train, we see a long, swift tracking shot which effectively releases our tightened viewpoint and disseminates the controlled intensity of the rather mechanically framed close-up views. That single thrust of energy, which we have seen held in and then let go, seems, within the film, to translate Lear's impulsive misjudgment and denial into a mammoth rushing movement which throws him headlong into the outside world.

In the same way, the opening scenes of Peter Brook's *A Midsummer Night's Dream*, characterized by extremely deliberate blocking and slow, careful treatment of the verse, further stylize and exaggerate the patterned, formalizing tensions already present in the text. Because this opening is so controlled, all energy gathers around and emanates from the verse, permitting and requiring increased attentiveness from both actors and spectators. As the performance builds, the early stilled poses of the actors reoccur—in the first moments between Lysander and Hermia, and in the initial meeting of Oberon and Titania—but gradually other playing styles—the sturdy, clumping comedy of the mechanicals; the fairies' seemingly effortless control over the stage, accentuated by the appearance of trapezes and by their watching positions on the catwalk surrounding the above-stage area; and the broadly physical comedy of Helena entrapping Demetrius with a series of tackles—activate increasingly larger areas of the stage. Then, as Titania's red feather "couch" lowers, she awakes and embraces Bottom, and he is suddenly raised aloft on the fairies' shoulders. One fairy thrusts an arm between Bottom's legs, forming an erect phallus; and as the fairies carry him off, the moment cues us into celebration: to the triumphant tones of the Mendelssohn wedding march, spinning plates and colored streamers zing out over the stage. Oberon swings across on a rope, nods to us and gestures to Puck, who begins to rake up the mess. The movement, excitement, surprise, and delight of these moments just preceding the interval effectively animate both stage and audience. The liveliness of the whole stage and the exaggerations of released energy seem exactly right, at this point, not only as the sharpest possible contrast to the subdued opening, but because the shifting performance styles have gradually prepared us to accept anything and everything.

At times, the contrast between held and released energies occurs even more quickly. In David Jones' recent revival of a 1973 production of *Love's Labor's Lost* (RSC), extremely stylized opening stage movements—Navarre and his fellow would-be "scholars" solemnly marching onstage, to a funereal melody, behind a coffin into which they throw, in turns, their courtly garments—prepares us for the further rituals of the verse. But just as we are becoming used to thinking in terms of artifice, Ian Richardson's Berowne mocks the repetitive tensions of the verse:

> *Light*, seeking *light*, doth *light* of *light* be*guile*;
> So ere you find where *light* in *dark*ness *lies*,
> Your *light* grows *dark* by *los*ing of your *eyes*.
>
> (I. i. 77–79)

The lines are spoken rapidly and easily, all in one breath, with a slight pause and rising emphasis marking the end rimes; Richardson points each "light" by a gesture of his hand, as if to distinguish between them; finally, he stumbles forward, as though speaking the lines required an overwhelming effort. By calling attention to his own artificiality, Richardson's Berowne asks us to accept the self-irony of the character and to understand his artificiality as a condition of the play which he, as an actor, finds rather ridiculous. The double acknowledgement releases our own energies to focus upon other dramatic signals.

In each of the performance sequences above, theatrical choices emphasize certain of the accessible dramatic signals, highlighting precise shifts of tension. In the *Lear* film, the rigidly patterned confrontation between father and daughter seems to cause a direct release of plot energy into action as Lear leaves the court; in the *Dream*, the careful verse speaking and the contrasted playing styles enliven particular moments of the text, asking for quickly fluctuating responses; Richardson's playing of Berowne characterizes the deliberate mannerisms of the play's language, allowing us to relax into its contrivances. Significantly, none of these choices represents a "right," a "wrong," or an "only" way to play the moments: each simply reflects a decision to give performance value to specific areas of the text.

As we look back to the text from such moments of performance, we are freshly aware of the signals available for focusing attention upon changing levels of presentation. Terry Hands speaks of rehearsing *Henry V* as a "why-how-result process . . . endlessly regenerating the next stage of character and narrative evolution."[8] Following his lead, we might explore levels of focus within a "what-who-how" framework, thus revealing the process through which Shakespeare's various dramatic signals direct our perceptions, lead us from one stage image to another of equal complexity, and ask us to evaluate a moment both on its own terms and in the light of other moments which may present resemblances or echoes.

Within the *what* of a particular moment, the event itself acts as a kind of structural support for other kinds of communication. Often, a primary focus upon an event as some sort of special occasion demands realization within a stage picture; what we see on the stage will often clarify and settle the significance of the moment in our memory, usually through directing our attention to formalized spectacle—as, for example, in *Richard II*, I. iii., the lists at Coventry—or through some comparably "imagic" level of presentation, such as the wedding masques in *As You Like It*, V. iv. and *The Tempest*, IV. i; the Ghosts in *Richard III*, V. iii.; or the witches in *Macbeth*, I.i., I. iii., and IV. i. But in other moments, such as *Macbeth*, I. v., the letter scene, focus rests primarily upon the *who* of a moment. In general terms, the "what" focus tends to widen and distance our perception and to make one level of meaning easily available through sight alone. On the other hand, the "who" focus particularizes our attention and demands not only a closer observation of facial expressions, gestures, and movements, but a more careful awareness of the language. Obviously, in each of the scenes mentioned above, meaning is not confined to a single level of focus. Since Shakespeare tends to measure sight by sound, an initially eloquent display based primarily upon visual and spatial energies may dissolve flexibly into the deeper ranges of meaning conveyed by various types of language—language which may direct and accentuate one or several gestures, either specifically indicated or implied by the text; and which may control the relative stasis or activity of the stage. Ultimately, the potential range of both energy and meaning—the *how* of a moment—becomes available to the spectator only through practical theatrical decisions made by actors and directors. The way toward the stage realization, however, entails a careful study not only of all the signals within a moment itself but of those signals preceding it, of those that it generates, and of what echoes it produces. The duologue between Antony and Enobarbus in *Antony and Cleopatra*, I. i. 131-197 offers an example for analysis.

The moment occurs toward the end of the first short rhythm of the play—the first "Egyptian" sequence—and it is one of the initial private encounters in the play. We have seen and heard Antony and Cleopatra together in public in the opening scene, where we have been told that we will see "the triple pillar of the world transform'd/ Into a strumpet's fool." And although we have seen a brief illustration of the "strumpet's fool," as yet our only image of Antony as a "pillar" is as Cleopatra's pillar; but she has just avoided his presence (I. ii. 87). Coming to this moment, Cleopatra has seemed in control of shaping the play; her quick exit with Enobarbus and her train releases our attention for Antony's presence. The speech rhythms have shifted from the easy prose of the servents' joking over the soothsayer's fortune-telling back to verse when Antony enters with a messenger. And as a second messenger enters, bringing Antony the news of Fulvia's death, the scene continues in verse, indicative of an increasing formalization in these essentially narrative moments which Antony, alone on the stage, defines even further by soliloquizing upon his wife's death. Our expectations center on and with Antony at this moment, and are unsettled, hesitant: focus is intense, subjective, and inward, resting primarily upon language and upon developing character—the *who* of the moment. And because this is the first moment of significant visual stasis thus far into the action, perceptually we may sense a pause, a possible resolution. As for Enobarbus, he perhaps comes to Antony a bit drunk (inferred from line 12) and slightly bemused by Cleopatra's command to him to seek Antony, by her sudden reversal, and by his exit with her (being swept along with her train?). Once Enobarbus joins Antony (I. ii. 130), verse gives way once again to prose, suggesting informality, "naturalism," and a relaxed intimacy. These reduced tensions within the language signal a matching ease within the stage image—Antony and Enobarbus close enough together to permit this "locker-room" talk. Twice, before Enobarbus' entrance, Antony has said that he must break with Cleopatra; his first words to Enobarbus are "I must with haste from hence." Everything that he says thereafter, aside from repeating the news of Fulvia's death, indicates an intention to go; yet he stays to listen to Enobarbus and (probably) to chuckle with him. Thus Antony's very presence speaks against his intent: and if Antony's split between "must go" and "needs stay" is capitalized upon, as in Trevor Nunn's 1974 television production (RSC), by the sight of Antony and Enobarbus reclining lethargically on cushions, then we see a stage picture which realizes fully a possible comic overtone. Enobarbus' bawdy punning further centers the comedy of the moment; yet underneath the fun of appreciating this language for its own sake, we carry away from the scene a reinforced sense of Cleopatra's control. Antony must "get her leave to part"; he justifies his decision at some length, choosing to formalize and intensify that decision by speaking in verse, and seems to turn the matter over to Enobarbus. Essentially, the moment confirms our sense of Cleopatra's power over Antony; but this is in turn qualified by Antony's reaction to Fulvia's death; and our expectations remain open, awaiting some resolution in the promised encounter with Cleopatra. And this happens almost immediately; for, in the ensuing moments, we see a "sick and sullen" Cleopatra, about to "die."

As for the echoing effects, we can identify several "feeling analogues" within the play: I. v. and II. v., where Cleopatra is dreaming to her women about Antony (moments which are themselves re-seen in V. ii., when Cleopatra tells Dolabella that she "dreamt there was an Emperor Antony"), and the closing moments of II. ii., where Agrippa and Maecenas pump Enobarbus about "what Egypt was really like," pick up the "locker-room" tone initiated here. But of course the most obvious reverberations occur toward the end of the play: Cleopatra's faked death (IV. xiii.) draws us back to these moments when death was only a joke; Antony's suicide on his sword (IV. xiv.) is an ugly tragic pun on Enobarbus' "light answers"; and Cleopatra seems, at the last, to exemplify passions that are indeed "the finest part of pure love." Thus a seemingly innocent comic moment resolves itself into the system of the play, becoming an urgent prophecy of future tragedy. And in a sense, this kind of metamorphosis governs not only the energies of moments within the play but the energies of our responses as well.[9]

In explaining the *how* of this moment, we have been looking primarily at the sense of the language—what is being said and why—and at the techniques of utterance—the formality of verse, the more relaxed tensions of prose—as signals which channel the energies of both actors and spectators. Such verbal signals often seem to dominate and direct the playing of individual moments; we have also seen that they provide clues for the management of stage space.

When a scene depends, in part, upon distinguishing formalized relationships—a king seen in relation to his court, for example—these ceremonial spatial relationships, usually broadly indicated by stage directions and further ordered by the language, register important areas of meaning. The opening and closing scenes of *Richard II* illustrate a significant patterning of such spatial energies. Both are formal court scenes in which Richard and Bullingbrook, surrounded by "other nobles and attendants," share the center of attention. In each scene, too, the King's uncle is present—John of Gaunt in I. i.; the Duke of York in V. vi. Gaunt speaks a few lines; York is a silent presence—a change which registers, in little, both onstage and offstage reaction to the events of the play. The opening scene, with Richard in command as Bullingbrook pleads for the occasion to prove Mowbray's treason, is deliberately patterned toward ceremony:

its 205 lines separate into speeches of nearly equal length as
Mowbray and Bullingbrook accuse each other. Richard, here,
questions and comments upon their speeches, so that although
our attention focuses now on Bullingbrook, now on Mowbray,
we are always centered again by Richard's control, which he
reinforces by cuing both his own language and that of the others
into rhyming couplets at line 156: "Forget, forgive, conclude and
be agreed,/ Our doctors say this is no month to bleed." Thus two
opposed energies play against each other: although we realize
that no decision has been made, the heavy rimes of the language
contribute a sense of distance, finality, and closure.

At the end of the play, all seems changed: Bullingbrook is
King; and the first half of this short (52 lines) scene is busily
interruptive, as Northumberland, Fitzwater, and Harry Percy
(with the Bishop of Carlisle) enter in quick succession and King
Henry assigns praise or doom. In part, we will perceive this
patterning as characteristic of Henry's informality and ease, so
that comparing these moments to the play's opening gives us a
final register for comprehending the shift from Richard's verbal
excesses and parentheses (and those of others when he is in
control) and his indecisiveness to Bullingbrook's more direct
speech and action. But once Exton enters with attendants bearing Richard's coffin, we become aware of further expressive
links—both verbal and nonverbal—between the opening and
closing moments, at once reinforcing and qualifying a sense of
constancy. Mowbray and Exton are parallel figures—both have
committed similar deeds. Mowbray will be banished in I. iii.;
Exton is summarily sent from court (although he does not leave)
in V. vi. And as Bullingbrook banishes Exton and expresses his
grief and his intent to make a pilgrimage to the Holy Land, he
now speaks in successive rhyming couplets, suggesting that he
has, at least for the occasion, taken on Richard's earlier verbal
formality.

If at times Shakespeare exercises rigid control over stage
space, at others the definition of spatial relationships remains
"free"—in the hands of the actors. In *Macbeth* I. v., for example,
Lady Macbeth, after reading Macbeth's letter and receiving news
of the King's arrival, sinks into a violent invocation as she summons "spirits that tend on mortal thoughts." Macbeth's entrance
interrupts her speech at mid-line; the moment offers a number of

potential choices. Does Lady Macbeth move toward him eagerly and immediately and embrace him? Or does she start toward him and stop short of an embrace, either because she is waiting for him to move or because she cannot bring herself any closer? Or does she only turn, perhaps startled by the sound of footsteps, but still so wrapt within herself that she seems unable to move? Each choice (and these are only a few of many possibilities) gives us a different Lady Macbeth. If we see the Macbeths as close at this point, their later separation will have one meaning; if we see either a hesitancy or a degree of inward reserve or isolation between the two here, each gesture may develop, within the continuum of performance, to emphasize other meanings. How does Macbeth himself react? Does he go directly to his wife and embrace her, without regard for whatever state she may be in? Or does he go toward her only to be stopped by her unresponsiveness? However managed, the space existing between the actors here is "poetic space," in itself communicating an image as essential to performance as are the images arising from language—such as the evocations of the Chorus in *Henry V* or the rapid succession of images comprising Clarence's dream in *Richard III.*, I. iv.—which ask us to imagine things, events, and spaces lying beyond the stage.

Consistently, Shakespeare creates a comprehensive spatial poetry which becomes an active presence within the play, clarifying and defining not only the actors' attitudes and responses but those of the audience as well. One dimension of spatial meaning in *The Winter's Tale*, for example, lies in both the literal and imaginative distance between Leontes and Hermione. They are together at the play's beginning, yet almost immediately they draw apart: Leontes sends Hermione to prison, she returns for her trial and "dies." Their separation, both physical and metaphorical, governs the middle emphases of the play, which illustrate other separations or possible separations, similarly involving both death and desire—Antigonus dies; Perdita is abandoned; Polyxenes and Florizel part; Florizel and Perdita are threatened with parting. Then, in the final moments of the play, as Hermione descends from her pedestal and moves toward Leontes, all meaning rests within the physical distance between them—once seemingly insurmountable and now gradually, inevitably, closing before our eyes, summarizing more surely than language the essence of the play's experience.

If the final dissolution of space between Hermione and Leontes shows us a tiny icon of renewal, the spatial poetry of *Romeo and Juliet* continually reminds both actors and spectators of the fragility of union. Broadly, Shakespeare conceives his play in terms of challenge and conflict, of harmony and disharmony of movement, energies which are further exaggerated by the central spatial fact upon which the action rests—the invasion of each family's "territory" by the other. Active spatial conflict dominates the opening moments: the Samson-Gregory and Tybalt-Benvolio fights confront us immediately with deliberately kinesthetic images of bodies in motion, moving toward each other only through conflict. But as the play develops, and Romeo and Juliet "confront" each other, we observe them in particularly static, though resonant situations—meeting at the ball in I. v., on the balcony in II. ii., and then at Friar Laurence's cell in II. vi. to be married; parting at dawn in III. v.; joining in death at the play's ending. Within each moment, the lovers speak an unusually charged poetry, expanding the quiet, "listening" confines of the space between them so that these "stock" situations seem measured by an electrifying lyricism.

Yet at the same time that speech draws the lovers together, their desire for physical contact is qualified, questioned, or prevented in each of the scenes they share: their union seems expressible only in terms of a spatial poetry of parting. When the lovers are apart, these dimensions of the poetry disseminate, spilling over into the other spaces of the play: following the balcony scene, Mercutio and Romeo indulge in verbal feud in II. iv., a feud which affirms their closeness; Romeo and Juliet's marriage receives its onstage consummation in the Tybalt–Mercutio battle. Thus the fluent, rhythmic concord established by the verbal energies of the lovers seems to receive expression in near-physical or physical conflict which both releases our desire for action and contributes to a tightened sense of the inharmonious harmony of physical contact. This double tension persists even in the closing moments of the play, so that our controlling impression, in spite of all else that we may have seen, is of a central duet, finally silenced but still containing the juxtaposed energies of impossible union. And as the mourning and guilts of the living receive expression, the final gesture—a handclasp—and the last promise—to raise fine golden statues of the lovers—hauntingly suggest how incompletely all have understood.

In both *The Winter's Tale* and *Romeo and Juliet*, spatial poetry is just one of many signals that ask us to reassess previous moments and to draw all that we have seen and heard together, assisting at a final synthesis. In each play, one area of meaning rests firmly upon the last moments—and more specifically so as they seem to echo back through the entire performance. Similarly, the final moments of *Much Ado About Nothing*, conventionally mechanical as they may seem, afford an opportunity to recall, in retrospect, most of the play. In spite of all the artificiality, disguising, and pretense preceding the "set-up" ending, the moments are essentially "realistic"—that is, the language approaches naturalistic discourse, quickly arranging narrative flow, pointing toward a conclusion. As Claudio accepts Hero and she unmasks, we may recall the earlier masked dancing at the ball in II. i. as well as the quick tragedy "masking" her former wedding and prompting the funeral rites. And just as this gesture asks us to review other parts of the action, and to see a concluding harmony, the final exchange between Beatrice and Benedick reviews their essential attitudes toward each other before the play resolves into concord. The dialogue moves toward resolution as Benedick asks, "Which is Beatrice?" She unmasks, inquiring, "What is your will?"—a question the Beatrice of I. i. would not, could not, have asked, except in jest. But now Benedick comes close to marring all: he does not state "I love you"; rather, his question, "Do not you love me?" returns us, and Beatrice, who replies, "Why no, no more than reason," to their initial Mexican stand-off. It is up to the others—Leonato, Claudio, and Hero—just as it was before, to affirm that Beatrice and Benedick love one another and to trick them so that they do take hands, and so that Benedick finally commits himself to a public kiss. But there is no more talk of love, only of "Benedick the married man," of friendship and kinship, of dancing and of music. The courtship seems still to be in progress, this time with the willing assistance of all involved—an assistance which affirms a reciprocal understanding that the energies released by the actors within the play may travel beyond it to reach the audience.

Just as Shakespeare manipulates the co-existence of opposite and conflicting energies within his playtexts, so must we, in practical terms, expect and demand opposed and contradictory approaches to co-exist within both our imagined and realized performances. Inevitably, identifying, understanding, and interpreting the various signals which direct the stage realization of a Shakespearean text will further validate the study of performance as a discipline, and freshen the ambivalence of our responses. Perhaps eventually we will find more precise ways to measure the signals of a particular moment; to assign a relative order of dominance of language, gestures, actions, and stage pictures, determining how each influences the spectator's perception; and to assess how, and to what extent, a scene builds into the comprehensive "system" of the play. Perhaps, too, we will be able to speak, as the film semiotician is learning to, of codes of color, shape, space, light, sound effects, and music within individual productions, relating these, in turn, to the text. Or, extending our questioning further, we may attempt to uncover the process of selection that orders individual plays or groups of plays—comedies, histories, tragedies, romances— giving them a special character. What, for example, are the general possibilities for meaning in an ensemble, or gathering scene? And what function does this kind of scene play when it is preceded or followed by a soliloquy, by a duologue, by movement, or by stasis? Is the effect different in different plays? Or is it always the same?

Whatever questions arise, and whatever procedures or schemata we may employ in order to find answers, we must guard against developing a method so "scientific" that it excludes affective perceptions and leads us to standardize and stabilize the conditions of "ideal" or "perfect" performance. Rather, our search for the performance present should become an effort toward opening up and realizing the various opportunities for expression at any one given moment within the performed play.

Notes

1. Quoted by Ronald Hayman, ed., in *Playback* (London: Davis-Poynter Limited, 1973), p. 95.

2. J.L. Styan, in *Drama, Stage and Audience* (Cambridge: Cambridge University Press, 1975) refers throughout to the "signals" present in a dramatic text; in some senses, I echo his use of the term.

3. Michael Goldman locates dramatic energies within the double awareness of bodies—the actors' and our own—which characterizes the dramatic experience, arguing that we must "grow separately sensitive to the presence of each of the strands of feeling that run between actors and audience." *Shakespeare and the Energies of Drama* (Princeton: Princeton University Press, 1972), p. 6. As I use the term "energy," I am attempting to give it "a local habitation and a name."

4. Bertrand Evans, *Shakespeare's Comedies* (Oxford: Oxford University Press, 1967).

5. All references to the plays follow *The Riverside Shakespeare* (Boston: Houghton Mifflin Company, 1974).

6. John Russell Brown, in *Shakespeare's Plays in Performance* (London: Edward Arnold, Ltd., 1966), broadly characterizes dramatic focus as either wide or intense. See especially pp. 129–130.

7. Harley Granville-Barker, in his *Prefaces to Shakespeare*, Vols. I–IV (Princeton: Princeton University Press, 1946–1963), was the first to speak of "movements" within a play. Recently, Emrys Jones, in *Scenic Form in Shakespeare* (Oxford: The Clarendon Press, 1971) has further extended the use of the term.

8. Terry Hands, "An Introduction to the Play," in *The Royal Shakespeare Company's Production of 'Henry V' for the Centenary Season at the Royal Shakespeare Theatre*, ed. Sally Beauman (Oxford: Pergamon Press, 1976), pp. 17–18.

9. Janet Adelman, in *The Common Liar* (New Haven: Yale University Press, 1973), speaks of this transforming process as a device which constantly requires us to reinterpret and reassess our experience of the play.

Poetry of the Theater

MARVIN ROSENBERG

Is there in fact, to use Cocteau's words, a poetry *of* the theater that can be distinguished from poetry *in* the theater? Is it possible to isolate in conventional drama a nonverbal symbolic structure that parallels the effects and architecture of verbal poetry?

Shakespeare offers the best laboratory to test the hypothesis. How the gestures of his dramatic language were shaped into poetic patterns has been often explored; what of the visual and aural gestures that intimately support the poetic scaffold? Of course Shakespeare, as poet in and of the theater, fused his imageries of word, sight, and sound much too tightly for any one of them to be known separately; but scholars and critics, myself included, have long been impudent enough to try to isolate his verbal poetry for study; I will here essay the visual-aural.

Consider this definition of the language of dramatic poetry:

> Dramatic poetry is an organic structure of verbal symbols, with associated sounds, rich in denotative detail and connotative reverberation and ambiguity, often presented in recurrent, rhythmic patterns and changing perspectives that accumulate and extend the power of the whole to stimulate feeling, thought, and kinesthetic response in its audience.

How does this definition apply to Shakespeare's visual imagery and, in association, the imagery of sound: the subverbal

This essay was previously printed in *Costerus*, III(1972), 211-219. A different version appears in Marvin Rosenberg's *The Masks of King Lear* (Berkeley: University of California Press, 1972), pp. 336-345. Reprinted with permission. Quotations follow, generally, the Arden edition of *King Lear*, ed. Kenneth Muir.

poetry of cries, howls, barks, trumpets and similar music? The best way to approach Shakespeare's composition in spectacle is to imagine a play—I will use *King Lear* as an example—as a *mime*, with only those non-verbal sounds that are linked to the action. This will enable us to discern, in relief, something of the poetry of Shakespeare's gestures.

For an easy bridge to this imagining, I will concentrate on a single motif in the *Lear* language: the familiar motif of seeing. Every literate reader of *Lear* has followed the orchestration of the idea through the network of such words as *see, sight, blindness, look, looking-glass,* and has sensed the growing reverberative implications for perception, understanding, insight, knowing, and their opposites. These implications converge in Gloster's focal speech

I see feelingly.

On one level, the blind man actually reaches out to Lear, and so sees him in his touch. But Gloster's way of seeing, as well as his words, suggests that he feels he has insight, he understands what is not visible, he does so with his feelings, and he does so very well. A further shadow persists—Gloster does not, even inwardly, really see well. The words say some of this, but words are often seen to fail in *Lear* (and elsewhere in Shakespeare), and sight-sound imagery must complete the communication, especially when latent, subconscious impulses must be conveyed.

The scene resonates with visual, as well as verbal, echoes. Shakespeare has created a string of "speaking pictures," every line and shape of which say something to the mind. We in this century are learning to demonstrate experimentally what visual artists like Shakespeare have always understood: that the eye *thinks*, it selects what things or what parts of things it will see, and brings to their interpretation a tremendous store of funded information and preconception. The hieroglyph, the pictograph, in our day the cartoon, more relevantly the Elizabethan emblem are examples of single visual symbolic structures that carry implications far beyond their components. The very components are eloquent. A simple straight line implies one thing; torture the line, and it says something else. Once figures become representational, as in Shakespeare's work they are, they are burdened with social meaning. Some attempts have been made to reduce Shakespeare's speaking pictures to the terms of contemporary emblems; but as an artist he was always breaking and restructuring the familiar. Thus he provided many royal tableaux, but even in the histories they were visually tensed and discolored with ambiguities of character and situation. More: as the artist shifted perspectives with his startling visual designs, he also used these images—as he used verbal images—in rhythmic and recurrent patterns. The images changed in light, line, color, and shape; their implications and ambiguities widened as the plays progressed. Thus, in our *Lear* mime, the first royal tableau would be refracted in succeeding images that hollowed, mocked, and grotesquely inverted the initial experience.

Let us return to the specific visualized act of seeing. In our life, the act is so central to our way of knowing our world, and particularly the people in it, that any theater representation is charged with allusion. Shakespeare exploited the act from his very first plays. In *Comedy of Errors*, many "see" words and acts help centrally to complicate and solve the puzzle of mistaken identity. In later plays, as deception grows inward, and more inward, words of seeing and insight are more subtly mated and polarized, and associated with visual images that confuse reality and appearance. The "ocular proof" Iago promises is meant to deceive. Macbeth's speech to the knife is loaded with *see* words—he finally knows the knife is there because he *sees* it—but it is not there. On the stage, the simple visual act of *looking* may be powerfully dramatic. For one character to lock eyes with another, or avoid this, in silence or in speech, may be rich in ambiguity, stir deep responses. No words are needed to convey the potential of an exchange of speaking looks, as—to give an obvious example—between Edmund and Goneril. In a great actor's face, the complex of feeling can converge in such singleness of passions as to be frightening; conversely, his fluid face may reveal multiple-layered, struggling impulses. For Lear to look, to see, to try to understand and identify, is peculiarly characteristic; and each seeing adds to the others, extends the implication of the act.

In the first scene this will become apparent as Lear glances at the other characters, while addressing them. Here the playwright is partly, as craftsman, identifying the characters for the audience; but he is also saying something about them, and their relationship to Lear; and he is developing Lear's special way of scrutinizing those he addresses—Lear himself will have something to say about that later on. In his madness, asked if he is the king, he notes a distinguishing characteristic:

> Ay, every inch a king.
> When I do stare, see how the subject quakes.

At some level of his consciousness, Lear always tests, with his look, the submission of his subjects. This will be apparent, without words, in the special and different way he looks in the first scene at the subservient Gloster, the "fiery" Cornwall, the uncertain Albany, the masked Regan and Goneril, the withdrawn Cordelia. His act of scrutinizing will set off ripples of ambiguity in the recurrent motifs of appearance and reality, of disguise and disclosure, of the success and failure of this primary way of knowing.

In a *Lear* mime, we would observe at once a quality that actors of Lear have sometimes accentuated in the play—the mystery of Lear's seeing—by seeming to look at the court about them, and all else, with an almost painful intensity, as if indeed Lear's physical capacity to see was strained—as in fact it would fail. Some actors have also seemed to look beyond what they saw, as if trying to discern something not present, as if looking into another world. In the first scene, our mime audience does not need Lear's words to know that Lear will believe what he sees: and that what he sees in Goneril and Regan satisfies him. What he sees in Cordelia—however hard he looks—does not satisfy him. Then he makes a negative seeing gesture, often to be repeated—*out of my sight*. He will look elsewhere, cover his eyes, wave away what is present—if he does not like it, he will not see what is there.

On the other hand, he will look upward toward invisible powers, and seem to command them, as he would command the people around him. Here, he seems indeed to see into a world beyond reason—a vision that will be inverted ironically later.

The visual imagery of Lear's scrutiny of his world will be echoed and orchestrated in mimes with the disguised figures he encounters: first the banished Kent, whom he examines so closely in Act I, Scene iv. Shakespeare's design of suspense includes the possibility that Lear will recognize this disguised old friend, now called enemy, who must die if discovered: so the scrutiny functions in the action as well as the character. The seeing symbolism partly is extended by Lear's need to assure himself of *his* identity, to know *he* is there. This is central to his confrontations with Oswald, Fool, Goneril. *Who am I, sir? Dost thou call me Fool, boy? Does Lear walk thus? Speak thus?* In our mime, we know, without speech, that he is *looking* for some assurance of who he is. It is himself he is trying to see.

Slowly Lear's way of seeing changes; the rhythm alters. When he banished Cordelia, he looked confidently to unseen powers of night and day to endorse his oath of excommunication. When he calls on the unseen to curse Goneril, he looks with appeal, and his eyes are misted now; physically he cannot see so well because of tears, his eyes betray him, he may be seen to threaten them with plucking out; and yet on his face a new seeing begins to be visible, that reflects, "I did her wrong."

Charged as his glance is with anger and contempt, as when in Act II, Scene iv, he confronts Kent in the stock, as when Gloster servilely keeps him outside the castle door, he yet looks with some insecurity at the approach of Regan, and with even more when Goneril appears. His face reflects many ways of seeing at once because he is designed to experience many feelings at once. He is reduced to glancing helplessly from one to the other daughter as they beat down the number of the knights; and when next he speaks to the unseen powers, he is much less certain, his questing eyes beseech support. Again these organs of his sight cloud with tears; but we see that Lear has nevertheless begun to see reality beneath surfaces.

In the storm, he defies the invisible powers, but also defends himself against them, asks for pity—"you see me here," he gestures—for what he sees as himself: poor, weak, infirm, despised. Raindrops join teardrops in blurring his sight; and yet a better vision becomes possible to him, the light of it shows on his face, and he kneels to pray. For a moment we see that in this dark night Lear sees better.

Then his eyes find Mad Tom, and he slides into madness; and the mime emphasizes a curious, ironic change that happens in his seeing. He sees things no man else sees, but he seems to see them more sharply, more craftily than he ever saw before. The base of his knowing, and of ours, as we experience with him, is altered—herein lies much of the power of mad scenes. Lear examines Mad Tom with the same care he gave to the scrutiny of Kent; yet he sees him in a different way. The uncertainties of the rational seeing are replaced by the certainties of the irrational. With this, values are reversed. Where before we saw that Lear saw beauty in robes and furred gowns, he now discovers it in rags and nakedness.

Before, he spoke to invisible powers he saw in space; now, mad, he speaks to invisible hallucinations he sees in space. Handy-dandy—a god or hallucination—is one any more real than the other? And behind this ambiguity lurks another; the eyes that seem to see Edgar, and then Gloster, for what they are *not* may, on some level, in fact see them for what they are. The line between reason and unreason may dissolve in cunning, or accident, or naturally. These uncertainties are latent in the text; they are made visual in Lear's looking, for instance, at Gloster in Act IV, Scene vi; the face to face searching of the bloody sockets as Gloster peers sightlessly—seeingly—into Lear's eyes. What is it that the empty eyes see that shocks Lear into admitting some awareness of reality?[1] Silences—those punctuation marks of visual language that are often more powerful than any words or acts in the dramatic art—accent the process of Lear's mad seeing. His staring.

Ay, every inch a king.

This is a mock king, a fool king, in a crown of weeds; one subject now, Gloster, may quake before him. When he was a real king, the subjects he wanted to quake did not. The stare, now, stirs ironic reverberations of the earlier unavailing look.

The mad king weeps, but the tears do not clear his sight now. Only when the great rage is stilled can he open his eyes in reason again; and then he can hardly believe what he sees. He touches Cordelia's weeping eyes, in an echo of his gesture to Gloster—eyes are for weeping, as well as seeing, whether blind or not. He must try to reestablish a base in knowing, try to see himself again, try to believe the hands he holds up before his eyes are his own. When Cordelia is dead, at the very end, his sight in fact begins to fail, he can hardly see what to believe, cannot recognize an old friend. A dull sight.

He dies on an ambiguity. He sees something—points—(we don't need the words, *Look there, look there*—) and only the visual and subverbal poetry sustains the action now, all else fades away. What Lear sees in Cordelia's face—vision, illusion, joy, horror, or a mixture of all of them—can be known *only* by what his face tells us his eyes see. And somehow, this will be another refraction of the whole preceding, accumulating visual imagery of seeing-knowing.

Seeing involves an act. Some inanimate visual images in the play carry a heavy load of symbolism almost by themselves. One of these is the crown. It is hardly mentioned; and yet it is a centrally significant image in the ironic reversal in which the most powerful are seen to be degraded, robes and furred gowns exchanged for rags, the regal gestures once made with a royal sceptre now parodied by a disheveled madman with a baton of straw. In the complex interweaving of change and loss of garments, where fugitives disguise themselves downward to lower station or divest themselves of opulence while upstarts take on the gorgeous dress and ornaments of higher rank, the crown is a pivotal symbol.

Lear wears it in the first scene. He might continue to wear it as one of the "additions" to a king, and if so, with so much more irony does he carry this ornament charged with authority, now meaningless. More likely he does not wear it again, hunting, or riding in the night toward Regan; he dashes out into the storm, and runs unbonneted. The next reference is to the weedy circlet he will be seen to wear in Act IV, Scene vi.; but there may be other visual allusions to it. To one great Russian actor of Lear, the crown's presence was felt most in its absence; after the first scene, when he let it go he would reach up, in a habitual gesture, to reassure himself that it was there—and it was not. A German actor, in the trial scene, Act III, Scene vi., took up a three-legged copper pot, and put it upside down on his head, so that its legs simulated a crown, a simulated power image for simulated authority. The flowered madman's crown, made of plants related to mindsickness, is the primary visual symbol of the irony of surface values. Lear's gestures as he asserts his mad kingship may be exactly the same as those he made in Act I, Scene i.—gestures of magnanimity, authority, power, rage—but now they make only a grotesque charade.

The reappearance and shifting of the real crown can convey the ambiguities of power's meaning, as we could not help but see in a wordless mime. Cordelia may restore a crown to Lear in Act IV, Scene vii. — she is concentrating on making him feel his royal strength again. He may wear it in the brief passing over with the army at the beginning of Act V, before he and Cordelia are captured. Then Edmund, their captor, will take it, and try it—and in this gesture make visual the whole scheme of the king's fall intersecting the bastard's rise to within one planned murder—Albany's—of a kingship. The crown will fit Edmund; but Albany will take it from him, and again a resonant symbolic visual act will be performed: Albany will try to give the crown back to Lear, but now to the true king the piece of metal is as nothing. Albany will momentarily try it himself; but being, as the Quarto has Edmund say, *full of abdication and self-reproving*, he will offer to divide it between two rulers, Edgar and Kent: a ghastly repetition of the first scene—as indeed the whole ending is visually a symbolic reprise of the assembled court at the beginning. Edgar will accept reluctantly the ultimate symbol of power; in the context of this royal tableau of corpses, he is king of the dead.

None of these kaleidoscopic "speaking pictures" can be taken as moral or philosophical statements. They are poetic images, open ended, reverberant, ambiguous. The crown is real, and carries real authority; it may also be utterly without value, or dangerous, blinding, subversive. The very power the crown symbolizes is, in its absoluteness, disastrously linked to infantile fantasy: anyone but a child can see that he is not everything. Yet the crown must be worn.

For discussion, I have isolated the developing images of a symbolic act and of a symbolic thing. In fact, they cannot be separated from each other, as they cannot be separated from the interwoven verbal images. Lear's seeing is one aspect of a total character design that reflects a larger design in the play: the necessity and difficulty of seeing to know. Characters strain to see in the dark, in the storm. Again and again they look off to see what mystery, what danger, approaches. No language is needed to convey to us the persistent alarm as to identity: *What's he? Who's there? What are you there?* One of the oldest techniques of the theater craftsman, to compel the actors—and hence the audience—to look toward an entrance in anticipation or dread, is repeatedly employed, in appearances by Edgar, Goneril, Regan, Mad Tom, Gloster, Gentleman. All the actors, like Lear, try to look, see, know. What they see may, in a purely visual stroke, defeat their hopes: Albany, in a prayerful gesture to the gods, begs Cordelia's safety, Lear enters bearing her corpse. In the theater, Lear sometimes dies with his eyes open, unseeing and someone must close them—a final irony.

Seeing and knowing are never certain in *Lear*, for the play's dialectic insists on ambiguity. Lear's character design, sustained by conflicting and even contradictory qualities, emerges in all his visual manifestations. In a clear light of mime we would see that Lear sees and does not see. He wishes others banished from his sight, and he wishes them by him. When sane, he sometimes looks as if mad; when mad, as if sane. His gestures—as well as his words—would be qualified by what we see him do: when his refusal to see is frustrated—as it invariably is—it is associated with another pervasive visual image: of flight. Men constantly flee pursuit in *Lear*, but he who flees most is Lear himself, who first ordered Kent to fly. A mime would stress how much Lear flees, phychically as well as physically. Lear tries to banish resistance from his sight but, failing, he always flees confrontation—until finally Cordelia has caught him, and they kneel to each other.

Each repetition of a visual image takes on new meaning in a context that becomes more dense and complex as perspectives accumulate. How Lear kneels in serious prayer refracts the implications of his daughters' initial kneeling to him, of the kneeling of his courtiers, of his mock kneeling to Regan, of Gloster's blind kneeling to him, of his kneeling with Cordelia, of his kneeling over her dead body. So with other symbolic acts, such as putting on or off clothes, weeping, threatening, playing animal, fleeing pursuit, suffering pain, dying.

These images then, and their associated sounds, support an organic structure of symbols rich in denotative detail and connotative reverberation and ambiguity, in rhythmic and recurrent patterns and changing perspectives that accumulate and extend the power of the whole to stimulate feeling, thought, and kinesthetic response in its audience. They can only be known in performance: the minds eye, imagining *Lear*'s physical action, can never recreate the totality of the visual poetry that the eye's mind, in the theater, experiences and organizes.

Notes

1. Gloster's own failure to see is powerfully visual. He does not, in fact, see feelingly. Without eyes, he is seen to be nearly helpless. He cannot tell the identity of his guide, cannot know high ground from low, can be led anywhere, deceived anyhow. Edgar for ambiguous purposes of his own deliberately baffles Gloster's attempts to perceive reality through ears and body sense. If eyes are no guarantee of seeing, neither is blindness.

Choreography and Language in *Richard II*

PHILIP C. McGUIRE

Richard II offers striking evidence of the insights generated by that intense focus upon the language of Shakespeare's plays which has been a salient feature of Shakespearean criticism for several decades. Clemen, Altick, and Suzman are among those who have persuasively linked patterns in the verbal imagery of *Richard II* to the play's major concerns, and within the past few years, Calderwood and Hawkes, following the example of Mahood, have directed attention to the possibility that in *Richard II* Shakespeare not only uses language with extraordinary effectiveness but also explores the nature of language.[1] However, the prevailing concern with language as instrument and as subject in *Richard II* has, despite the perceptions it has afforded, dulled our responsiveness to a different (but complementary) kind of "language" in the play: the non-verbal but nevertheless eloquent language of movement and gesture—of physical actions—which, shared with dance, sets drama apart from purely verbal modes of art. A play justifiably much studied for its verbal patterning, *Richard II* also offers unusually clear examples of how in drama, as in dance, specific physical actions are performed, repeated, and varied, thereby establishing what might be called choreographic patterns or motifs of movement. Even allowing for differences between individual productions of the play, such patterns—implicit in the words of the text but far more prominent in performance than in reading—prove to be as intricate and as revealing of central issues in *Richard II* as the verbal patterns which have received far more attention. An appropriate awareness of the gestural language of *Richard II* also permits us to see how, united in performance, words and actions take on a power that neither have separately, endowing drama in general and this play in particular with the capacity to clarify the past through enacting it.

The choreographic patterns that emerge during *Richard II* are composed in some instances of actions (such as exits and entrances) that are a virtually inescapable feature of any drama and in other cases of actions such as exchanging gages and kneeling and rising that are more specific to *Richard II*. Consider the patterning of entrances and exits during the scene in which we first see Bolingbroke after his return from exile. He and Northumberland enter, their movements part of their travelling through "these high wild hills and rough uneven ways" (II. iii. 4)[2] of Gloucestershire. Pausing in their journey towards Berkeley Castle, they are intercepted by Percy, who enters having travelled, as Northumberland remarks, "from my brother Worcester, whencesoever" (l. 22). Soon after, Ross and Willoughby, whose hurried departures to meet Bolingbroke at Ravensburgh concluded the scene (II. i) in which Richard seized the possessions of Lancaster, finally catch up with him, arriving "Bloody with spurring, fiery red with haste" (l. 58). Their arrival is shortly followed by the separate entrances—from a direction different from the others—of Berkeley and York, each coming from Berkeley Castle rather than towards it. The patterning of the entrances underscores that we are watching characters in the process of moving from one place to another encountering others who are also engaged in journeying, and the scene concludes with all those whom we have seen arrive singly and in pairs from various directions resuming, together, as a group, the movement towards Berkeley Castle initiated with the entrance of Northumberland and Bolingbroke. Enacting journeys which are suspended, then resumed, the sequence of entrances followed by a common group exit conveys the tidal force of Bolingbroke's power, which, pausing only to increase, sweeps with it all whom it encounters, including, most prominently York, whose will and purpose waver and change during this scene in the same way that his entering movement away from Berkeley Castle is turned back upon itself. Having entered to confront Bolingbroke, he departs in his company, pondering Bolingbroke's invitation to join him in another journey—". . . go with us/ To Bristol castle" (ll. 163–164). Through its entrances and exits the scene establishes a pattern of confluence and augmentation—of initially separate individuals and pairs pooling themselves into a group—which is a visual analogue to Scroop's subsequent description of Bolingbroke's uprising as a flood:

> Like an unseasonable stormy day
> Which makes the silver rivers drown their shores
> As if the world were all dissolv'd to tears,
> So high above his limits swells the rage
> Of Bolingbroke, covering your fearful land
> With hard bright steel and hearts harder than steel.
>
> (III. ii. 106–111)

Another—considerably more intricate—choreographic pattern emerges from how *Richard II* associates the entrances and exits typical of drama with the journeys to specific places which characters repeatedly undertake during the course of the play. We watch characters depart for or arrive at a variety of destinations: Plashy, Coventry, Ravensburgh, Berkeley Castle, Bristol, Flint Castle, London, France, and Pomfret. The movements of actors on and off the stage and of characters from place to place become during *Richard II* choreographic analogues to, if not metaphors of movement for, that process of personal and societal change which is the paramount experience that characters confront during the play.

Richard II contains numerous exits (often solitary ones) which—in contrast to the group exit that completed the process of augmentation enacted in Act II, Scene iii—mark moments of leavetaking and, frequently, moments of what the characters involved know is a final farewell. The parting of Gaunt and his widowed sister-in-law, the Duchess of Gloucester, is the first such exit (I.ii.), and during the tournament scene which immediately follows, Mowbray and Bolingbroke twice take final leave of their relatives and friends. Before the combat is to begin, Bolingbroke declares,

> . . . Mowbray and myself are like two men
> That vow a long and weary pilgrimage.

Then let us take a ceremonious leave
And loving farewell of our several friends.

(I. iii. 48–51)

Farewells are repeated after the combat is stopped and banishment decreed. Sentenced to lifelong banishment which he explicitly compares to "speechless death" (l. 172), Mowbray takes what he knows is his last leave, while Gaunt delays the moment of what he, like the Duchess of Gloucester from whom he parted in the previous scene, knows[3] will be a final separation from Bolingbroke: "Come, come, my son, I'll bring thee on thy way" (l. 304). Occurring against a backdrop of final separations and departures which intensifies during the course of the play, the movements of Gaunt and Bolingbroke as they exit together embody the link between them as father and son which neither royal decree nor death can sunder. Their bond contrasts with the increasing isolation in time of Richard, who is both fatherless and childless. One of the most powerful visual expressions of that isolation occurs when the embittered departures first of Gaunt and then of York—the last of Richard's living uncles—frame Richard's seizure of the Lancastrian possessions (II.i.), an act which violates the bond linking Gaunt to Bolingbroke, past to present.

Gaunt's departure in that scene is, like many others in the play, fraught with a sense of finality:

Gaunt.
Convey me to my bed, then to my grave:
Love they to live that love and honour have.

[Exit]

Richard.
And let them die that age and sullens have;
For both hast thou and both become the grave.

(II. i, 137–140)

Similar finality resonates through the farewells which Bushy, Green, and Bagot exchange after learning that Bolingbroke has landed:

Green.
Farewell at once, for once, for all, and ever.
Bushy.
Well, we may meet again.

Bagot.
    I fear me never.

(II. ii. 148—149)

We next see Bushy taking final leave of Bolingbroke and his followers before being removed, with Green, for execution: "More welcome is the stroke of death to me/ Than Bolingbroke to England. Lords, farewell" (III. i. 31—32). His leavetaking follows soon after that of the Welsh captain, who speaks for an entire army when, convinced that "These signs forerun the death or fall of kings," he announces to Salisbury, "Farewell" (II. iv. 14).

The final act of the play is punctuated by a series of leave-takings and departures which also ring with finality. During Richard's meeting with the Queen—the starting point for new and separate journeys for each—he counsels her, "Think I am dead, and that even here thou tak'st,/ As from my death-bed, thy last living leave" (V. i. 38—39). The play concludes with Exton departing, as Mowbray did earlier, into unending exile and with Bolingbroke, as he looks upon Richard's corpse, vowing to undertake a journey to the Holy Land and ordering the court to join him in following Richard's coffin: "March sadly after; grace my mournings here/ With weeping after this untimely bier" (V. vi. 51—52). Like the endings of most tragedies, this last movement of characters off the stage is resonant with finality, but in *Richard II* the resonance of that exit is amplified because it is the last of a series of similarly resonant exits during the play.

The numerous moments during *Richard II* when characters depart to begin a journey contrasts with those during which we witness the arrival of characters completing a journey. The tournament scene, which ends with banishments and departures, contains two arrivals which can receive unusual emphasis in performance because audience as well as characters can be compelled to wait for them to occur. The sense of waiting which precedes Richard's arrival is made explicit: "Why, then, the champions are prepar'd and stay/ For nothing but his Majesty's approach" (I. iii. 5—6). Once Richard arrives, there is a further wait (its duration depending upon the discretion of the director) as he and his attendants settle themselves, a wait which ends when, summoned in turn, Mowbray and Bolingbroke enter prepared for combat. Since the opening scene, we and the characters have waited for "St. Lambert's day" (I. i. 199), and now that that day has come, we and they wait again—for Richard's arrival, for the appearance of the lords appellant, and for the beginning of the long-anticipated trial by arms. That beginning never comes, leaving unresolved the accusations which they have voiced and leaving unfulfilled the waiting in which audience and characters have been engaged since the opening scene.

The tournament scene is not the only time that the play compels both audience and characters to wait. Act II, Scene i opens with characters—this time York and Gaunt—again waiting for Richard to arrive; "Will the King come," Gaunt asks, "that I may breathe my last/ In wholesome counsel to his unstaid youth" (II. i. 1–2). Their waiting—and ours—ends when, sixty-six lines later, Richard enters, completing a journey begun with a haste which he had hoped would prove "too late" (I. iv. 64).[4] In Act IV, Scene i, we wait again, this time with Bolingbroke and his court, for Richard to arrive, and once he has arrived, we wait again for him to acquiesce in the transfer of royal authority to Bolingbroke. Richard's invitation to Bolingbroke—"Here, cousin, seize the crown" (IV. i. 181)—proves to be not the act of surrender which the words on first hearing seem to imply and for which we and the assembled characters have been waiting but an eloquent prelude that makes us and them wait longer for the moment when Richard does give up the crown. The Queen, who waits in Act V, Scene i for Richard to pass by on his way to the Tower, embodies that sense of waiting in which the play repeadly and self-consciously involves characters and audience alike. We watch her, during the first scene in which she speaks, anxiously awaiting the arrival of a moment, an event, which she intuitively fears and knows to be imminent:

> Yet, again, methinks,
> Some unborn sorrow, ripe in fortune's womb,
> Is coming towards me, and my inward soul
> With nothing trembles.
>
> (II. ii. 9–12)

Her waiting ends with the arrival of news that Bolingbroke has landed.

The waiting which often precedes arrival in *Richard II* serves several functions. It sharpens our awareness of how Richard, for whom we and the characters repeatedly wait, becomes during the course of the play a man who is himself waiting. From the instant of his perception that ". . . within the hollow crown/ That rounds the mortal temple of a king/ Keeps Death his court" (III. ii. 160-162), Richard awaits, sometimes in dread, sometimes with eagerness, that moment which, with Exton's arrival in his cell, he knows is come at last: "How now! What means death in this rude assault" (V. v. 106). By making us wait the play also subjects us to something like the royal indolence at which the play's opening lines hint as Richard asks whether Bolingbroke is present "Here to make good the bois'trous late appeal,/ Which then our leisure would not let us hear" (I. i. 4-5). That indolence is one facet of Richard's pervasive failure—acknowledged in the solitude of his cell—to act in timely fashion: "I wasted time, and now doth Time waste me" (V. v. 49).[5] That failure also manifests itself in his barely but fatally premature departure for Ireland and his slightly tardy but equally fatal return to his realm "One day too late . . ." (III. ii. 67). The language describing the Londoners' response to Richard after the newly crowned Bolingbroke has passed by invites us to link Richard's ill-timed departures and arrivals with the exits and entrances of actors:

> As in a theatre, the eyes of men,
> After a well-grac'd actor leaves the stage,
> Are idly bent on him that enters next,
> Thinking his prattle to be tedious;
> Even so, or with much more contempt, men's eyes
> Did scowl on gentle Richard.
>
> (V. ii. 23-28)

Drama consists of actions that require timing, and the properly timed exits and entrances of actors during *Richard II* become a measure, embodied in the very performing of the play, of that mistiming (particularly in arriving and departing) which is a prominent feature of Shakespeare's characterization of Richard.

The arrivals and departures scattered through *Richard II* intertwine with particular intricacy in Act II, Scene i. Richard, long awaited, arrives, and Gaunt soon after departs, going to his deathbed, then to his grave. When Richard remains resolved to sieze the possessions of Lancaster, York also departs: "I'll not be by the while. My liege, farewell" (*l*. 211). Having ordered preparations made for his own imminent departure for Ireland,

Richard exits with the Queen, urging her, "Be merry, for our time of stay is short" (*l.* 223). Immediately after his exit, we learn that Bolingbroke's arrival in England is as imminent as Richard's departure from it. The scene concludes with a trio of departures, as Ross, Willoughby, and Northumberland race off to meet Bolingbroke at Ravensburgh—departures which anticipate the race to reach Bolingbroke which York, his Duchess, and their son Aumerle undertake at another moment in the play (V. ii.) when allegiances to king and to family are again in conflict with one another. In this scene the physical movements of people coming from and departing to other places swirl around the long speeches of dying Gaunt and palsied York, and their exits—slow, pained, enfeebled—sharpen our sense of the pervasiveness of the motion in this scene by showing us even the oldest, least agile of the characters caught up in the flux of arrivals and departures.

One of the distinctive features of arrivals and departures in *Richard II* is the frequency with which they interlock to present both the beginning and the end of specific journeys. We watch Richard leave to visit the dying Gaunt (I. iv.) and see him come into his presence (II. i.). When Ross and Willoughby encounter Bolingbroke near Berkeley Castle (II. iii.), they complete a journey which began with their departures for Ravensburgh at the end of Act II, Scene i. We are shown the Queen commencing (III. iv.) and concluding (V. i.) her journey to London, just as we soon after watch York, his Duchess, and Aumerle begin (V. ii.) and end (V. iii.) their race to Bolingbroke. In the ensuing scene, Exton begins his journey to "The King at Pomfret" (V. iv. 10), and the completion of that journey (V. v.) becomes the starting point of the journey back to Bolingbroke which we see concluded when Exton enters Bolingbroke's presence (V. vi.) to announce Richard's death and present his corpse. Each such completed journey, occurring within the broader flow of arrivals and departures, yields a momentary sense of completion, of stasis, which then dissolves as other movements, other journeys, commence or continue, thus heightening visually the predominant impression of flux breaking through structures—social as well as personal—established to contain it.[6] The completion of Exton's journey to Bolingbroke, for example, becomes, when Bolingbroke banishes him forever, the starting point of a journey which has no destination and therefore no possibility of completion.

The meeting between Richard and Bolingbroke in the base court of Flint Castle marks the conclusion of two separate journeys which began with Bolingbroke's departure into exile and Richard's decision to leave for Ireland. The play presents both men in the process of making those journeys. We are shown Richard landing in Wales and setting out for Flint Castle and Bolingbroke as he approaches Berkeley Castle and again as he moves into Wales after executing Bushy and Green at Bristol. The conclusion at Flint Castle of their separate journeys becomes the starting point for another which they make together: to London, with Richard in Bolingbroke's custody.

The play concludes with another journey, as Bolingbroke and the court follow Richard's coffin off the stage. That final exit constitutes a last, powerfully visual declaration of the link between departures and dying developed earlier, most forcefully with the Duchess of Gloucester's departure from Gaunt and with Gaunt's departure out of Richard's presence and into his deathbed. That link helps *Richard II* to establish the movement of characters from place to place—their motion through space—as an analogue for, almost an extension of, their movement through time and towards death. Even the banishments that compel characters to undertake journeys out of England are endowed with a temporal dimension, for Bolingbroke remarks to Mowbray after Richard orders their exile:

> By this time, had the King permitted us,
> One of our souls had wand'red in the air,
> Banish'd this frail sepulchre of our flesh
> As now our flesh is banished from this land.
>
> (I. iii. 194–197)

Mowbray, too, compares banishment to death, arguing that both deny him the exercise of his gift of speech:

> That language I have learn'd these forty years,
> My native English, now I must forgo;
> And now my tongue's use is to me no more
> Than an unstringed viol or a harp,[7]
> . . . .
> What is thy sentence then but speechless death,

Which robs my tongue from speaking native breath?

(I. iii. 159–173)

The report of Mowbray's death in exile also correlates motion through space and through time. Mowbray's wanderings from battlefield to battlefield and his retirement to Venice become—as the Bishop of Carlisle reports them—the equivalent of his journey towards death:

> Many a time hath banish'd Norfolk fought
> For Jesu Christ in glorious Christian field,
> Streaming the ensign of the Christian cross
> Against black pagans, Turks, and Saracens;
> And, toil'd with works of war, retir'd himself
> To Italy; and there at Venice gave
> His body to that pleasant country's earth,
> And his pure soul unto his captain Christ,
> Under whose colours he had fought so long.

(IV. i. 92-100)

The correspondence between spatial and temporal movement is strengthened by the motif of the pilgrimage, which is developed verbally and choreographically during *Richard II*. Before the trial by combat Bolingbroke speaks of his and Mowbray's movement onto the battlefield and towards death as a pilgrimage: ". . . Mowbray and myself are like two men That vow a long and weary pilgrimage" (I. iii. 48–49). After Richard exercises his royal power by removing four years from the term of Bolingbroke's exile, Gaunt uses the metaphor of pilgrimage to declare that Richard is powerless to prolong a man's movement through time: "thou canst help time to furrow me with age, But stop no wrinkle in his pilgrimage" (I. iii. 229–230). The motif of pilgrimage emerges again in Richard's response to Gaunt's death, a response which explicity links movement through time and space: "The ripest fruit falls first, and so doth he;/His time is spent, our pilgrimage must be" (II. i. 153–154). Looking upon Richard's corpse, Bolingbroke vows—immediately before his final departure from the stage—to undertake a pilgrimage to the Holy Land.[8]

Richard II also elaborates the motif of pilgrimage choreographically by means of the intricate association of entrances and exits with the beginning and conclusion of journeys to specific destinations. Each of the numerous journeys thus demarcated—particularly those which we see both beginning and ending—serves to re-enact, in miniature as it were, that vaster pilgrimage which every character in the play is making as he moves through space and time towards the moment and the place of his dying. Both the specific journeys presented during the play and the fact of pilgrimage to which they visually attest are themselves facets of a broader, more pervasive phenomenon central to *Richard II*: the process of change, of flux, manifesting itself in the bodies, the minds, and the values of individual men as well as in their relationships, their institutions (particularly kingship), and their society.[9]

Richard is the character whose experience of change is most profound, and his pilgrimage is the most moving of the journeys, spatial as well as temporal, which we see completed during the play. As Richard makes that pilgrimage which, as he acknowledges on learning of Gaunt's death, "must be," the space within which he moves continually contracts and his control over when he moves and to where dwindles. The man who early in the play moves freely through his dominions and orders others into exile becomes—following the meeting with Bolingbroke at Flint Castle—a man whom we see moving under guard, travelling to destinations which Bolingbroke fixes, appearing at his command, departing with his permission, changing direction (from the Tower to Pomfret) as Bolingbroke's wishes vary. The imprisonment which precedes Richard's assassination is the antithesis of the exile which he imposed upon others. Richard finds himself confined to a single area, the space enclosed by the walls of his cell, while those whom he banished find themselves not restricted to but excluded from a single, sharply demarcated place: England. Those banished are free, as Mowbray declares before departing into exile, to move to any place but one: "Farewell, my liege, now no way can I stray;/ Save back to England, all the world's my way" (I. iii. 206–207). In his cell, with his movement through space most restricted, Richard comes to see himself as Bolingbroke's timepiece—"his Jack o' th' clock" (V. v. 60)—reduced to moving in time, as he has been moving in space, according to Bolingbroke's preferences. The moment of death which terminates Richard's movement through time also imposes the final limit on his movement through space.

Richard's pilgrimage culminates in his being carried by other men and confined, motionless, within a coffin.

In addition to the complex choreographic patterns presented through the acts of entering and leaving the stage, *Richard II* establishes comparably intricate patterns through actions which are not common to virtually all drama: the gestures of kneeling and rising and of exchanging gages. Those actions entail movement in a vertical rather than a horizontal plane, motion particularly appropriate for the multi-level stage of the Elizabethan public play house. Such movement also makes possible a visual rendering of the *de casibus* theme of the fall of great men widespread in the literature and drama of the English Renaissance. One of the most extensive and most frequently described patterns in the verbal imagery of *Richard II* arises from references to motion upwards and downwards, and the thematic ramifications of Richard's descent from the walls of Flint Castle to its "base court" are well known.[10] But the patterns which emerge from the numerous occasions in *Richard II* when characters kneel and then rise are equally extensive, intricate, and important.[11] The opening scene contains at least one such occasion: Mowbray kneels as he pleads to be permitted to keep Bolingbroke's gage. Two scenes later Bolingbroke, before receiving his lance to do battle with Mowbray, asks, "Lord Marshall, let me kiss my sovereign's hand/ And bow my knee before his majesty" (I. iii. 46–47). Before departing into exile, Mowbray and Bolingbroke both kneel before Richard to swear that during their mutual banishment they will never "reconcile/ This louring tempest of your home-bred hate" (l. 187).

Act II, Scene ii, in which entrances and exits were organized to present a pattern of confluence and augmentation, illustrates the complexity of the choreographic motif of kneeling and rising, particularly the way in which that motif calls upon a director to choose between a range of diverse, in certain respects contradictory possibilities. The script of *Richard II* explicitly requires that Bolingbroke kneel to York in this scene (III. ii. 83–84), but it does not specify what young Percy does upon learning that he is in Bolingbroke's presence. In John Barton's 1973–1974 production of *Richard II* for the Royal Shakespeare Company, Percy does not kneel to Bolingbroke but remains seated upon his horse while Bolingbroke stands beside him. Percy's failure to kneel anticipates the refusal of his father, who is also mounted during this scene, to kneel to Richard in Act III, Scene iii. In a play which repeatedly shows men kneeling to those who are their elders or who are superior to them in rank or in power, the failure of Percy to kneel to Bolingbroke and of Northumberland to kneel to Richard heralds the rebellion against Bolingbroke's authority as king which Richard predicts[12] and which *1* and *2 Henry IV* portray. If, however, a director chooses—as David Scase did in his 1974 production of *Richard II* at the Library Theatre (Manchester, England)—to have Percy kneel to Bolingbroke,[13] a different set of relationships emerges from the choreographic pattern. As young Percy kneels to Bolingbroke and Bolingbroke in turn kneels to the aging Duke of York, the last of his living uncles, their actions complement one another, conveying the deference owed by younger men to their elders, the deference which Richard's treatment of Gaunt in the previous scene has violated. The acts of kneeling which occur in Act II, Scene ii also demonstrate the potential ambiguity of such ceremonial gestures, which in *Richard II* sometimes are and sometimes are not consistent with the facts of who holds power. A possible correspondence between such gestures and the possession of power is established during Act I, as we watch Mowbray and Bolingbroke individually and then jointly kneel before their annointed king. That correspondence is both confirmed and broken if this scene is played with Percy kneeling to Bolingbroke. Percy kneels, as Mowbray and Bolingbroke did earlier, to a man superior to him in rank and in power, while Bolingbroke, showing a knee "Whose duty is deceivable and false" (II. iii. 84) kneels before a palsied York whose powers—both his own and those of his forces—are in fact too weak to check Bolingbroke's advance.

The same dichotomy between gestures of submission and the actualities of power manifests itself when Richard and Bolingbroke meet—for the first time since Bolingbroke knelt before Richard with Mowbray before departing into exile—in the "base court" of Flint Castle. On that earlier occasion, Bolingbroke, before taking up his lance, had asked permission to kiss Richard's hand and kneel before him in farewell, and Richard had deigned, in the fulness of his royal power, to come down from his seat: "We will," he declared then, "descend and fold him in our arms" (I. iii. 54). At Flint Castle, however,

Richard, now like the palsied York too feeble in himself and in his forces to withstand Bolingbroke, finds himself compelled to assent to another request from Bolingbroke that he descend. When Richard reaches the base court, Bolingbroke, in a gesture whose significance is highlighted by the attention given to Northumberland's failure earlier in the scene to kneel in Richard's presence, sinks to his knee before Richard as he had earlier knelt before York, ordering those with him to follow his example: "Stand all apart,/ And show fair duty to his majesty" (III. iii. 187–188). Richard interrupts Bolingbroke's declarations of loyalty—as York did earlier—to point out that Bolingbroke's gesture of submission is inconsistent with the power that he now commands.

> Fair cousin, you debase your princely knee
> To make the earth proud with kissing it.
> . . . .
> Up, cousin, up; your heart is up, I know,
> Thus high at least, although your knee be low.
> (III. iii. 190–195)

When Bolingbroke, responding to Richard, rises from his knee, that upward movement condenses into a single metaphorical gesture—his ascent to power. As we watch a kneeling subject rise to become the custodian of his king, we see enacted in miniature one facet of the broader phenomenon of change as it manifests itself in the shifting relationships of rank and power among men.

The gestures of other men subsequently confirm Bolingbroke's possession of power and royal authority. After Bolingbroke concludes the deposition scene by fixing the date of his coronation, we next see him, three scenes later (V. iii.) receiving a sequence of people—Aumerle, York, and the Duchess of York—who kneel before him as he and others had earlier knelt before Richard. Their kneeling to Bolingbroke, in addition to suggesting the totality of the political, ocial, and personal changes which have occurred, marks the emergence of a new order—what York calls "this new spring of time" (V. ii. 50)—in which ceremonial gestures are once more aligned, however precariously, with the facts of power, authority, and rank.[14]

The play also utilizes Richard's and Bolingbroke's acts of kneeling and of coming in touch with the ground as a means of conveying visually the importance of the relationship between the soil of England and its ruler. The moment when Bolingbroke departs into exile is juxtaposed against the moment of Richard's return from Ireland. Bolingbroke bends or kneels to touch the ground, declaring: "Then, England's ground, farewell; sweet soil, adieu;/ My mother and my nurse that bears me yet" (I. iii. 306–307). Richard, returning from his Irish expedition, employs the same analogy but reverses its terms, envisioning himself as a mother and the "dear earth" as his child:

> As a long-parted mother with her child
> Plays fondly with her tears and smiles in meeting,
> So weeping, smiling, greet I thee, my earth,
> And do thee favours with my royal hands.

(III. ii. 8–11)

Richard also repeats Bolingbroke's gesture of stooping or kneeling to touch the soil, but those identical gestures become parts of choreographic patterns which enact the difference in each man's relationship to the land. The moment in Act I, Scene iii when Bolingbroke touches the ground marks the nadir of his fortune, and his rising to depart into exile anticipates the trajectory of his subsequent growth in power. We next see him (II. iii.) returned from exile and greeting those who have come to join their powers with his. Once Bolingbroke has returned from exile, his acts of kneeling become a choreographic affirmation of the bond between him and the land. Each time after his exile that Bolingbroke kneels upon "England's ground," he rises with his powers enlarged. He kneels to York near Berkeley Castle and rises to merge York's forces with his own; he kneels to Richard in the base court of Flint Castle and rises to exercise control over the king's movement and person; finally, in the deposition scene, he can—if the director so chooses[15]—kneel once more, to receive the crown of England and to rise as England's acknowledged king. This particular choreographic pattern makes visible to the theater audience the process by which, just as the Queen sinks to the ground in metaphorical childbirth to "bear" Bolingbroke as her "sorrow's dismal heir" (II. ii. 63), so the soil of England—"This nurse, this teeming womb of royal kings" (II. i.

51)—"bears" or gives birth to Bolingbroke's power, increasing it each time his knee and the earth touch.

Richard's act of greeting the earth with his hand is the first of several times after his return from Ireland that he sinks to the ground. Later in the same scene, he sits upon the ground to "tell sad stories of the death of kings" (III. ii. 156), and during the deposition scene he sits again as he studies himself in the mirror. He also kneels or sits upon the ground during his final parting with the Queen and as he struggles to make "populous" (V. v. 3) the solitude of his cell. Taken together, such movements contribute to a choreographic pattern which conveys in actions the validity of Gaunt's warning to Richard that "Thy death bed is no lesser than thy land" (II. i. 95). Each time that Richard sinks to, kneels, or sits upon the ground after his return from Ireland, he rises weaker than before. The same earth which "bears" Bolingbroke after his exile, augmenting his power whenever he comes in touch with it, drains Richard's will and strength after his return from Ireland. The land whose riches Richard is accused of wasting while unchallenged king now works to waste and dissipate his power each time that he touches it. This particular choreographic pattern enacts how Richard himself becomes the victim of that "senseless conjuration" which he directed against Bolingbroke when, after greeting "my earth" with his hand, he called upon it to harass and "Throw death upon thy sovereign's enemies" (III. ii. 23, 10, 22). Each act of coming in touch with the earth also traces the broader motion of Richard's decline from power and his descent—his "pilgrimage"—into an "earthy pit" (IV. i. 219).[16] The process of wastage and decline culminates when Richard sinks mortally wounded to the earth, with his life's blood draining into and staining "the King's own land" (V. v. 110). The two patterns of growth and wastage, of bearing and draining, coalesce in the moment when Bolingbroke kneels or stands over Richard's corpse—a tableau that signifies his bond with the very land which has consumed Richard, its landlord king.

In addition to giving rise to a variety of specific choreographic patterns, the numerous acts of kneeling and rising in *Richard II* serve as visual analogues, recurring through the play, of the well-known verbal imagery of scales and buckets moving upwards and downwards in reciprocal motion.[17] Those actions take on—individually and collectively—the function of choreographic emblems or metaphors which enact, rather than describe, the dynamics of change which moves men upwards and downwards in relation to one another during the course of the play. In Act V, Scene ii, for example, we watch Aumerle, York, and the Duchess of York in sequence enter Bolingbroke's presence, kneel, and then rise once Bolingbroke exercises the royal power to punish or to pardon treachery which was Richard's at the start of the play. Their movements three times re-enact the process of rising and falling which has lifted Bolingbroke to the throne of England, a process condensed into a single metaphorical gesture each time a character kneels and rises during the play.

The various acts of throwing down and picking up gages come to have a similarly metaphoric function in *Richard II*. During the opening scene Mowbray bends to pick up the gage which Bolingbroke has thrown down, then straightens to declare his defiance and hurl his own, which Bolingbroke takes up in turn. Their actions are repeated and amplified in Act IV, Scene i, when Aumerle, Fitzwater, Percy, Another Lord, and Surrey throw down and pick up gages in interlocking sequences that leave Aumerle empty-handed and asking for something to throw: "Some honest Christian trust me with a gage" (IV. i. 83). Each time a gage is thrown down and picked up in *Richard II*, we watch a man sink and then rise in response to another man's actions. Performed as many as nine times during the course of the play, that specific action becomes a pattern of movement and, like the act of kneeling and rising, serves as a choreographic metaphor for the phenomenon of relationships among men in the very process of shifting and re-aligning. This is strikingly evident in Act IV, Scene i, where the relative decorum that marked the exchange of gages in the opening scene gives way to the spectacle of seven gages being thrown down in rapid, perhaps even frantic succession, after which we watch the deposing of England's "annointed king" (III. ii. 55), a change in social and political relationships so profound that its consequences will touch groomsman as well as peer, man not yet born as well as those living.

The throwing down of gages in *Richard II* has additional implications. Gages are thrown down in *Richard II* when language alone no longer functions effectively as an instrument or medium for clarifying the past. Mowbray and Bolingbroke resort to the exchange of gages leading to trial by combat after their accusations of treachery in Act I, Scene i. cancel one another, and the ritualistic formality of the words each employs when called upon to "Speak truly" (I. iii. 14) immediately before the trial by combat further testifies to the failure of language. While Mowbray asserts that he appears in arms to prove Bolingbroke "A traitor to my God, my king, and me—/ And as I truly fight, defend me heaven" (I. iii. 24—25), Bolingbroke declares with equal fervor that he enters the lists to prove Mowbray "a traitor, foul and dangerous,/ To God of heaven, King Richard, and to me—/ And as I truly fight, defend me heaven!" (I. iii. 39—41). The symmetry between their words accentuates the falsehood one or the other must be speaking. The five men who exchange gages in Act IV, Scene i, do so after their words—like those of Mowbray and Bolingbroke earlier—fail to establish the identity of the killer of Thomas of Woodstock, Duke of Gloucester. Theater audiences frequently laugh as the gages rain down during this scene, but far from being a problem for a director to overcome, such laughter, if it occurs, is an appropriate response to the futility, at this moment, of trying to clarify the past by means of ritualistic gestures.

In *Richard II* the throwing down of gages marks the moment when men resort to acts rather than words in an effort to make past events—specifically, the slaying of Woodstock—intelligible. However, the trials by combat to which the characters resort when language fails to make sense of the past never occur. Richard, who was unable to reconcile Mowbray and Bolingbroke by words in the opening scene, stops their impending combat, not by speaking but by wordlessly throwing down his warder,[18] and Bolingbroke's decision to fix a day for a trial by combat between Mowbray, whom he himself accuses of killing Woodstock at the start of the play, and Aumerle, whom we heard four others accuse of the same crime once Bolingbroke is in power, is negated by the news that Mowbray has died in Venice. "That honourable day," the Bishop of Carlisle observes, "shall ne'er be seen" (IV. i. 91). The possibility of discovering the truth about Woodstock's murder through the speechless actions of a trial by combat lies buried with Mowbray, swallowed by time as the events themselves have been. The truth which the accusations and the aborted trials by combat seek to establish never emerges within the play. The question of whether Shakespeare's original audiences—or, for that matter, today's audiences—did or did not know who Woodstock's killer was is irrelevant, since what any audience of *Richard II* sees on stage is characters trying but failing to find that out. How they fail is significant. In *Richard II* neither words divorced from actions nor actions divorced from words succeed in answering the question of who killed Woodstock.

The futile attempt to discover the circumstances of Woodstock's death has a self-reflexive function within *Richard II* comparable to that of the play-within-the-play in *Hamlet* and *A Midsummer Night's Dream*. The efforts of characters in *Richard II* to come to an accurate understanding of an event which occurred in their recent past mirrors Shakespeare's attempt to probe more distant past events and make them comprehensible by means of—through—the medium of drama. The "divorce" of words from actions typical of the characters' fruitless attempts to determine who killed Woodstock stands in contrast to and thereby heightens the integration of words and of actions which every performance of *Richard II* accomplishes. That integration manifests itself in the way in which the choreographic patterns of exchanging gages and of kneeling and rising augment the verbal pattern of scales and buckets in vertical motion, thus "marrying" the action which the audience see with the words they hear. Another aspect of that integration is demonstrated when the distinction between words and actions is by-passed during the performing of a play, when speaking is itself one kind of action in which actors are engaged. As it integrates words and actions—a process which much criticism, with its preoccupation with the verbal, tends to ignore, if not violate—*Richard II* succeeds where its characters fail: in finding and conveying a vision which makes past events intelligible.

In this play which presents futile efforts to learn what has happened in the past, Richard and the Gardener are two characters sharply aware of the importance of remembering and of being remembered. For Richard the process of remembering is predominantly verbal. Told of the executions of Bushy, Green, and the Earl of Wiltshire, he calls upon those assembled to defend his cause to join him, not in actions, but in recalling the deaths of the kings: "For God' sake, let us sit upon the ground/ And tell sad stories of the death of kings" (III. ii. 155–156). Richard's inclination to indulge in words rather than undertake actions is an aspect of his character which manifests itself at other points in the play and which on this occasion moves the Bishop of Carlisle to rebuke him: "My lord, wise men ne'er sit and wail their woes,/ But presently prevent the ways to wail" (III. ii. 178–179). The ways in which Richard asks his retinue to remember the fall of other kings anticipates the instructions on how he is to be remembered which he gives to the Queen at their final parting:

> In winter's tedious nights sit by the fire
> With good old folks and let them tell thee tales
> Of woeful ages long ago betid;
> And ere thou bid good night, to quite their griefs,
> Tell thou the lamentable tale of me,
> And send the hearers weeping to their beds.
>
> (V. i. 40–45)

The Gardener, on the other hand, relies on actions rather than words in his effort to make certain that future ages will remember the Queen's suffering:

> Here did she fall a tear; here in this place
> I'll set a bank of rue, sour herb of grace.
> Rue, even for ruth, here shortly shall be seen,
> In the rememberance of a weeping queen.
>
> (III. iv. 104–107)

Participating in the seasonal rhythms of growth, decay, and renewal which Richard in his capacity as "gardener" of the kingdom has neglected, the rue plant has the potential to endure in time and to offer wordless but effective reminder of past suffering.

Through the different modes of remembering to which Richard and the Gardener resort, *Richard II* presents a variation of the divorce between words and actions typical of the efforts of other characters to clarify the past. But in the very process of being performed, the play unites Richard's impulse to tell tales with the Gardener's preference for commemorative action. The events which Richard calls upon the Queen to *tell* to her fire-side audience are those which the play *enacts* before a theater audience. *Richard II* itself is an act of corporate memory,[19] but it is also a process of remembering that draws upon and exploits qualities unique to the medium of drama. Peter Brook describes those qualities in his discussion of drama as representation in *The Empty Space:*

> A representation is the occasion when something is represented, when something from the past is shown again— something that once was, now is. For representation is not an imitation or a description of a past event, a representation denies time. It abolishes the difference between yesterday and today. It takes yesterday's action and makes it live again in every one of its aspects—including its immediacy. In other words, a representation is what it claims to be—a making present.[20]

Richard II employs actions performed in the present in order to make present—to "re-present"—actions that have occurred in the past. For the play's original audiences, the actions thus represented were excruciatingly pertinent. The Elizabethan audiences of the first performances of *Richard II* were the off-spring, the "children yet unborn and unbegot" (III. iii. 88), of those who had endured the War of the Roses which issued from events presented during the play and which brought the first of the Tudor monarchs to the throne of England. In addition, the first performances of *Richard II* re-enacted a past transfer of royal authority before audiences who were themselves conscious of the certain but nevertheless unsettling prospect of a change in dynasty as the childless Elizabeth, the last of the Tudors, grew older. The early stage history offers further evidence of its prickly topicality. Its performance on February 7, 1601—apparently the first in some time—has been linked by some to the outbreak of Essex's rebellion the next day, and Elizabeth herself is reported to have remarked, "I am Richard II, know ye not that?"[21]

As the first audiences of *Richard II* shared in the theater the present enactment of past actions which once threatened to fragment English society, their very presence affirmed that society's capacity to endure change, a capacity which the increasingly imminent expiration of the Tudor dynasty threatened to test again. Today, of course, the past actions which the play re-presents do not touch us as directly, but the distance imposed by the intervening centuries accentuates another feature of the play. During those moments of performance when *Richard II*, uniting words and actions, flowers into the awareness of a present-day audience, the play eludes the temporal limitation of mortality which negated the possibility of determining the identity of Woodstock's killer by means of the actions of a trial by combat. Like the bank of rue which the Gardener resolves to plant, *Richard II* exists in time but does not succumb to the limits upon man's actions which death imposes, for the actions of which the play is composed have the capacity to be performed again and again, in different eras and places, each time illuminating the past by making it present. For us today, the play—which during performance moves through space and time—is perhaps less an act of remembering than a witness, rendered through actions integrated with words, of that pilgrimage through space and time which individuals and societies continue to make and to bear.

Notes

1. Wolfgang H. Clemen, *The Development of Shakespeare's Imagery* (1936; rev. rpt., Cambridge, Mass.: Harvard University Press, 1951), pp. 53–62. Richard D. Altick, "Symphonic Imagery in *Richard II*," *PMLA*, 12(1947), 337–365. Arthur Suzman, "Imagery and Symbolism in *Richard II*," *SQ*, 7(1956), 355–370. James L. Calderwood, *Shakespearean Metadrama* (Minneapolis: University of Minnesota Press, 1971), pp. 149–186. Terence Hawkes, *Shakespeare's Talking Animals: Language and Drama in Society* (London: Edward Arnold, Ltd., 1973), pp. 73–104. M.M. Mahood, *Shakespeare's Wordplay* (London: Methuen and Co., 1957), pp. 73–88. For a discussion of *Richard II* which considers its theatrical dimensions, see John Russell Brown, *Shakespeare's Plays in Performance* (London: Edward Arnold, Ltd., 1966), pp. 115–130. [An All-University Research Grant from Michigan State University helped to meet the expense of preparing this essay for publication.]
2. Quotations and their numbering are according to *The Complete Plays and Poems of Shakespeare*, ed. William Allan Neilson and Charles Jarvis Hill, New Cambridge Edition (Boston: Houghton Mifflin, 1942). [Speech heads have been put on a separate line for uniform presentation.—*Ed.*]
3. I. iii. 216–224.
4. The brief scene (II. iv.) between Salisbury and the Welsh captain presents the moment when another period of waiting for Richard

ceases—for the only time in the play—not with his arrival but with the departure of those awaiting him.

5. For a persuasive discussion of the importance of time and timing as themes in *Richard II*, see Ricardo Quinones' *The Renaissance Discovery of Time* (Cambridge, Mass.: Harvard University Press, 1972), pp. 312–324. Also see Richard J. Montgomery, "The Dimensions of Time in *Richard II*," *Shakespeare Studies*, ed. J. Leeds Barroll, Vol. 4 (Dubuque, Iowa: Wm. C. Brown Co., 1968), pp. 73–85.

6. David Scase's 1974 production of *Richard II* at the Library Theatre (Manchester, England) extended this to include the structures of individual scenes by having the entrances of the characters to begin a scene slightly over-lap or intrude upon the ending of the previous scene.

7. Note the parallels between these lines and those in which Northumberland announces Gaunt's death: "His tongue is now a stringless instrument,/ Words, life, and all, old Lancaster hath spent" (II. i. 149—150).

8. That pilgrimage proves to be one made through time rather than space, for in 2 *Henry IV* (IV. v. 232–240), Bolingbroke is carried off the stage to die in a place called the Jerusalem room without ever having reached or even set out for the city of Jerusalem.

9. In *Shakespeare's History Plays* (New York: Macmillan, 1946), E. M. W. Tillyard argues that *Richard II* portrays "the medieval world being superceded by the more familiar world of the present" (p. 259). Quinones (p. 324) comments on the importance in *Richard II* of the principle of organic change which Richard, in his rigidity, resists.

10. Examples of such imagery include I. i. 82–83; I. ii. 49–53; II. i. 153–154; II. iv. 18–22; III. ii. 36–53, 217–218; III. iii. 62–67, 178–179, 183–184, 194–195; III. iv. 85–89; IV. i. 111–112, 184–189, 195, 260–262, 317–318; V. i. 55–56; V. v. 87–89, 111–112. Also see S. K. Heninger, Jr., "The Sun-King Analogy in *Richard II*," *Shakespeare Quarterly*, 11 (1960), 319-327.

11. Paul A. Jorgenson discusses some of these movements in his "Vertical Patterns in *Richard II*," *The Shakespeare Association Bulletin*, 23(1948), 119–134.

12. V. i. 55–65.

13. In I. iii. 242–246 of 1 *Henry IV* Percy recalls this meeting with Bolingbroke as one "where I first bow'd me knee/ Unto this king of smiles, this Bolingbroke...."

14. These observations hold whether the scene is played somberly (as in the Scase production) or comically (as in the Barton production).

15. As Barton did.

16. It is also possible—David Samuelson has pointed out to me—to see Richard's decline as a growth towards and into the ground, much as the untended plants which the Gardener mentions in III. iv. 29–32 bend towards the ground. The Duchess of York, pleading for Aumerle's life, tells Bolingbroke: "Our knees still kneel till to the

ground they grow" (V. iii. 106)—an observation that proves true of Richard as he spends more and more time kneeling and in touch with the earth.

17. III. iv. 84–89; IV. i. 184–189.

18. This act of throwing down the warder can be linked to Richard's act of dashing to the ground the mirror which enables him to "see the very book indeed/Where all my sins are writ, and that's myself" (IV. i. 274—275). Just as the gages thrown by Mowbray and Bolingbroke led to Richard's throwing down his warder, so his throwing down of the mirror follows upon an exchange of gages more numerous, more frantic, and even more explicitly symptomatic of social disorder than the initial exchange. Richard's words to the Queen as they meet on his way to the Tower endow Richard's acts of throwing down with additional significance by associating those gestures with the wastefulness which weakened his kingship. "Our holy lives," he tells her, "must win a new world's crown/ Which our profane hours have here thrown down" (V. i. 24–25).

19. See Hawkes' discussion of this point in *Shakespeare's Talking Animals*, p. 125.

20. London: MacGibbon and Kee, 1968, p. 139.

21. This frequently cited remark occurred during a conversation between Elizabeth and William Lambarde, the Keeper of the Records of the Tower, in August, 1601 (E.K. Chambers, *The Elizabethan Stage*, 4 vols. [Oxford: The Clarendon Press, 1923], II, 206, no. 4, quoting John Nichols, *Progresses...of Queen Elizabeth*, 3 vols. [London, 1823], III, 552). Elizabeth's identification of herself with Richard perhaps explains the absence of the deposition scene from all surviving editions of the play printed during her reign.

Richard II at Stratford:
Role-Playing as Metaphor

MIRIAM GILBERT

The report that John Barton's production of *Richard II* would feature Richard Pasco and Ian Richardson alternating as Richard II and Bolingbroke[1] immediately raised questions: What would such a switch do to the meaning of the play? What would happen when we were asked to think of Richard and Bolingbroke not only as equals but as interchangeable? Some similarities *are* inherent in the text, especially when one thinks of Bolingbroke as the future Henry IV, a monarch plagued by the rebellion of Northumberland and Hotspur, men who support him in *Richard II* and turn against him in *Henry IV, Part 1*. Bolingbroke's rise, as traced in *Richard II*, then becomes merely the upward turn of the inevitable downward spin of the wheel of fortune, dramatized in *Henry IV, Parts 1 and 2*. And even in *Richard II*, Bolingbroke faces, as Richard did, lords arguing about who was really responsible for Gloucester's death (IV. i.) and, later, (V. iii.) an incipient rebellion.

But even in these moments, one usually thinks of the differences rather than the similarities of the two men. The standard critical reading of the first section of IV. i. is that Bolingbroke smoothly and efficiently deals with a situation that Richard could not handle in I. i. and I. iii. without ineffectual pleading and whimsical decision-making.[2] And it is true that Bolingbroke cuts off the rebellion of Aumerle and others before it gets very far, though the loyal town of Ciceter in Gloucestershire *is* "consumed with fire" (V. vi. 2).[3] Thus the usual, and I would say, obvious strategy in performing the play is to find men who represent widely different qualities, both physically and emotionally. Barton's decision to use the same actors alternating in the major roles becomes then a crucial break with the patterns set up by previous productions.

The dominant interpretation of Richard in this century probably stems from Frank Benson's performance at Stratford in 1896 and from C.E. Montague's comments on that performance, comments both descriptive and prescriptive:

> Still it is well to see what Shakespeare meant us to, and we wonder whether anyone who hears Mr. Benson in this part with an open mind can doubt that Shakespeare meant to draw, in Richard, not only a rake and muff on a throne and falling off it, but, in the same person, an exquisite poet; to show with one hand how kingdoms are lost and with the other how the creative imagination goes about its work; to fill the same man with the attributes of a feckless wastrel in high place and with the quite distinct but not incompatible attributes of a typical, a consummate artist.[4]

So effective and persuasive were both the performance and the commentary that most twentieth-century Richards seem to be variations of that interpretation. John Gielgud, probably the most famous Richard of our century, was "a tall willowy figure in black velvet, surmounted by a fair head, the pale agonized face set beneath a glittering crown."[5] This was in 1929 at the Old Vic, a season in which he also played Hamlet, another agonized figure in black. Alec Guinness played Richard II at the Old Vic in 1947; his picture shows us a blond, impassive monarch, possessing "fine-cut elegance."[6] Ronald Pickup, who is also slender, frail-looking, and blond, played the role for the National Theatre in 1972. And there are even more extreme versions of the "weak king." Michael Redgrave's 1951 Richard was described as a "portrait of a wayward weakling, painfully cockering himself up to exhibitions of arbitrary power,"[7] while Harry Corbett's 1955 Richard was summed up as a "senile Osric."[8] In the list of famous actors associated with the role, Laurence Olivier's name is conspicuously absent; a coincidence, perhaps, but Olivier's dark, virile, athletic qualities may have seemed much too forceful for the prevailing interpretation of Richard as a poetic weakling.

Against such Richards, the tendency has been to play a dark, strong, cold Bolingbroke. (There has also been, unfortunately, a tendency for some Bolingbrokes to seem so unmemorable as not to be mentioned in reviews at all.) The physical contrast may take several forms: sometimes it is light versus dark (Donald Madden and Charles Cioffi in Stratford, Connecticut, in 1968, or Ronald Pickup and Denis Quilley at the National Theatre in 1972); sometimes slender versus stocky (again Pickup and Quilley, or Ian McKellen and Timothy West in 1969-1970); sometimes unbearded versus bearded (McKellen and West). Although the contrast of light with dark may be suggested by the sun image so constantly associated with Richard, it also implies a conventional distinction between good and evil. The other physical differences suggest inexperience contrasted with experience, the poet instead of the warrior, and frequently effeminacy opposed to manliness. The characters are made to seem polar opposites, whether we consider their physical or psychological makeup: Richard is vain, selfish, whimsical, self-pitying, dramatic, uncontrolled, poetic, while Bolingbroke is courteous, cautious, scheming, controlled, reserved, silent.

John Barton's production creates a new tradition by beginning with almost faceless similarity rather than striking contrast. The details of the set and of the "introduction" to the play signal to the audience that this is a world of role-playing. Walking into the theater, I see a space boxed in by black curtains, overhung with a starry sky, a huge golden sun stretched over the center of the "heavens." A pyramid of five steps occupies the center of the dark-carpeted stage; on the top level stands an iron scarecrow, its face a golden mask beneath a golden crown. Over its outstretched arms hangs a circular golden robe. Everything is symmetrical, hierarchical. The lights dim; and a figure, vaguely like Shakespeare, with balding head, pointed beard, trim mustache, and dressed in an all-brown "Jacobean" doublet over long trousers, walks in holding a large book. He smiles at us, raises a hand, and, to the accompaniment of drums and trumpets, two lines of actors all wearing the same brown costume, all anonymous, not individually distinguishable, stride in and line the two sides of the stage.

Now two more men, also in the brown costume but younger, unbearded, and with the red-gold hair of the Plantagenets, come forward, bow to each other, then go to the man with the book and take it from him. They bend their heads together over it—actors consulting the script—while the Shakespeare figure goes up to the top of the steps and brings down the crown. The quiet drums grow louder as he takes back the book and holds out the crown. They both seize it, standing as they will in the deposition scene, and Shakespeare nods to the one on his right. Tonight, that actor is Richard Pasco; and he smiles, as if to say, "All right, I'll do it." Lights come up full and the stage swirls into the action of actors preparing to go on. Pasco sits on the steps, checks his boots, looks at a long blond wig one man offers to him but waves it away, looks at his face in a circular mirror (another foreshadowing of the deposition scene). The music becomes a coronation march as Pasco kneels center, facing upstage; the golden robe is draped over his shoulders, the crown placed on his head. He walks up to the top of the steps as the rest of the men chant "God save the king," "Long live the king," "May the king live forever." And the all-gold figure, with the golden mask now covering his face, responds "May the king live forever." Golden curtains are drawn over the black ones as Pasco sits down on the top of the pedestal, takes off the mask, hands it to a servant, and opens the large book placed on his lap. He checks the opening lines—still an actor getting into his role—but with the line, "Old John of Gaunt, time-honored Lancaster," we are suddenly into the words, and the world of the play.

This opening devised by Barton is essential for setting up the rules by which the world of *Richard II* will operate in this production. It is a formal, military, symbolic world with brown uniform-like costumes—costumes that are also uniform in the sense of resembling each other so that switches of identity are easily possible because everyone looks alike. The stage picture, so carefully symmetrical, with the lords in the background and Richard center stage, steps higher than anyone else, presents to us an image of this hierarchical society. Rank is determined by place; tomorrow night, when Ian Richardson walks in and stands to the right of the Shakespeare figure, *he* will wear the crown. It is a deliberately theatrical world, where we watch people get into their roles; for a play where people seem constantly to be acting parts, the theatricality is another way of expressing that role-playing. And, most of all, we are asked to see this as a world in which Richard and Bolingbroke are amazingly alike. When the two leading actors walk in, I scan them carefully, trying to figure out which is which; is the taller one Pasco or Richardson? Only the deep circles under Pasco's eyes, almost hidden by the makeup, let me recognize him and that knowledge is mine only from having seen him in other productions, not from my current experience of this production. The two men respond to each other as equals—the friendly bow in the opening moment, a little salute from Pasco when Richardson is chosen to play the King that night. Both men and therefore both characters are seen as role-players, and the theatrical choices of the production emphasize the fact that Shakespeare's nod could easily go to *either* man.

This relationship, verging on identity, of Richard and Bolingbroke continues throughout the evening. When Bolingbroke returns from exile (II. iii.) he is bearded and looks older. When Richard returns from Ireland (III. i.), he too has grown a beard. By the end of the play, both men age even more; and their hair begins to grey. The physical ageing underlines the likeness of their patterns of sorrow and suffering. Richard's is longer, and more obvious, from the return to England through the deposition scene; but Bolingbroke is given Henry IV's soliloquy from *Henry IV, Part 2*, "How many thousand of my poorest subjects/ Are at this hour asleep," in order to show us that Bolingbroke's usurped crown is already keeping him from innocent sleep. Even without the addition of the soliloquy, however, the interpretation of V. iii., in which Aumerle, York, and the Duchess of York beseech Bolingbroke to forgive Aumerle's plot, stresses Bolingbroke's own need of forgiveness for his crime against Richard. When Bolingbroke says, "I pardon him [Aumerle] as God shall pardon me" (V. iii. 131), he is not just trying to quiet the Duchess, but expressing his true hope for God's pardon. Bolingbroke's repetition of the Duchess's phrase, "That sets the word itself against the word" (V. iii. 122) may at first seem an arbitrary choice. But his repetition underlines the phrase and so, in the following scene, when Richard in prison, struggling to express his inner feelings, compares his problems to the inconsistency of divine teachings, we become more conscious of hearing him use the same phrase:

> The better sort
> As thoughts of things divine, are intermixed
> With scruples, and do set the word itself
> Against the word.
>
> (V. vi. 11—14)

Thus, both visually and verbally, the two men mirror each other, a production strategy which seems to grow out of the central image of the deposition scene, the mirror which Richard calls for and which he then shatters. We see the mirror effect in the opening of the play when the stance of the two actors, holding the crown, is an early mirror of the deposition scene itself. The mirror turns up as an actual object when Richard admires himself in a white-plumed helmet as he plans to set out for Ireland. He wears the circular frame of the shattered mirror around his neck when he says good-bye to the queen (V. i.). And in the next-to-last scene of the play, the mirror becomes the symbol of identity between the king and the man who deposed him. In a daring move, prepared for by the sympathetic playing of Bolingbroke and by all the similarities set up between the two men, Barton sends a disguised-voiced, black-hooded-and-gowned Bolingbroke into Richard's prison to offer him the groom's words of comfort, and a white toy horse, an emblem touching in its childishness. Richard accepts the gift, recognizing the love behind the clumsy toy; but he then breaks out into fierce condemnation of both himself and the new king: "I was not made a horse;/ And yet I bear a burden like an ass,/ Spurred, galled and tired by jauncing Bolingbroke" (V. v. 92—94). Just as his angry voice bitingly clips the sharp syllables of "Bolingbroke," the black figure kneeling opposite him throws back his hood to reveal the new king's face. In the silence of recognition, Bolingbroke lifts the circular rim of the shattered mirror from Richard's neck and holds it up between them so that they literally mirror each other. Their hands touch on the mirror's frame and Richard speaks in a low voice, full of suppressed understanding, "If thou love me, 'tis time thou wert away," to which Bolingbroke replies, in an equally low tone, "What my tongue dares not, that my heart shall say" (V. v. 96—97). The words are Shakespeare's, here utterly transformed by the presence of Bolingbroke instead of the groom. This substitution, like the inclusion of a soliloquy from *Henry IV, Part 2* is aimed at increasing our sense that Bolingbroke is painfully aware of his own guilt. Now that he is finding out that being king in no way protects him from personal and political problems (hence, the importance of V. iii.), he can better understand Richard, both as man and as king. The meeting in prison becomes, in theatrical terms, the obligatory scene which this production, with its emphasis on the mirroring patterns traced by the two men, must give us—even though, we, like Richard, are surprised to see Bolingbroke there.[9] The scene as written is about love to Richard, "a strange brooch in this all-hating world" (V. v. 66). The scene as played asks us to imagine a Bolingbroke who, while acknowledging his tongue-tied state,[10] can still confess his sense of emotional involvement to the man he has trapped in a literal prison.

Bolingbroke's own imprisonment and the connection between the two men is made even clearer in the production's final scene. Shakespeare shows us a Bolingbroke appalled by Exton's deed, vowing a pilgrimage of repentance. At Stratford, the coffin containing Richard's body is lowered into the ground, as Gaunt's was earlier, and everyone on stage now wears a long black robe over the brown uniform. The familiar drum roll and coronation fanfare is heard once more, but with a strangely ominous quality; for the third time in the play we see a coronation, as the golden robe and the crown-mask encircle Bolingbroke, kneeling with his back to us. The golden figure once more ascends the central steps but when he turns around, the face is that of a skeleton; now indeed "keeps Death his court." Then the two hooded figures at the bottom of the steps throw back their hoods to reveal Richard and Bolingbroke, Pasco and Richardson, standing there together, *both* subject to the rule of Death (a sleight-of-actor move substitutes another actor for Bolingbroke underneath the wide robe). So the play ends as it began, with the two men standing together. They take their curtain calls together, hand in hand, reminding us once again that the external circumstances of this production—two leading actors switching the two main roles—is an exact counterpart of the production's interpretation of this play. *How* the play is performed and *what* it means are inseparable.

One of the major reasons the mirror strategy works is that the opening of the production, and indeed many moments throughout, cue us to accept a symbolic gesture as true. On the almost empty stage with everyone at first wearing the same costume, each prop and each article of clothing takes on a strong symbolic importance. We see Richard in the golden coronation robe, in a golden gown confronting a dying Gaunt already shrouded in white, in a brilliantly gleaming pleated golden robe which enables him to look indeed like "glist'ring Phaeton," and then at last in a black penitential gown; the golden robes become increasingly elaborate, almost as if Richard is hiding from the truth by more expensive costumes, until finally he is reduced to stark simplicity. Gesture and movement are reduced to a minimum in many scenes. Northumberland, Ross, and Willoughby stand in a straight line, ritually cross themselves as Gaunt's coffin is lowered into a grave, and then, without moving, comment as a chorus on Richard's inadequacies as king (II. i.). The following scene in which the queen is "comforted" by a chorus of Bushy and Bagot is played in a series of triangle poses, with the two men standing on either side of the kneeling queen. The Welshmen (II. iv.) appear in darkness—we see only Salisbury at the vertex of a triangle of shadowy figures, hear only voices which fade away.

This highly non-naturalistic staging was not, in spite of the cues of the opening, always interesting; at moments, such as II. ii. where Bushy and Bagot comfort the queen, it seemed uncomfortably static. But I began to understand its force—and to look for the moments where the formality was set up either to be broken, or to push the scene to striking emotional heights. The breaking of formal patterns happens throughout the play. I remember particularly the tournament (I. iii.) with the two knights dressed for battle, each one wearing/riding a harness/horse, Bolingbroke's trimmed with red, Mowbray's with blue. The highly patterned speech of the challenges is a cover for the tenseness of the occasion: Bolingbroke and Mowbray make little speeches to the king, each receiving ritually polite applause. The king's platform, held high by four servants, circles into position; and then, in mirroring moves, Aumerle leads the helmeted Bolingbroke slowly into his upstage position. The drums roll, the lances are lowered, the men and horses begin to gallop—and the king, watching for the exact moment, throws his baton down to stop the combat. As the king consults with his councillors upstage, the two knights, down center, are helped first out of their armor and then, out of their horses. Not only has the pattern on stage been broken, but suddenly I, as an audience member, am thrown into an uncomfortable situation. My acceptance of costume conventions is suddenly challenged. Of course those aren't horses and wasn't I silly to think they even might be. I experience, through the breaking of theatrical "reality," what Bolingbroke experiences within the play; as Richardson plays him, he peevishly strikes one of the side poles with his gloves, clearly thinking to himself, "what a fool I've been to think that the king would ever take this seriously."

Sometimes the breaking of patterns is simpler, a move from a highly formal impersonal mode of gesture and speech to a highly personal one. The deposition scene is full of these moments, both for Richard and Bolingbroke—let me cite two of Richard's. Richard comes into the scene and immediately begins to accuse everyone of betrayal; he must be *both* priest and clerk, and he ends with a bitter couplet, "God save the king! although I be not he;/ And yet amen, if heaven do think him me" (IV. i. 174–175). Then he remembers what is going on and asks, "To do what service am I sent for hither?" and York reminds him, in a slightly fussy voice and with an over–anxious overstatement:

> To do that office of thine own good will
> Which tired majesty did make thee offer—
> The resignation of thy state and crown
> To Henry Bolingbroke.

(IV. i. 177–180)

So Richard takes the crown and then, as if calling a dog, says, "Here, cousin," waving the crown as if it were a bone. The change of tone is so sharp and so unexpected that it is funny. I even giggle a little at Richard's cleverness, though I find myself shocked by his frivolity—and then, in yet a third reaction, I see the joke as a defense, the only way he can get through this bitter time.

By the end of the scene, Richard has almost run out of jokes and sarcastic inflections, and one of the most moving moments of the play comes when he can restrain his feelings no longer. After breaking the mirror, he asks for one favor; and he and

Bolingbroke exchange short lines: "Yet ask." "And I shall have?" "You shall." "Then give me leave to go." "Whither?" And Richard finally crumbles, shouting painfully, desperately, "Whither you will, *so I were from your sights*" (IV. iv. 310–315, italics mine). He has taken all that he can and the effect of this public breakdown is the greater because we have not before in the production seen Richard so trapped, so tired, so vulnerable.

The other major effect of the non-naturalistic staging is to add power to metaphoric moments—I have already cited the use of the mirror and the repeated coronation scenes with the golden mask finally being replaced by the face of Death. But the most striking of all these moments occurs, for me, in III. iii., the scene at Flint Castle, where the returning Bolingbroke comes to confront the king. Trumpets sound to call forth the king, but only bird cries answer back. The trumpets sound again, and we hear in the distance an answering flourish. Then, out of the mist which surrounds upstage center, the pyramid of steps slides forward, with Richard standing on the top step; he is uncrowned, but wears a glittering golden robe, brighter than any he has worn before. Bolingbroke's description, "See, see, King Richard doth himself appear,/ As doth the blushing discontented sun/ From out the fiery portal of the east" (III. iii. 62–64) is given visual force; Richard *does* seem to be the sun emerging from "the envious clouds." Throughout the scene Richard plays with the golden robe, first unfastening it when he says "Must he lose/ The name of king? A' God's name, let it go!" (III.iii. 145-146) to reveal a white beggar's gown underneath. (That was Pasco's timing; Richardson made the gesture seem even a little more calculated by waiting to list the things he would give up, and slipping off the robe on "My gay apparel for an almsman's gown"). Then Richard puts the robe back on as he regathers his self-possession and uses it proudly as he descends the stairs. The music which heralded his entrance blares out again and his voice soars over the music. He stretches out his arms to display the circular robe to its fullest: "Down, down I come, like glist'ring Phaeton," (III. iii. 178); the line is no longer a dramatic overstatement, but with this staging, visually true.

The metaphor of Phaeton's fall is restated once more at the very end of the scene (which is also the end of the first half in this production). Richard and Bolingbroke step over the crumpled golden robe which Richard discarded when he finally came down the steps, and the stage is empty save for the sound of Bolingbroke's triumphant trumpets. Then the huge golden sun stretched over the center of the heavens suddenly detaches itself and falls, billowing to the floor; a single spotlight catches the fall, and then goes out, leaving us in darkness. It's a vividly strong playing of the metaphor—obvious, if you will—but justified by the style of the production and completely unforgettable. Richard *is* larger than life and the symbolic staging gives both the actor and the emotion that size.

What I have been describing so far are essentially the choices of John Barton, the director, and it could be argued that the interpretation of the play was formed before he knew that he would use two actors alternating in the roles of Richard and Bolingbroke. It may even be true, as Ian Richardson suggested in an interview,[11] that the original motivation behind the casting and the switching of roles was economic; the offer of the dual roles might have been a useful way to get both actors at Stratford for the season. Nonetheless, the theatrical reality does, to some extent, create the interpretation,[12] and there are important questions which arise out of the switching of roles: What happens to the playing of Bolingbroke? What happens to the playing of Richard? And what happens to the audience seeing both versions of the play?

To deal with the most obvious effect first, the sympathetic playing of Bolingbroke as a figure who follows his own tragic curve from buoyant young challenger to banished exile to hesitant usurper to guilty and limited-in-power king is enhanced considerably by the presence of a strong and charismatic actor. Most previous productions of *Richard II* have relied on only one magnetic force—Richard himself, and the theatrical attractiveness of the actor playing him. Even when Bolingbroke is seen as strong and forceful, he is, as I have mentioned, frequently and deliberately played as unsympathetic, cold, and unglamorous. But since this production begins with Richard and Bolingbroke so alike, so equal, we cannot really choose which man we prefer. Richard's outrageous behavior in the opening scenes actually swings our emotional response to Bolingbroke. And Bolingbroke's calm control when he hears the sentence of banishment, "This must my comfort be—/ That sun that warms you here shall shine on me" (I. iii. 144–145) seems an attractive alternative to Richard's moment of hysteria in response to Bolingbroke as he threatens to strike him with the baton he carries.

Moreover, the production explores an interesting subtext for one of the notable features of Bolingbroke's character, his silence, by showing it as Bolingbroke's increasing helplessness under the growing power of Northumberland. When Bolingbroke returns from exile in II. iii., he is disguised as a pilgrim and is on foot, while armed Northumberland towers above him in a black-and-silver-draped war horse, frightening in its size and totally unlike the red-trimmed toy horse Bolingbroke wore in the tournament (I. iii.). In III. i., Bolingbroke breaks off his reading of the indictment against Bushy and Green, obviously drawn up by Northumberland, either in disgust (Richardson) or incredulity (Pasco), and finally says, in a strangled voice, "My Lord Northumberland, see them dispatched;" while execution drums roll, a single spot illuminates the satisfied face of Northumberland. In IV. i., it is Northumberland who quietly waves on the sequence of accusers of Aumerle, much as a commanding officer signals to the firing squad. Later in the scene, when Richard is about to appear, everyone, including Bolingbroke, retreats upstage to sit inconspicuously out of sight—but Northumberland arrogantly lounges on the central platform of stairs leading to the throne.

Throughout the deposition scene itself, Bolingbroke seems unable to cope. Richard's self-dramatizing switches of mood confuse and embarrass Bolingbroke. He is forced to kneel and submit to Richard's grandstand gestures of resignation, performed by Pasco with the chanting tones of a priest, by Richardson with a formal measured pace. Once Bolingbroke is crowned and seated on the throne he is, paradoxically, even weaker. Now that Bolingbroke is physically separated from his victim, Northumberland can attack directly, paying no attention to Richard's plea against further confession: "Must I do so? And must I ravel out/ My weaved-up folly?" (IV. i. 228–229). When Richard protests that tears blind his eyes so that he cannot read the articles of self-incrimination, Northumberland sardonically hands him a huge handkerchief. And in response to Richard's attack on Northumberland, verbally by Pasco, physically striking him with the handkerchief by Richardson, the crowned king can only ask wearily, "Go some of you and fetch a looking glass," (IV. i. 268). Bolingbroke's real powerlessness is finally revealed when Northumberland once again urges, "Read o'er this paper while the glass doth come" and after Richard replies, "Fiend, thou torments me ere I come to hell!" the agonized king can bear it no longer and desperately screams, "Urge it no more, my Lord Northumberland." But the new king's evident distress cannot stop the practical Northumberland, "The commons will not then be satisfied" (IV. i. 268–272). Only the appearance of the looking glass and Richard's once more taking over the center of the stage bring Northumberland's pressure to a halt.

The interpretation of Bolingbroke as a figure who increasingly feels both his guilt and the weight of the crown is textually valid, especially if we accept as sincere his wish to do penance through a pilgrimage to the Holy Land. Barton's additions and his conception of Northumberland as the real Machiavel stress Bolingbroke's trap. But the interpretation also works as well as it does because at Stratford there are two strong actors to make it compelling. Because Pasco and Richardson are both capable of engaging an audience's attention, and of doing so in the opening scenes of the play, Bolingbroke more easily becomes a figure who attracts our allegiance and sympathy. Even though he has many fewer lines than Richard, the force of the actor makes his torment involving.

The alternation of roles also has a noticeable effect on the playing of Richard—in general—although I must add that Pasco and Richardson differ far more in their Richards than in their Bolingbrokes. Neither Richard makes the mistake of underestimating his opponent who is, on alternate nights, played by himself; that is, the experience of creating a strong and attractive Bolingbroke leads the actor to find an equally compelling Richard. And the quality that distinguishes these two Richards from many of the previous productions and prevailing critical readings is a sense of real power and fierce anger when that power is threatened. For once, Richard seems to fall not because he is weak but because he arrogantly abuses the very real power he has. Not only does he arouse Bolingbroke's wrath by seizing Gaunt's lands, but he alienates any possible help from his uncle York by his reckless justification of that action. Moreover, this production makes it clear that Richard is taking personal revenge on Gaunt for Gaunt's verbal and physical attack on him; in II. i., the dying Gaunt is angry enough to grab Richard's golden gown and drag him to his knees, in an attempt to make Richard realize his carelessness. Anger is the dominant emotion for both actors, whether expressed in Richardson's disgusted attempts to turn away from Gaunt or in Pasco's more frantic evasions. And even after Richard has lost his crown, he retains a savage ironic command, whether aimed at himself, as when Richardson's king throws the handkerchief over his head on the line, "O that I were a mockery king of snow," (IV. i. 260), or at others, as when Pasco's Richard looks straight at the audience with fierce condemnation on "Nay, all of you that sit [the text reads "stand"] and look upon/ Whilst that my wretchedness doth bait myself" (IV. i. 237–238). It is anger, coupled with pride, which keeps Richard from breaking down when confronting his weeping queen in V. i.; after all, Northumberland looms in the background, like a hawk about to swoop down on its prey (a visual metaphor emphasized by huge silver wing-like sleeves). And in his last moments Richard possesses both strength and fury: though surrounded by a stage full of murderers, he forces the poisoned cup on one, then seizes a crossbow and kills another before he is finally pulled up on a harness and shot as he hangs crucified in the air. That final image seems constructed out of Richard's earlier comparison of himself to Christ (IV. i.); like the falling sun, it is a visual literalization of Richard's words, "Mount, mount my soul" (V. v.111) and is either accepted in that context, or dismissed as a director's extravagance. Yet, extravagant or not, it is of a piece with the whole conception of a Richard who manages to dominate through his angry power, even in death.

Perhaps the most fascinating effect of the switching of roles lies not in a single viewing or in the consideration of a single character, but in the experience of the play as a series of palimpsests. As soon as you have seen the production once, your mind immediately begins to work with the other possibilities—what will it look like with the roles reversed? When you do see the switch, then four characters take the stage instead of two: Pasco's Richard and Richardson's Richard are both visible, no matter which man is wearing the crown, and the same is true for Bolingbroke. We are treated to a production in which we can actually see, from our memory of the previous night, several choices at once. Does Richard decide to go to Ireland because he looks so marvelous in his white plumed helmet (Pasco's playing) or in spite of the helmet's feathers tickling his nose (Richardson's choice)? Is Bolingbroke being a Machiavellian liar when he promises York that he does not really mean to bring civil war to England (III. iii. 44–48) as in Richardson's reading; or is that a reassurance that he himself believes (Pasco)? Is Richard's entrance in the deposition scene in the long white gown of a penitent prisoner, that of a Christ-figure (Pasco): or, in the open-to-the-waist white shirt and brown trousers, that of the now-humanized and unregal Richard (Richardson)? Is Bolingbroke in V. iii. amused at the prospect of seeing the loudly penitent Duchess of York, giving an ironic inflection to "dangerous" as Richardson orders, "My dangerous cousin, let your mother in," (V. iii. 81); or is he suddenly dubious of his own position? "Our scene is alt'red from a serious thing,/ And now is changed to 'The Beggar and the King'" (V. iii. 79–80); Pasco takes a long pause before he says "the king," as if he does not quite believe that he really *is* the king. The choices are many, existing on every level from costume detail to gesture to vocal inflection to line interpretation. Obviously, one develops preferences, and since I saw the version with Pasco as Richard and Richardson as Bolingbroke first and more often (five out of seven times), I tend to find that series of choices more convincing. With Pasco, I always saw the king and felt his profoundly deep sorrow when the man loses the symbolic power which was, for him, his identity. With Richardson, I saw the man, delighting in playing the king, but with less to lose, with less emotional involvement in an image from which he would be torn.

But, in either version, the point is that seeing both performances made me see the variety of choices possible. We often say to our students that there are many interpretations of a text, but this series of performances made me believe what I had been saying. Barton's production, with its constant variations on itself, including small, but noticeable changes in the period of two months during which I saw the production, makes us aware of several motives for any action, several subtexts for any line.

Moreover, he gives us a new perspective on the play. Just as Peter Brook's doubling of Theseus and Oberon, Hippolyta and Titania, gave his controversial production of *A Midsummer Night's Dream* a new unity by suggesting that Theseus and Hippolyta work through the problems of marriage before they celebrate the ceremony, so Barton's decision to use both Pasco and Richardson, in both roles, forces us to see how much this play depends on role-playing. The production makes us constantly aware that Pasco and Richardson play each other's roles—and so we see too the play's insistence that Richard and Bolingbroke are each king and usurper, king and beggar. Richard, after all, sums it up in prison: "Thus play I in one person many people."

Notes

1. First staged by the Royal Shakespeare Company at Stratford in 1973, then produced in Brooklyn in the spring of 1974, and restaged for Stratford and London in late spring, summer, and fall of 1974. I saw the 1974 Stratford version, which had a conspicuously simpler set (no ladders) than the earlier productions.

2. See, for example, Irving Ribner, *The English History Play in the Age of Shakespeare* (Princeton: Princeton University Press, 1965), pp. 160–161; M.M. Reese, *The Cease of Majesty* (London: Edward Arnold, 1961), pp.252–253; James Winny, *The Player King* (London: Chatto & Windus, 1968), pp. 72–73. Even Norman Rabkin, who argues convincingly in *Shakespeare and the Common Understanding* (New York: Free Press, 1967) "the primary technique of *Richard II* is that of keeping our sympathies in suspense" (p. 86), goes on to make the point that Bolingbroke, unlike Richard, can deal "honorably and wisely with the assassin he has employed" (p. 90).

3. All quotations from the play are from *William Shakespeare: The Complete Works*, gen. ed. Alfred Harbage. (Baltimore: Penguin Books, 1969).

4. C.E. Montague, quoted in *The English Dramatic Critics*, ed. James Agate (London: A. Barker, Ltd., 1932), pp. 249–250.

5. Harcourt Williams, quoted in Richard Findlater, *The Player Kings* (London: Weidenfeld & Nicolson, Ltd., 1971), p. 174.

6. Audrey Williamson, *Old Vic Drama* (London: Rockcliff, 1948), p. 210.

7. Richard David, *Shakespeare Survey 6*, ed. Allardyce Nicoll, (Cambridge: Cambridge University Press, 1953), p. 134.

8. Kenneth Tynan, *Curtains* (London: Longmans, 1961), p. 89.

9. One might note that Richard Pasco, at least originally, shared the

reservations of many audience members about this staging. According to Eileen Totten, *Plays and Players* (June, 1973), "it was only when the scene was played as Barton wanted it in front of fellow actors, that their stunned reaction convinced Pasco that Barton and Richardson, at least theatrically, were perfectly right" (p. 28).

10. Rabkin, pp. 88–89, comments usefully on Bolingbroke's silence and mystery.
11. *Plays and Players* (June, 1973), p. 27.
12. My thinking on the relationship between performance and interpretation has been greatly helped by Thomas R. Whitaker, both in conversation and in his article, "Notes on Playing the Player," *Centennial Review*, 16 (1972), pp. 1-22.

Speculations on Doubling in Shakespeare's Plays

STEPHEN BOOTH

Your If is the only peace-maker; much virtue in If.

Cordelia and Lear's Fool never meet, and ever since Wilfred Perrett's *The Story of King Lear* in 1904 critics have often and persuasively argued that one boy actor played both parts. *If* that was indeed the case, then "And my poor fool is hang'd," the statement with which Lear begins his last speech, takes on an extra dimension in a scene and play notable for irreverence of definitions and ideational boundaries. Inasmuch as the possibility of such a dimension to *King Lear* has so long been a relatively tame familiar among Shakespearians, I hope that it may evoke some tolerance for the following pure but not wholly wanton speculation on phenomena of which "And my poor fool" may be the ultimate instance: Shakespeare's awareness and use of the dramatic potential in the fact of performance and the facts of particular performances.

The facts of playhouse, actors, costumes—all the accidents of performance—can never be absent from the mind of an audience; but in our willingness to suspend disbelief, we ordinarily maintain a separating membrane between our consciousness of the events portrayed and our consciousness of the actual theatrical events that convey the story. The partition is easily breached—by fat heroines, fire engines in the street, forgotten lines, inadequate props, an over- or under-heated theater, or the accidental pertinence of a word, line, or situation to some concern local to a particular time, place, or audience (I once saw a Petruchio who came back after intermission without his glass eye); but our minds ordinarily reject incursions of playhouse reality into the fiction. We simply amend performances in passage in much the way we automatically correct or delete linotypers' errors while we read a newspaper. We entertain two fused but distinct "realities" at once.

Shakespeare seems always to have been fascinated with the double consciousness inherent in watching actors on a stage and watching the characters they portray. His interest is most straightforwardly evident in the opening chorus of *Henry V*. More typically, however, Shakespeare likes to experiment with the unsettling but enriching effects to be had from making an audience's two incompatible consciousnesses indivisible. Take, for example, his inexhaustible delight in the fact of boys playing girls who are pretending to be boys (in *As You Like It* he treats us to the contemplation of a boy pretending to be a girl pretending to be a boy pretending to be a girl),[1] or such exercises as a scene where two actors playing antique Danes discuss a "late innovation" of the London theater *in* a London theater during a "war of the theaters" in which both speakers are combatants (*Hamlet*, II. ii. 323-365), or a scene where an actor playing a Danish prince gives an acting lesson to a group of actors playing actors (*Hamlet*, III. ii. 1-42). In the scene where Julius Caesar is murdered, the actor playing Cassius speculates on a future that is also the present: "How many ages hence/ Shall this our lofty scene be acted over/ In states unborn and accents yet unknown" (*Julius Caesar*, III. i. 111-113).[2] At the very end of *Antony and Cleopatra* the boy playing Cleopatra delivered this excellent description of the first scenes of the performance in which he spoke it:

> . . . the quick comedians
> Extemporally will stage us, and present
> Our Alexandrian revels; Antony
> Shall be brought drunken forth, and I shall see
> Some squeaking Cleopatra boy my greatness
> I' th' posture of a whore.
>
> (V. ii. 215-220)

In a scene where actors pretending to be Toby Belch, Maria, and Fabian mock the pretentious Malvolio by pretending they believe he is mad, Fabian says "If this were play'd upon a stage now, I could condemn it as an improbable fiction" (*Twelfth Night*, III. iv. 121—122). Even in *Henry V,* where the Chorus begins by carefully distinguishing between what the audience sees on the stage and what is represented there, he goes on to mock the distinction with a pun on real and metaphoric nausea:

> . . . the scene
> Is now transported, gentles, to Southampton;
> There is the play-house now, there must you sit,
> And thence to France shall we convey you safe
> And bring you back, charming the narrow seas
> To give you gentle pass; for, if we may,
> We'll not offend one stomach with our play.
>
> (II. Chorus. 34-40)

The general phenomenon probably reaches its ultimate complexity in Thisby's logically casual, joyously obscene "I kiss the wall's hole, not your lips at all" (*MND,* V. i. 200).

Shakespeare's demonstrable experimentation with unifications of performance and performed invites speculation on other and non-demonstrable experiments along the same lines— notably by means of doubling parts. We know of instances where Renaissance companies did double parts,[3] and we know from such things as the tracks of a tall blond boy actor and a short dark one in the early comedies that Shakespeare wrote with his casts in mind. We are also mindful of characters like Francisco, Philo, and Archidamus who appear in the first scenes of their plays, and vanish,[4] of characters like Poins and Casca who are important in the early parts of plays and absent thereafter, and of important characters like the Earl of Douglas, Octavius (in *Julius Caesar*), and Macduff, who do not appear until others have strutted their hours and departed. Speculation on doubled parts has traditionally served to explain such mysterious appearances and disappearances; it could also explain why *As You Like It* has two dukes named Frederick and two characters named Oliver (see Oliver Mar-Text's uncalled-for exit lines in III. iii.). Speculation on doubling might also lead to more far-reaching possible connections between Shakespeare's activities as writer and his activities as producer.

Consider the explosion of categories effected by the following exchange if the actors playing Titania and Oberon double as Hippolyta and Theseus:

Oberon.
Ill met by moonlight, proud Titania.
Titania.
What, jealous Oberon! Fairies, skip hence.
I have forsworn his bed and company.
Oberon.
Tarry, rash wanton; am not I thy lord?
Titania.
Then I must be thy lady; but I know
When thou hast stolen away from fairy land,
And in the shape of Corin sat all day,
Playing on pipes of corn, and versing love
To amorous Phillida. Why art thou here,
Come from the farthest steep of India,
But that, forsooth, the bouncing Amazon,
Your buskin'd mistress and your warrior love,
To Theseus must be wedded, and you come
To give their bed joy and prosperity?
Oberon.
How canst thou thus, for shame, Titania,
Glance at my credit with Hippolyta,
Knowing I know thy love to Theseus?
Didst not thou lead him through the glimmering night
From Perigouna, whom he ravished?
And make him with fair Ægles break his faith,
With Ariadne, and Antiopa?
Titania.
These are the forgeries of jealousy . . .

                     .   .   .   .   .

And through this distemperature we see
The seasons alter: hoary-headed frosts
Fall in the fresh lap of the crimson rose,
And on old Hiems' thin and icy crown
An odorous chaplet of sweet summer buds
Is, as in mockery, set. The spring, the summer,
The childing autumn, angry winter, change
Their wonted liveries; and the mazed world,
By their increase, now knows not which is which. . . .
                              (*MND*, II. i. 60-81, 106-114)

I begin with the example of the royal couples in *A Midsummer Night's Dream* for several reasons: (1) because the possibility that one pair of actors played both couples is specifically—though, I believe, arbitrarily—denied by William Ringler in the most sophisticated, recent, respectable, and respected of all studies of Shakespearian doubling;[5] (2) because doubling in those four roles (and in those of Philostrate and Puck) in Peter Brook's 1971 Royal Shakespeare Company production was so spectacularly workable and so spectacularly successful as to have since become a theatrical fad among less grand companies; (3) because in Brook's production the entrance of Theseus and Hippolyta at IV. i. 107, immediately after the same actors have exited as Oberon and Titania at IV. i. 106—the entrance that caused Ringler to say that the kings and queens could not have been successfully doubled—particularly delighted the two audiences I observed as they watched the Brook production and also seemed to delight the two actors (who strode back through the doorway grinning in apparent triumph at the transparent theatricality of their physically minimal metamorphosis); and—most importantly—(4) because the lines quoted above suggest that they were written to capitalize on and intensify the effect of planned theatrical doubling. The lines (which lead up to the dispute over the changeling boy), seem specially designed to hold a maximum number and variety of examples of changes and confusions of persona: Oberon and Titania dwell on identity (". . . am not I thy lord?" "Then I must be thy lady . . ."). Titania alludes to a magical metamorphosis in Oberon's shape and to the season's improbable changes of costume. She introduces the topic of Oberon's infidelity with Phillida, and that accusation merges muddily with the charge of infidelity with Hippolyta. Oberon accuses Titania of alienating Theseus's affections from three lovers whom he had abandoned in the past; the abandonments of Ægles and Ariadne are clearly documented in mythology, but in some accounts "Antiopa" is another name for Hippolyta herself (Plutarch calls her Antiope, and, in the course of recording the various and conflicting accounts of Theseus's campaigns against the Amazons, says this—here in North's version: "Clidemus the Historiographer . . . sayeth that . . . peace was taken betwene them by meanes of one of the women called Hyppolita. For this Historiographer calleth the Amazone which Theseus maried, Hyppolita, and not Antiopa").

Despite the scholarly enlightenment we have undergone

during the last hundred years, most of our thinking about Elizabethan casting is still based on the assumed universality of Ibsenian practices. Moreover, we show a narrowmindedness improbable in a century that accepted Charlie Chaplin as monochromatic, silent, twenty feet high, and flat. We are inclined, for example, to assume that young actors played young characters and that changes of costume and make-up were radical and time-consuming. What if characters "were to be known by garment, not by favor?" By analogy with the George Spelvins and Walter Plinges who used to skulk through the cast lists of twentieth-century barnstormers, we generally assume that Elizabethan companies doubled parts as a last resort when they were understaffed. We take it for granted that Laurence Olivier and John Wayne will always play the best parts in any productions in which they appear; we are untroubled that the General Burgoyne of this week's play was Othello last week and Archie Rice before that. What if Elizabethan audiences exercised the same habits of mind not only between play and play but between scene and scene so that a leading actor's assignments within a single play were limited by nothing but physical possibility and the egos of his peers? What if Bottom's ridiculous scheme for playing Pyramus and Thisbe and the lion were slightly less of an exaggeration of Elizabethan stage practice than it now seems?

I suspect that Shakespeare used the doubling of parts in performance adjectivally—to inform, comment on, and, perhaps, augment the events enacted. For example, although I do not accept the casual premises on which Ringler rejects the possibility of doubling the royal couples in *A Midsummer Night's Dream*, I am at least as much persuaded as Ringler himself is by his well-documented and carefully argued suggestion (pp. 133—134) that the four adult actors who played Flute, Snout, Starveling, and Snug doubled as Peaseblossom, Cobweb, Moth, and Mustardseed. The doubling of those two sets of different roles in production mirrors, underscores, and comments on the comically troublesome philosophic implications of the "doubling" of Flute, Snout, Starveling, and Snug—four "real" people—with Thisby, Wall, Moonshine, and Lion—the complexly and variously unreal creatures they personify in the play staged within the fiction.

Before I go further, I should acknowledge the fact that this essay has obviously invaded the traditional purviews of old-fashioned, hardcore literary scholarship; and—even though I have been, and will be, at pains to insist that my speculations are *only* speculations, that I do not pretend to be proving anything—I will pause to examine the validity of arguments inconvenient to my own which have been offered by earlier and more obviously qualified speculators, speculators who have believed themselves to have proved, or who have been believed to have proved, their cases. In picking at the work of my predecessors, I may seem to think I am discrediting it. I do not think that at all. I mean only to suggest that their arguments are as speculative as my own and are equally, and just as necessarily, selective and arbitrary both in their use of the sparse, inconsistent, and therefore inconclusive surviving evidence about Renaissance doubling practices and in their use of analogies from modern theatrical custom.

Inasmuch as I began with the case for doubling Cordelia and Lear's fool, and since I will conclude there also, arguments against that possibility make a good point of departure for a survey of previous speculation. This is the immediately relevant portion of Kenneth Muir's note on "And my poor fool is hang'd" in the New Arden *King Lear:* "Brandl, Quiller-Couch and Edith Sitwell have argued that the two parts of Cordelia and the Fool were taken by the same actor; but [Alwin] Thaler, *T.L.S.* 13 February, 1930 [p. 122], shows that the parts could not have been doubled."[6] In fact, Thaler shows only that he believes such a doubling would not have been to his taste. I say "believes" because the immediate occasion of Thaler's letter to *The Times* was an Old Vic production of *Julius Caesar* in which "forty-three speaking parts (not counting the mob) were done by twenty-five players"; Thaler, who "did not happen to get a programme until the play was over," was delighted because he failed to detect a dozen instances of doubling. However, although he assumes that audiences are inevitably displeased when they recognize one actor in two or more roles, Thaler seems to have been equally delighted by the experience of detecting the reappearances of one actor who played Decius Brutus, Lepidus, and Messala. "The good round *voice*" of that "gifted and versatile actor . . . gave him away; but the trouble (if trouble it was) lay also in the fact that he was called upon to double—or rather, to treble—in parts which repeatedly gave him almost the centre of the stage, though not nearly so much prominence, after all, as the storm and agonies of Lear give to the Fool and to Cordelia." The bases of Thaler's specific case against the doubling of the Fool and Cordelia are inferentially presented at the end of the foregoing excerpt; they are (1) that an audience would inevitably have been aware that the same actor played both parts, and (2) that doubling those parts or any others like them would therefore be aesthetically unsatisfying. I grant the first but not the second (with which Thaler himself seems uncomfortable; see his parenthetical "if trouble it was").

Thaler works also from a complementary set of casual and dubious assumptions about the desires and perquisites of actors, a set of assumptions which, like those about the likes and dislikes of audiences, had recently sustained the more prolix and more arbitrary speculations of William J. Lawrence in *Pre-Restoration Stage Studies* (Cambridge, Mass.: Harvard University Press, 1927), pp. 43-78. Both Thaler and Lawrence assume that, in Thaler's words, "doubling was, at best, a necessary evil." As they work through the perfectly inconclusive available evidence, that assumption is embodied in a succession of "have to" constructions (e.g., this from Thaler: "Dr. Greg's analysis has shown . . . that not a few sharers in Henslowe's companies did have to double . . . as, for instance, in certain performances of Peele's *Battle of Alcazar* in which twenty-six actors did sixty parts, and the 'burden of doubling fell mainly on the sharers.' This, of course, does not absolutely prove that the sharers in Shakespeare's company also had to double, though it may not be altogether beside the point to observe that the principals in modern productions of Shakespeare. . .do not escape entirely.") The foregoing example focuses on a distinction between sharers and hired players that is urgent to the arguments of Thaler and Lawrence, a distinction that is, I think, misconceived because it rests on the improbable assumption that actors do not like performing. In obedience to a variation on the kind of snobbish, temporary prejudice that had earlier led less sophisticated commentators to such grosser follies as the conclusion that a mere actor from Stratford could not have written the plays that bear his name and the conclusion that, if he did write them, he must have been an inept and unwilling actor who appeared as infrequently as possible and then only in small, genteel roles—Thaler and Lawrence assume that Renaissance actors did not like doubling parts, that the extra work of doubling would have been onerous to them, and that doubling would have demeaned the doubler. This is Lawrence explaining why he thinks "that the perfectly obvious 'doubles' in *Hamlet* were precisely those which were carefully avoided": "Though the necessary intermediate annihilation of a character might suggest to the dramatist how the services of the released actor might be further utilised, he would, I think, occasionally be given pause by the status of the actor. Polonius [whom 'modern barnstormers' often double with the First Gravedigger], and the Ghost [also a prime candidate for doubling], were important roles and must have been sustained by two sharers. . . . Personally, I cannot see sharers trenching on the pitiful prerogative of the hirelings" (pp. 71-72). Personally, I can.

Lawrence's adverbial admission and my own are unavoidable and must be of the essence of any study of this subject. The evidence is insufficient to allow for anything like objectivity. Even the hard evidence on Renaissance doubling practices is soft. Take, for example, the table of character distribution printed in the 1611 quarto of *The Fair Maid of the Exchange*. It purports to distribute twenty-one characters among eleven actors; its evidence suggests that doubling was not restricted to minor roles (the part of Barnard and three lesser parts are all listed "for one"); that actors doubled in very different roles (Barnard, an adult male, is listed for the same actor who plays two women and a boy); and that very fast changes were not considered impractical (the list demands that the actor who exits at line 601 as Bobbington, a thrasonical footpad, reenter three lines later as Mr. Berry, an elderly gentleman). However, although the list testifies that prospective buyers of the 1611 quarto would have been unsurprised by such doubles, the list calls for a demonstrably impossible production; as Lawrence points out (p. 75), both Barnard and Mr. Berry are on stage late in the play at the same time as characters whom the list says they double. The casting table is thus useful but treacherous evidence both for and against the belief that parts were freely doubled on the late sixteenth-century and early seventeenth-century London stage.[7] No conclusion can be other than speculative, and a speculator's direction necessarily reflects the brand of common sense that suits his personal aesthetic bias.

Thus, Lawrence—faced with one of the rare surviving cast lists, the Dramatis Personae published with the 1629 text of Massinger's *The Roman Actor*—treats the fact that a sharer in the King's company is listed for two roles as a mysterious deviation from custom: "fourteen players are shown taking sixteen characters [several characters are not listed], but curiously enough, though several hirelings played parts, the only doubling revealed fell to the lot of a sharer, T. Pollard, whose name stands opposite [those of two characters, Aelius Lamia and Stephanos]" (pp. 76-77). I, on the other hand, resist with difficulty an inclination to press Thomas Pollard's double duty into service as evidence for a hypothetical norm exactly opposite to Lawrence's. This particular speck of rare evidence especially appeals to me because it suggests that parts were doubled from choice as well as from necessity; Lawrence continues:

> This remarkable reversal of [what he assumes must have been] custom somewhat mystifies, but we have still another puzzle. Of the sixteen [listed] characters, four were sustained by boy players of women, though the adult players, sharers and hirelings, of the King's company certainly numbered more than twelve. Since the full manpower had not been drawn upon, what was the necessity for resort to doubling? It was not as if anything was gained by economizing in players: a sharer got his share even on days he did not act. (p. 77)

A similar divergence of interpretation results from contrary aesthetic perspectives on the "Induction" to Marston's *Antonio and Mellida*, where some boy actors discuss the parts they are about to play. When asked what part he is to act, one of them replies, "The necessity of the play forceth me to act two parts: Andrugio, the distressed Duke of Genoa, and Alberto, a Venetian gentleman, enamoured on the Lady Rossaline. . . ." Lawrence takes the speech as an "oblique apology," and, since doubling "cannot have been so rarely resorted to . . . as to necessitate any explanation or apology," he sees no reason for Marston to write the speech, "unless perchance it were that some exigency had compelled him to run counter to a recognized taboo and make the actor of so important a character as Andrugio double it with another" (p. 63). I, on the other hand, see the "Induction" as a sustained exposition—and exploitation—of the likenesses and unlikeness of the various kinds of doubleness inherent in all acting and particularly in acting a play in which actors pretend to be characters who pretend to be what they are not. The boys discuss their parts: one is to play a hypocrite; another will play Antonio, a young nobleman who disguises himself as an amazon (in order to woo a boy actor playing a heroine who disguises herself as a page); another, when asked what part he plays, says, "The part of all the world," and then explains away that improbability by saying that by "the part of all the world" he means "the fool"; a fourth plays "a modern braggadoch"; and a fifth plays Galeatzo, "a right part for Proteus": "now . . . as grave as a Puritan's ruff; with the same breath as slight and scattered in his fashion as—as—as—a—a—anything . . . now lamenting, then chafing, straight laughing, then . . ." In that group, the actor who says he plays two parts merely adds one more to a carefully baroque collection of doubles; and the inclusion of theatrical doubling in such a context suggests that at least one playwright saw (and, if only for the length of the "Induction" to *Antonio and Mellida,* expected an audience to see) thematic ramifications in accidents of production. Marston saw that theatrical doubling is akin to, has the same physics as, and is an exploitable auxiliary of the double identities that are the mainsprings of delight in all theatrical productions and most theatrical plots—delight in imperfectly blurred distinctions between such categories as fact/fiction, stage/fictional location, actor/character, child/adult, male/female, reality/disguise, honesty/hypocrisy, truth/falsehood, wicked lies/innocent deception. . . .

My sense of theatrical aesthetics says that Thaler and Lawrence base their common-sense arguments on assumptions that misunderstand the tastes of audiences and the temperament of actors. *My* common sense says that audiences have not changed much in four hundred years. The famous elegy on Burbage ascribed to "Jo ffletcher" suggests that, like us, Renaissance audiences delighted alternately and equally in being taken in by theatrical illusion and by seeing through it (and thus becoming party to it); the elegist revels both in listing contrasting characters in whom he has recognized Burbage ("young Hamlett, ould Heironymoe") and in the fact "that spectators . . . whilst he but seem'd to bleed,/ Amazed, thought even then hee dyed in deed." Similarly, actors seem always to have delighted in the virtuosity

involved in doubling—as Bottom and Holofernes, Shakespeare's
fictional amateur actors, testify; as Hamlet suggests, profession-
als too probably wanted to do more and not less than was required of them—wished to speak more than was set down for
them.

If I were to choose modern analogues, I would point (1) to
Lon Chaney playing bit parts in films—and sometimes in
scenes—where he played the star part; (2) to *Frankenstein Meets
the Wolf Man* (Universal Pictures, 1943) in which Bela Lugosi was
billed as, and in close-ups actually played, Frankenstein's
Monster; Lugosi was by then too weak to carry the costume, so
Lon Chaney, Jr. played both monsters through most of the film;
(3) to the fact that people who detect that instance of doubling are
delighted to do so and that, when they tell their friends, the
friends are equally delighted by having been fooled; (4) to the
London stage in 1957; in that year Robert Morley appeared in a
play he seems to have rewritten for the specific purpose of
playing a portly middle-aged man and his portly young nephew
(who at one point met each other in a doorway: one departed—
balding and in a three-piece gray business suit—just as the other
entered with bright red hair and wearing a sporty checkered
jacket); in the same year Richard Attenborough appeared in a
play that hinged on whether the central character did or did not
have a criminal twin brother (once Attenborough exited, rear
stage right, and—in what seemed less time than it would have
taken him to run diagonally across the stage—sauntered from the
wings at the front of the stage on the other side, totally recos-
tumed as "the brother"); (5) to the fact that those two ridiculous
plays offered nothing to Morley, Attenborough, or their audiences except delight in impossibly quick changes; and (6) to the
fact that that was quite enough to satisfy all parties.

If it is now thoroughly understood how genuinely speculative the enterprise must necessarily be, I will proceed to offer
some possibilities for Shakespearian doubles that would thematically enrich the plays in which I propose them and that *might*
have been not only anticipated but exploited as Shakespeare
wrote. Each, like the doubles employed by Brook and those
proposed by Ringler in *A Midsummer Night's Dream*, takes its
particular play one step further in that play's own direction.

Consider the effects on two plays that dwell on the inconclusiveness of murder if the actor murdered as Julius Caesar returns not only as Caesar's ghost in IV. iii., but also as his nephew Octavius in IV. i. and V. i., and if the actor murdered as Duncan does indeed wake Duncan with his knocking by returning as Macduff to discover his own body.[8]

Consider the quite differently ironic effect if in II. i. of *Richard II* the scrupulous Gaunt is helped off the stage at line 138 and the same actor returns at line 146 in the person of the unscrupulous Northumberland, Bolingbroke's political foster father, to announce Gaunt's death:

> *Northumberland.*
>   My liege, old Gaunt commends him to your majesty.
> *King Richard.*
>   What says he?
> *Northumberland.*
>   Nay, nothing; all is said.
>   His tongue is now a stringless instrument;
>   Words, life, and all, old Lancaster hath spent.
>
> (146-150)

Northumberland next speaks seventy lines later when he and his fellow conspirators are left alone on the stage:

> *Northumberland.*
>   Well, lords, the Duke of Lancaster is dead.
> *Ross.*
>   And living too; for now his son is Duke.
>
> (224-225)

In *Romeo and Juliet* Shakespeare belatedly labels Mercutio and Paris as "a brace of kinsmen" to Prince Escalus (V. iii. 293-294). The carnage among the prince's relatives demonstrates that the woe said to be generated by the feud extends to a family of bystanders innocent of even blood ties to the Montagues and Capulets. However, the family relationship among Escalus, Mercutio, and Paris is so haphazardly and casually established within the fiction, that it may have been registered only as the formal incorporation of a link already obvious to an audience that saw all three played by one actor.[9]

Dolabella, Cleopatra's last conquest and the character addressed in the last sentence of *Antony and Cleopatra*, appears

at the beginning of V. i. where Caesar sends him to treat with
Antony ("Go to him, Dolabella, bid him yield"). Then Dercetas
enters to report Antony's death to Caesar. The dying Antony
gave Cleopatra one piece of specific advice: "None about Caesar
trust but Proculeius"(IV. xv. 48). The scene that began with
Dolabella's embassy to Antony ends with the introduction of
Proculeius, whom Caesar sends on a parallel mission to
Cleopatra:

> *Caesar.*
>> Come hither, Proculeius. Go and say
>> We purpose her no shame. Give her what comforts
>> The quality of her passion shall require,
>> Lest, in her greatness, by some mortal stroke
>> She do defeat us. For her life in Rome
>> Would be eternal in our triumph. Go,
>> And with your speediest bring us what she says,
>> And how you find of her.
>
> *Proculeius.*
>> Caesar, I shall. [*Exit.*]
>
> *Caesar.*
>> Gallus, go you along. [*Exit* Gallus.] Where's Dolabella,
>> To second Proculeius?
>
> *All.*
>> Dolabella!
>
> *Caesar.*
>> Let him alone, for I remember now
>> How he's employ'd; he shall in time be ready....
>>> (V. i. 61–72)

Caesar's lapse of memory seems gratuitous at best; all it does is
emphasize the parallel between Proculeius and Dolabella, remind us that Dolabella's employment is a mission to a dead man,
and give Dolabella special prominence. In the next scene, the last
of the play, Proculeius immediately demonstrates the error of
Antony's trust by objectifying the perfidy inherent in the instructions we have just heard Caesar give. After Proculeius has
tricked and captured Cleopatra, Dolabella, the one man about
Caesar who turns out to warrant Cleopatra's trust, enters and
takes charge of the prisoner. When he and Cleopatra are alone,
Dolabella's first concern is with his own identity. That concern
re-emphasizes the parallel between himself and Proculeius
(whose interview Cleopatra began by asking his name).

Dolabella, however, stresses his identity with an intensity that seems curious—but would be justified and dramatically powerful if the actor we saw in our own dream of an Antony were now before us as Dolabella. The doubling of the parts would also give a special falsehood and a more special truth to "Gentle madam, no":

Dolabella.
    Most noble Empress, you have heard of me?
Cleopatra.
    I cannot tell.
Dolabella.
                  Assuredly you know me.
Cleopatra.
    No matter, sir, what I have heard or known.
    You laugh when boys or women tell their dreams;
    Is't not your trick?
Dolabella.
                I understand not, madam.
Cleopatra.
    I dreamt there was an Emperor Antony—
    O, such another sleep, that I might see
    But such another man!
Dolabella.
                If it might please ye—
Cleopatra.
    His face was as the heav'ns, and therein stuck
    A sun and moon, which kept their course and lighted
    The little O, the earth.
Dolabella.
              Most sovereign creature—
Cleopatra.
    His legs bestrid the ocean....
    ...realms and islands were
    As plates dropp'd from his pocket.
Dolabella.
                  Cleopatra—
Cleopatra.
    Think you there was or might be such a man
    As this I dreamt of?
Dolabella.
            Gentle madam, no.
                        (V. ii. 71–82, 91–94)

In the great restitution at the end of *The Winter's Tale* two losses are irrevocable: Mamilius and Antigonus are dead and gone. I suspect that, although they are not restored in one dimension of the play, its story, they were restored in a second dimension, the performance. Mamilius's death was reported in III. ii.:

Servant.
   ...The Prince your son, with mere conceit and fear
   Of the Queen's speed, is gone.
Leontes.
                     How! Gone?
Servant.
                            Is dead.
                           (142–143)

In the final scene Mamilius is all but forgotten. Two scenes earlier, when the fugitive Florizel and Perdita are about to be brought before Leontes, Paulina brings up Mamilius:

Paulina.
            Had our prince,
   Jewel of children, seen this hour, he had pair'd
   Well with this lord; there was not full a month
   Between their births.
Leontes.
      Prithee, no more; cease. Thou know'st
   He dies to me again when talk'd of. Sure,
   When I shall see this gentleman [Florizel], thy speeches
   Will bring me to consider that which may
   Unfurnish me of reason.
                     (V. i. 115–123)

Mamilius remains a recurring topic for the rest of the scene. For instance, Florizel and Perdita enter during Leontes's response to Paulina, and Leontes immediately addresses Florizel in words that echo lines spoken earlier to and about Mamilius and Perdita:

            They are come.
   Your mother was most true to wedlock, Prince;
   For she did print your royal father off,
   Conceiving you.
                     (V. i. 123–126)

The ensuing dialogue is too rich a jumble of real, feigned, assumed, past, present, and potential identities to describe here and is too long to quote. Suffice it to say that, if the actor who played Mamilius were now playing Perdita, the jumble would be sufficient nearly to unfurnish an audience of reason. *If* the actor who played Mamilius also played Perdita, then, when Leontes said, "What might I have been,/ Might I a son and daughter now have looked on,/ Such goodly things as you!" (176–178), he would have been doing so in three very different ways: Perdita is the daughter he thinks dead; Florizel, "paired well with" Perdita rather than Mamilius, will be Leontes's son by marriage; and this seeming lady, the boy dressed as Perdita, would—in theatrical fact—be Leontes's lost son Mamilius. Such intercourse between fictional and theatrical reality could make Mamilius's subsequent fall from the characters' memory more palatable.

Antigonus is not forgotten. At the very end, after everyone else has been brought to a fairy tale prospect, Paulina says:

> Go together,
> You precious winners all; your exultation
> Partake to every one. I, an old turtle,
> Will wing me to some wither'd bough and there
> My mate, that's never to be found again,
> Lament till I am lost.
>
> (V. iii. 130–135)

Thereupon, in the last speech of the play, Leontes suddenly makes dramatically impromptu restitution for Paulina's loss:

> O, peace Paulina!
> Thou shouldst a husband take by my consent,
> As I by thine a wife. This is a match,
> And made between's by vows. Thou hast found mine;
> But how, is to be question'd, for I saw her,
> As I thought, dead, and have, in vain, said many
> A prayer upon her grave. I'll not seek far—
> For him, I partly know his mind—to find thee
> An honourable husband. Come, Camillo,
> And take her by the hand, whose worth and honesty
> Is richly noted and here justified
> By us, a pair of kings....
>
> (135–146)

Five lines later Leontes concludes the play in a specifically theatrical metaphor:

> Good Paulina,
> Lead us from hence, where we may leisurely

Each one demand and answer to his part
Performed in this wide gap of time since first
We were dissevered. Hastily lead away.

(151—155)

The pairing of Paulina and Camillo (whose function as Leontes's chief courtier is taken on by Antigonus after Act I) would have seemed less arbitrary, less an act of mere authorial tidiness, to an audience that saw one actor play Antigonus in Acts II and III and Camillo in the other three acts. Such an audience would have seen the story line of this winter's tale, this old wives' tale, conclude with Leontes getting his old wife back and the theatrical event conclude with Paulina getting her old husband back.[10]

In *Twelfth Night*, Maria is the only major character who fails to appear in the final scene. The reason may be that the actor playing Maria was on stage as another character. It is tempting to think about the dramatic implications if Maria (whose handwriting is nearly indistinguishable from Olivia's, and who is thus a mainspring of one plot line), and Sebastian (whose likeness to Viola powers another) were really indistinguishable in theatrical fact. The entrances and exits of Maria and Sebastian in III. ii., iii., and iv. require them to trip over each other in the wings, but those scenes comment on one another, and, given producers and audiences attuned to conventions other than ours, the doubling would give the themes of *Twelfth Night* an appropriate extra dimension and extend them into the actual experience of the audience.

Twelfth Night could be described as a collection of variations on the word "suit." Although the characters take no note of Maria's absence from the last scene, they do have need of the sea captain who rescued Viola. He appears only in I. ii.—where he performs a necessary and demanding task of exposition by laying out all the givens of Illyrian society, and where Viola's suggestion that she become a follower of Olivia leads into this exchange:

Viola.

O that I serv'd that lady,
And might not be delivered to the world,
Till I had made mine own occasion mellow,

> What my estate is!
> *Captain.*
> > That were hard to compass,
> > Because she will admit no kind of suit—
> > No, not the Duke's.
> *Viola.*
> > There is a fair behavior in thee, Captain;
> > And though that nature with a beauteous wall
> > Doth oft close in pollution, yet of thee
> > I will believe thou hast a mind that suits
> > With this thy fair and outward character.
> > I prithee, and I'll pay thee bounteously,
> > Conceal me what I am, and be my aid
> > For such disguise as haply shall become
> > The form of my intent. I'll serve this duke....
> *Captain.*
> > Be you his eunuch, and your mute I'll be;
> > When my tongue blabs, then let mine eyes not see.
> *Viola.*
> > I thank thee. Lead me on.
>
> > > > (41–55, 62–64)

In the last scene, when occasion is so mellow that only Malvolio's problem remains to be solved, and nothing lets to make the lovers happy except Viola's "masculine usurped attire," she says this:

> The captain that did bring me first on shore
> Hath my maid's garments. He, upon some action,
> Is now in durance, at Malvolio's suit,
> A gentleman, and follower of my lady's.
>
> > > > (V. i. 266–269)

What if Shakespeare wrote both parts for one actor who wore one suit as the Captain in I. ii. and thereafter changed his clothes to become Malvolio (whose tongue blabs, who changes his clothes as the letter instructs him, and who is bound in a dark room)?

Cymbeline begins with two gentlemen who furnish exposition that establishes both the thematic and narrative bases for the play. The two gentlemen are interchangeable in all respects save that the first has information for which the second catechizes him. Throughout their seventy-line conversation they insist on, inquire about, assert, attempt to establish, and inadvertently dissolve various kinds of *uniqueness*—a concept always near the surface of their talk and also embedded either positively or negatively in their syntax ("You do not meet a man but frowns"—I. i. 1) and diction ("his wife's sole son," "None but the King," "Is she sole child to th' King?" —5, 10, 56). Above all, the First Gentleman insists that Posthumus is uniquely superior to all other men; but at the passionate height of his admiration, he introduces (47–50) the altogether appropriate and altogether subversive notion of Posthumus as, in Ophelia's terms, "the glass of fashion." Not surprisingly, the first gentleman's insistence on the difference between Posthumus and all other creatures relies heavily on assertions that Posthumus is beyond compare *and* on comparisons between him and other men— notably Cloten, his fellow foster-child to Cymbeline and his rival for Imogen. Consider this passage, which delivers its sense perfectly straightforwardly but is variously confusing, confused, and self-defeating in its structure:

> He that hath miss'd the Princess is a thing
> Too bad for bad report; and he that hath her—
> I mean that married her, alack, good man!
> And therefore banish'd—is a creature such
> As, to seek through the regions of the earth
> For one his like, there would be something failing
> In him that should compare. I do not think
> So fair an outward and such stuff within
> Endows a man but he.
>
> (16–25)

There are intriguing, but by no means definitive, signs that *Cymbeline* was written with the expectation that the substantively accidental facts of its performance would supplement—and provide a harmonious running commentary on—the themes, ironies, and texture of the play. Since the most spectacular double would be Posthumus/Cloten, consider the non-spectacular matter of the doubtful departure of the banished Posthumus. In his first substantial speech, the First Gentleman invites us to assume that Posthumus has already left Britain ("[Imogen is] wedded;/ Her husband banish'd, she imprison'd"—7–8); but Posthumus and Imogen enter with the Queen at I. i. 70 (I. ii. 1 in modern editions that follow the Folio's scene division). Both women urge Posthumus to depart quickly, and sixty lines later

Posthumus does in fact set out for Rome. Thirty lines after that
we hear that, within moments of Posthumus's departure from
the stage, Cloten met him and challenged him, and that the two
have for the last few minutes been fighting just off stage from the
place where Imogen bade Posthumus farewell, and where she
has remained to lament their parting. Then, after a conversation
among Imogen, the Queen, and Pisanio about Cloten and Posthumus (a conversation that includes Imogen's deeply ambiguous "I would they were in Afric both together;/ Myself by with a
needle, that I might prick/ The goer-back"—167–169 [Folio, I. ii.
97—99]), the stage clears, and Cloten makes his first entrance—
with two lords, the first of whom opens the scene (I. ii. or, Folio,
I. iii.) by saying "Sir, I would advise you to shift a shirt." If the
actor who, as Posthumus, has finally departed from Britain has
now changed his costume and remains to play his rival, then the
First Lord's suggestion takes on an extra dimension that does not
intrude upon the fiction but complements it.

There is neither space here nor probable need to rehearse the
events of *Cymbeline* in order to demonstrate that the play lends
itself to production with one actor in the insistently contrasted
roles of Posthumus and Cloten—or to spell out the various ways
in which that production device would lend something appropriate and positive to the play. A few reminders should be
enough: *Cymbeline* dwells persistently on the frailty of eyesight,
on the frailty of judgment, on the ricketiness of all evidence, and
on the limited capacity of clothing to transform its wearer or
deceive those who see him. The parallel between the invaluable
Posthumus and the worthless Cloten culminates in IV. ii. when
Imogen awakens beside the headless corpse of Cloten and recognizes it as Posthumus—not only by its borrowed clothing but by
"the shape of's leg...his hand,/ His foot Mercurial, his Martial
thigh" (310–311) and so on. Imogen's error is echoed in the last
scene of the play when Posthumus fails to recognize Imogen and
throws her violently aside as he abuses her in a sustained theatrical metaphor: "Shall's have a play of this? Thou scornful page,/
There lie thy part" (V. v. 228–229).

Instead of laboring a case for doubling Posthumus and Cloten, I want to return to the two gentlemen in Scene One to offer
token support for the more complex and less immediately interesting proposition that the fusion and confusion of absolutely

distinguishable identities is so of the essence of *Cymbeline* and of an audience's experience of its smallest details that the grosser manifestation in theatrical doubling is all but an aesthetic inevitability.

The gentlemen's opening conversation, concerned as it is for absolutes, dwells on two major examples of contrasting but confusable pairs in addition to Posthumus and Cloten, pairs that get confused in and by the gentlemen's syntax and diction: appearance as opposed to inward truth (I. i. 1–3, 9–14, 22–25) and the family of Sicilius Leonatus (of whose three children only one survives) as opposed to that of Cymbeline (of whose three children only one is known to survive). The three major contrasts coexist with and overlap with several incidental pairs (Cloten is the Queen's "sole son," and Imogen is "sole child to th' King"; the Queen and Imogen—among others—nearly become confused in lines 4—7: "His daughter, and the heir of's kingdom, whom/He purpos'd to his wife's sole son—a widow That late he married—hath referr'd hershel Unto a poor but worthy gentleman. She's wedded . . ."; and so on).

Of these incidental confusions the most incidental, most complicated, and most emblematic occur in the following lines on Posthumus's "name and birth"; the passage focuses on names, and is so precise in its details that its distinctions become indistinct:

> I cannot delve him to the root; his father
> Was call'd Sicilius, who did join his honour
> Against the Romans with Cassibelan,
> But had his titles by Tenantius, whom
> He serv'd with glory and admir'd success,
> So gain'd the sur-addition Leonatus. . . .

(28-33)

The syntactic and ideational physics of the subordinate clause modifying "Sicilius" present Cymbeline's two royal predecessors in such a way as to make the pairing feel like a contrast and—illogically—to imply an opposition between them—an opposition that the clause does not in fact assert: consider the fleeting false signals inherent in the mere presence of *Against*, the inversion of the unambiguous, normal sentence structure (which would be "did join his honor with Cassibelan against the

Romans"), and the implications of reversal and of Tenantius as the reverser in the use of "by" (the words "But" and "by" here beckon the listening mind toward some such conclusion as "But had his titles by Tenantius revoked"). Similarly, almost as incidentally, but even more complexly, Posthumus's father is named to us in a way that minimizes the definition naming is designed to provide. Posthumus's father "was called Sicilius" ("was" is a simple preterite, appropriate because, and indicating that, Sicilius is dead); but Sicilius later "gained the sur-addition Leonatus" (so "was," now five lines in the past, acquires a syntactically posthumus addition, the sense "was originally").[11] Confusion by means of names—by means of labels that fix identity—continues into the next generation and, thus, into the body of the play: Posthumus Leonatus is sometimes called Posthumus, sometimes Leonatus; and an audience has slight but constant difficulty jumping from one label to another. A variation on the phenomenon occurs on a larger scale in Imogen-Fidele and in Guiderius-Polydore, Arviragus-Cadwal, and Belarius-Morgan. Finally—in the prophecy that is miraculously delivered to Posthumus during his dream (V. iv. 133–143)[12] and is later read again and interpreted by the soothsayer (V. v. 435–457)—the play-long network of labels that fail to define because they overdo their specificity flowers luxuriously into the clarifying confusions of a series of overlapping puns and arch etymologies: "piece"—*woman*, "piece"—"branches," "piece"—"peace," "tender air"—*tender heir*, "Leonatus"—"lion's whelp," "lopped"—"clipped about," "piece of tender air"—"mollis aer"–"mulier" . . . .

The list of possibilities for doubling is long and tempting. For instance, I have said nothing about the thematic expansion that could result from doubling Ægeon and Dr. Pinch in *The Comedy of Errors* (see V. i. 294), or about the potential mental fireworks to be had by doubling Desdemona (Othello's innocent but falsely slandered white wife) and the urgently named Bianca (the white—the hoar—whore); but I will do well to return to *King Lear*, where the grounds for speculation are at least relatively firm.

Nahum Tate's sense that by all the laws of fiction Cordelia and Edgar are meant to marry might once have been fulfilled outside the fiction in what the audience actually saw on the stage; the actor who played the King of France in Scene One may have played Edgar thereafter.

Doubling of parts would also have added dimension to the "clothing" theme in *Lear*.

But the intriguing topic remains Cordelia and the Fool.

From the beginning of the play to the end, Shakespeare emphasizes the parallel between Kent and Edgar and between Cordelia and both. In Scene One Lear's rejection of his blunt-spoken daughter is intertwined with his rejection of the blunt-spoken Kent, who says he loved Lear "as my father" (I. i. 140). The likeness between Lear's wronged child and Gloucester's is obvious and directly stated several times. In the last scene the parallel between Edgar and Kent is underscored when we hear that they have exchanged accounts of their activities in disguise (V. iii. 210–215). The pairing of Kent and Cordelia recurs in the lines over Cordelia's body where alternation between certainty that Caius is dead and certainty that he is living interrupts Lear's series of similar alternations about Cordelia's state. In complement to the paired banishments of Kent and Cordelia in Scene One, the introduction of the disguised Kent in Scene Four flows into and fuses with Lear's call for the Fool. The first specific information we get about the Fool not only links him with Cordelia but also presents the Fool's condition as contingent on the presence or absence of Cordelia (in the following passage, note the general confusion about who is who, who is being sent for, and who answers):

> *Lear.*
> ...But where's my fool? I have not
> seen him this two days.
> *Knight.*
> Since my young lady's going into France,
> sir, the fool hath much pined away.
> *Lear.*
> No more of that; I have noted it well.
> Go you and tell my daughter I would speak
> with her. [*Exit an Attendant*] Go you,
> call hither my fool. [*Exit another Attendant.*]
>   *Re-enter* Oswald.
> O, you sir, you! Come you hither, sir. Who am I, sir?
> *Oswald.*
> My lady's father.

Lear.
    'My lady's father'! my lord's knave!

(I. iv. 70–79)

Kent and Edgar spend the body of the play succoring Lear and Gloucester. Each is disguised, and each is disguised as a kind of fool (Edgar as mad Tom; Kent as Caius, who sounds like, and whom Lear treats like, a professional clown—see I. iv. 9–43, 94). Cordelia leaves England for France, leaves Lear, leaves the play; but, though the character goes, the actor may have stayed behind to maintain the parallel between Cordelia and the two victims who disguise themselves to provide kind nursery for their erring oppressors.

I should say one more time that this essay does not pretend to add to our knowledge of Renaissance stage practices. At most it questions some assumptions by which our thinking has been arbitrarily bound and offers some directions in which informed ignorance may justly but tentatively range. There could, however, be some solid, practical use to this essay if it were to encourage modern directors to follow Brook in exploiting the theatrical energy inherent in the doubling of parts by companies that revel in the practice and, like their audiences, revel in the theatricality of theater. We might also get more productions of *Cymbeline* if it were taken to contain two star turns—not only Imogen but Posthumus/Cloten; and we might get better productions of *As You Like It* if a producer could lure a first-class character actor into the double role of the two dukes by means of a single, and therefore large, salary and the temptations of a professionally rewarding theatrical vehicle.

Notes

1. Compare the last scene of Jonson's *Epicoene* where a member of a boy company playing an adult male snatched away Epicoene's wig so that a stage full of boy actors playing characters of all ages and sexes could see for themselves that Epicoene is not a woman but a boy. Shakespeare, writing for an adult company, exploits similar metaphysics in the induction of *The Taming of the Shrew* when he presents an actor playing a boy dressed as Christopher Sly's lady and then presents a group of male actors playing male actors who play men and women in a story that focuses on real and imagined distinctions between masculine and feminine behavior.

2. Citations from Shakespeare are to *The Complete Works*, ed. Peter Alexander (London: Collins, 1951 and New York: Random House, 1952).

3. The early evidence is well presented and sensibly discussed in David Bevington's *From Mankind to Marlowe* (Cambridge, Mass.: Harvard University Press, 1962). On the subject of doubling on the London stage during Shakespeare's professional lifetime, see W.W. Greg, *Dramatic Documents from the Elizabethan Playhouses*, 2 vols. (Oxford: Clarendon Press, 1931) and the studies by William J. Lawrence, Alwin Thaler, and William A. Ringler, Jr. cited below.

4. At American county fairs it always used to take a brave and highly skilled master of ceremonies to quiet an audience and focus its attention long enough to begin an open-air program in daylight. The men I remember had trouble, even though they had loudspeakers and little brass bands to help them. Moreover, audiences at county fairs always doubted that the Hollywood star (perhaps the former comical sidekick to a singing cowboy) was actually there as advertised. The same conditions now obtain at supermarket openings and, in the mid-1960's, developed in the face of the awesome technological credentials of national television: The Beatles were to appear on *The Ed Sullivan Show*; the studio audience would not quiet down for the supporting acts that led up to the star turn next-to-closing; when the Beatles were scheduled again, Sullivan did what M.C.'s do at county fairs and suburban supermarkets; he showed the Beatles to the audience for a minute at the beginning, and the audience, assured that it would get what it came for, sat with reasonable patience through forty preliminary minutes of night-club comics and dancing mice.

    Shakespeare may have created Francisco, Archidamus, and Philo, characters who speak the opening lines of their plays and never appear after Scene One, for the specific purpose of allowing Burbage or an actor of similar stature to quiet the audience by his talent and, perhaps, reassure them by his presence.

5. William A. Ringler, Jr., "The Number of Actors in Shakespeare's Early Plays" in *The Seventeenth-Century Stage*, ed. Gerald Eades Bentley (Chicago: University of Chicago Press, 1968), pp. 110–134. Ringler says that *A Midsummer Night's Dream* has "four women characters who cannot double—Helena, Hermia, Titania, and Hippolyta (Helena, Hermia, and Titania are on stage together at IV. i.1; and though Titania exits at 106 while the other two remain, Hippolyta immediately enters at 107, so none of these four parts can be doubled)" (p. 133). By Ringler's logic, Oberon (who exits with Titania at IV. i. 106), and Theseus (who enters with Hippolyta at 107), could not be doubled either.

6. London: Methuen & Co. Ltd., 1952; revised ed., London and Cambridge, Mass.: Methuen & Co. Ltd. and Harvard University Press, 1959, p. 217. Like most recent editors, Muir glosses "fool" in "And

my poor fool is hang'd" as "a term of endearment" applied to Cordelia. Although the word "fool" was regularly applied to innocent creatures as a term of pity and/or endearment, although Shakespeare often uses the word to refer to children and to animals ("fool" here is followed immediately by "a dog, a horse, a rat"), and although that information suffices to explain all Renaissance uses of "fool" where the meaning "innocent" is clear from context and a scholarly footnote functions primarily as a historical persuader against student ingenuity—this is not such a context, and no comforting footnote can dispel the impression that "my poor fool" refers to Lear's Fool as well as to his daughter. The context that dictates that "fool" refers to Cordelia—Lear's position over her body, the pronoun "thou," her death by hanging, and the echo of two earlier cycles of grief and hope—coexists with the context provided by a play in which one character is a fool, a professional clown, who has vanished noiselessly during Act II, and by a scene punctuated with six reports of off-stage deaths; moreover, the syntactic habit of the word "and" is to introduce material relatively extraneous to what precedes it. One sentence, "And my poor fool is hang'd," makes— and cannot be reasoned out of making—two distinct and yet inseparable statements. See Arthur Eastman's "King Lear's 'Poor Fool'" (*Papers of the Michigan Academy of Science, Arts, and Letters,* XLIX [1964], 531–540).

　　Muir properly ignores a possible line of argument based on a rather new but well-entrenched tradition that says that Robert Armin played Lear's Fool (and would not have played the obvious boy's role or Cordelia); there is no evidence whatever that Armin played Lear's Fool (nor, of course, is there any proof that he did not).

7. Of plays printed during Shakespeare's career, the only other known distribution tables occur in the 1598 and 1610 quartos of *Mucedorus.* They are incomplete and less interesting than the one in *The Fair Maid of the Exchange,* but, for the parts they do distribute, they are workable. See Lawrence, pp. 58–59.

8. The doubling of Duncan and Macduff is possible if one takes the Folio's opening stage direction for I. vi. (*Enter King, Malcolme, Donalbaine, Banquo, Lenox, Macduff, Rosse, Angus, and Attendants*) as a literary embellishment. Only Duncan, Banquo, and Lady Macbeth speak in I. vi. Moreover, the stage directions in early texts are notoriously casual and notoriously independent of physical necessities dictated in dialogue. Still, it is well to remember that the doubling of Duncan and Macduff can be conjectured only if one allows oneself the arbitrary luxury of ignoring stage directions that indicate the presence of a character who does not speak and is not mentioned as present in the dialogue.

　　The same liberty allows—and casts doubt on—the inviting possibility that the actor who appeared as the shipmaster in I. i. of *The Tempest* played Prospero thereafter. The master, who is the first

character to speak in *The Tempest*, exits after his second speech and
never speaks again. The master has Prospero-like superiority both
metaphorically, in his office, and literally, in that the fourth speech
of the play suggests that the master is then on an upper stage—
invisible to the boatswain and mariners, but perhaps visible to the
audience (that speech also generates an incidentally suggestive
confusion between the master and the storm):

> *Boatswain.*
> Heigh, my hearts! cheerly, cheerly, my hearts!
> yare, yare! Take in the topsail. Tend to th'
> master's whistle. Blow till thou burst thy wind,
> if room enough.

But Prospero specifically lists the master as one of the two mariners
he sends Ariel to fetch in V. i. (97–101), and the stage direction at
line 216 calls for Ariel, the boatswain, and the master to enter. Still,
the master has no lines in Act V, and the boatswain speaks of him in
a manner appropriate to someone not then on stage (the *we* of the
boatswain's last sentence could refer to any token mariner brought
on with the boatswain and chosen from the mute supernumeraries
who appear as mariners in I. i.):

> *Boatswain.*
> …We were awak'd; straightway at liberty;
> Where we, in all her trim, freshly beheld
> Our royal, good, and gallant ship; our master
> Cap'ring to eye her. On a trice, so please you,
> Even in a dream, were we divided from them,
> And were brought moping hither.
>
> (V. i. 235–240)

9. Here again, there is genuine but inconclusive evidence against the
possibility I propose: Paris's dying words to Romeo are "Open the
tomb, lay me with Juliet" (V. iii. 73); Romeo says he will do so, and
then apparently does ("lie thou there, by a dead man interr'd"—87).
In modern production, Romeo never takes "with Juliet" to mean
"along side"; he reserves that position for his own corpse; in most
productions Paris's body is dragged to the rear and is often actually
invisible when Friar Lawrence says "Thy husband in thy bosom
there lies dead;/ And Paris too" (155–156). The lines do not make my
suggestion probable, but they do not make it impossible.

10. Since all of this is so obviously speculative, it may be unnecessary to
note that the doublings I suggest are not the only ones that could be
proposed. For instance, the case for one actor playing the phonetic
triplets Archidamus, Antigonus, and Autolycus is at least as good as
the one for doubling Antigonus and Camillo; as Northrop Frye has
shown us (in *A Natural Perspective*, New York: Harcourt Brace

Jovanovich, 1965, p. 115), Antigonus's shoulder-bone (III. iii. 97) and Autolycus's shoulder-blade (IV. iii. 77) join the two like Siamese twins.

11. Note that "sur-addition" contains the sound of "Sir"—a post-Roman British counterpart of honorary epithets like "Leonatus"—and that "Leonatus" contains the idea of birth—the general and specific topic of this speech on Posthumus's "name and birth," a speech in which "So gain'd the sur-addition Leonatus" is an urgently non-essential incidental detail, a sur-addition by a garrulous gossip.

12. In this context there is hardly need to mention that the five actors needed to play the five characters in Posthumus's dream (V. iv. 30–122) are likely candidates for doubling and that the play itself points to actors whose use in those parts would underscore rhyme-like contrasts and/or equations: Guiderius and Arviragus as the Leonati; the Queen (Cloten's mother) as Posthumus's mother; Cymbeline (or Belarius) as Posthumus's father; and Belarius (or Cymbeline) as Jupiter.

Changeable Taffeta: Shakespeare's Characters in Performance

J.L. STYAN

For some years now, we have been trying not to talk about Shakespeare's characters, as if they were eccentric old aunts whose manners we do not trust in public. Bradley had his say; historical critics and old new critics took him to task; and then we got on with other, obviously more important matters of themes and images. But the characters will not go away; and it is all the more embarrassing that when they do come up in conversation, we are still Victorians at heart, and assume their well-bred motivation and a decorous conformity of manner: we hope they will behave themselves properly. It is the result of our training. Consistency in character is a law of the realistic drama, and actors and audiences have been living too long in the shadow of Ibsen and Chekhov, Stanislavsky and Freud, exposed to the limited kind of dramatic style which has been unnaturally perpetuated by the proscenium arch and the photographic actuality of cinema and television. For an aside on TV is all but impossible, and a wink at the audience in the theater is unforgivable. So actors get "A's" if they stay in character, and critics seem always to write as if there were a definitive characterization called, say, Hamlet or Lear. It remains the common assumption, just as in the nineteenth century, that "the end of drama is the exposition of

---

Line references are from the Pelican Shakespeare in the one-play-a-volume format. The punctuation is my own, intended for acting.

character and that all other elements are contributory to this end."[1]

It is certain that a sense of character is central to the dramatic experience. Plays need characters: actors need them, audiences need them. A play employs actors with voices, legs, and other human attributes, in order that characters may be recognized by their audience. An actor may need a comforting consistency of character in order to be able to impersonate. An audience, however, is obliged to complete the human image on the stage, since the playwright can supply only imperfect clues to work with: Hamlet and Helena wear black — we judge them to be in mourning. Nor is it entirely improper for an audience to talk about a character as if he were alive after the play is over: it is as natural as talking about a party after the guests have all gone home. However, during the performance itself, an audience perceives, not a character, but a live actor and his impersonation, which are sometimes the same thing, and sometimes different, according to the conditions and conventions of the play and the playhouse.

It is also certain that Shakespeare is past master at helping an actor do his job. He wonderfully helps the boy actor who is charged with playing a complicated part like Cleopatra, helping him to set up a careful sequence of character images, loyal and quixotic, sensitive and sensual, noble and shrewish, symbolic and realistic, picking his way from one contrasting scene to another, in order to create the many-sided creature we know. And Shakespeare is masterful in constantly supplying those fine little realistic details of sight and sound, little pegs to hang a mask upon, even to his smallest assignments. Poor Feeble, the ragged recruit of *Henry IV, Part II*, may be a walking skeleton, but, bless him, he will "bear no base mind" (III. ii. 227). Capulet's bully of a First Servant is also partial to marzipan and Susan Grindstone (*Romeo and Juliet*, I. v. 8–9). Beatrice must steal closer to her friends "like a lapwing . . . Close to the ground" (*Much Ado*, III. i. 24–25). Preparing to meet Troilus, Cressida fetches her breath "as short as a new-ta'en sparrow" (III. ii. 32). It wonderfully humanizes King Henry IV to have him envy a ship-boy who can fall asleep up in the crow's nest (*Henry IV, Part II*, III. i. 18–21). Cordelia must touch her sleeping father's "white flakes" and caress his "thin helm" (*King Lear*, IV. vii. 30, 36). It is a commonplace that Shakespeare can get a character in a line or two. But this extraordinary gift can be deceptive.

There are occasions when Shakespeare *refuses* us insight into character, as if he wanted the audience itself to supply the possible reactions of the actor. The method is to hold the character in silence, forcing us to complete the equation set up on the stage. Such a moment comes when Juliet remains "speechless" for thirty lines when Lady Capulet rationally and the Nurse lasciviously propose that she marry the County Paris (*Romeo and Juliet*, I. iii.). After there has been no clue to Juliet's feelings, we are grateful to hear her mother ask directly, "Speak briefly, can you like of Paris' love?" But Juliet's slow, ambiguous answer is not helpful: "I'll look to like, if looking liking move." The effect of this stagecraft is to force the audience to receive the proposal for an arranged marriage as a personal questioning of its own values, and even suggests that we should not see Juliet's face during the questioning. For another instance, the scene in which Beatrice of *Much Ado about Nothing* eavesdrops upon Hero and Ursula urges the audience itself into action as she is fed false information of Benedick's love (III. i.). The tone of the scene differs in several respects from the previous one of Benedick's eavesdropping, but it is fundamentally different in that Beatrice remains wonderfully silent until the end, so that we scrutinize her features for her feelings as her friends castigate her, until we are forced to supply them ourselves. The device involves us directly in the action, but in so doing temporarily refuses us the comfort of straightforward "characterization."

Many warning signs should tell us that definitive and consistent characterization is a false target. For one, it is another commonplace that the characters have many lines which are "out of character:" in Maurice Charney's words, "Shakespeare's characters sometimes speak not for themselves but for the play."[2] He reminds us of Caliban's lyrical lines about his magic island, and about Enobarbus's glowing account of Cleopatra's barge. E.P. Nassar[3] points also to Juliet's unexpected wit when she learns of the death of Tybalt:

> Come, cords; come, nurse; I'll to my wedding bed;
> And death, not Romeo, take my maidenhead.
> (*Romeo and Juliet*, III. ii. 136–137)

We do not have to explain this joke away by reference to lusty young Elizabethan womanhood, or by Juliet's precociousness. Professor Nassar argues that Juliet is merely "stepping out of character when she delivers those lines." She does so by using an actor's many choices of inflection and gesture, and the audience senses the switch immediately. Such lines could speak for the play; and in spite of them, Juliet's character remains continuous and unblemished. In effect, Juliet is not the sum total of all the lines given to her. Similarly, Iago seems repeatedly to condemn himself out of his own mouth:

> I have't. It is engender'd. Hell and night
> Must bring this monstrous birth to the world's light.
>   (*Othello*, I. iii. 397–398)

But Iago is not schizophrenic when he talks like this. He requires us simply to separate what we might call the inner action of the play from the commentary upon it from the stage itself. As long ago as 1930, Wilson Knight rejected the very term "character" because it seemed to him to encourage criticism to try to control and limit the turbulent images of the poetic stage.[4]

Because every new actor's personality must interact with his part, the study of stage history insists that we should no longer look for definite characterization, but rather for the spectrum of a character. Every performance study I have read has shown that the great Shakespearian actors have given us different experiences when playing the same part, without necessarily deviating from the text by one syllable. Lady Macbeth, for example, has ranged from a kind of fourth witch to a siren temptress, from sweet Victorian femininity to a fiery little vixen. The truth is that the fiction known as Lady Macbeth can embody all these qualities, although we should not be disappointed if any one actress can not manage them all by herself. It is as if Shakespeare were intent upon helping the actress to help herself for the sake of keeping the play immediate and alive for each new audience. A "character" is an open invitation to work towards a personal extension of the lines, as it were an improvisation upon a theme, and one gratefully received by actor and spectator alike. We can imagine a perfect Hedda Gabler or Mme. Ranevsky, but never a final Lady Macbeth. A Shakespearian character is shifting and elusive, and capable of endless possibilities. To be in vogue, perhaps we should speak of the "parameter" of a part and the "tolerance" of a performance.

Another line of argument is one based upon our growing sense of the Elizabethan stage and the kind of theatrical experience it fostered. Open stage production in the last twenty years has confirmed that characters need not always be seen as realism, but sometimes as role. The extra-dramatic behavior of characters in Shakespeare was encouraged by plays which were peppered with prologues and epilogues, soliloquies and asides, all kinds of direct address both explicit and implicit. No doubt the Elizabethan stage shared with that of the Restoration its joy in bows and curtsies to the audience, "takes" and "ad-libs." These elements of mutuality in performance between actor and audience serve to remind us that earlier theaters cared little for the imperatives of illusion. The players often seem more concerned to manipulate the responses of the audience by using any device to open or close the aesthetic gap between illusion and reality, between the stage and the house. On the open stage the actor is free to move in and out of the inner play, taking the spectator with him. Schücking found these techniques "primitive," but he was quite right to suggest that the Elizabethans went for the immediate effect before any consistency of character.[5]

Any acting is conditioned by the conventions of a particular playhouse; the image of the character an actor assumes is similarly conditioned. We do not find the Greek theater primitive because the use of *cothurni* restricted the play to static, stylized characterization, nor presumably was the Greek actor troubled when he had to change from a man to a woman at the drop of a mask. The extensive practice of doubling parts in the Elizabethan period seemed to worry no one; whereas, with our modern realistic presuppositions, we grow very knowing if Oberon doubles with Theseus, or Perdita with Hermione, and critics explode in a frenzy of insights. In the past, such devices implied a happy conspiracy between actor and audience in the mutual pleasure of putting on a play. Acting then was role-playing, and no doubt it would have been unnatural not to address the audience; so that, if soliloquies and asides had not existed, some actor would have had to invent them. It would come as no surprise to learn that Elizabethan audiences were at one and the same time aware of both the actor and the character he was playing; indeed, we are not past thinking like this when we go to a play today ("Olivier is not at his best as Shylock tonight"). All this is characteristic of what Peter Brook has recently identified as the "rough" theater: "A popular audience," he asserts, "usually has no difficulty in accepting inconsistencies of accent and dress, or in darting between mime and dialogue, realism and suggestion. They follow the line of story, unaware of the fact that somewhere there is a set of standards which are being broken."[6]

The question is, then, whether a character like Hamlet or Polonius, Lear or Leontes, Cleopatra or Capulet, is complex because of its psychology in depth, or because it has more than one job to do; whether it is contained remorselessly within the inner play or is an agent exercising the audience for the greater occasion. Such an audience, Brecht might argue, is intelligent and self-aware, engaged by consent in the proper business of imaginative theater. By the hint, "Edgar I nothing am", the wronged son of the Duke of Gloucester is to serve the play as a highly ironic chorus to the blind father and the mad king. By the simple assumption of a friar's habit, the Duke of Vienna can be man of God and man of state both, a play-acting duke of dark corners. By stepping out of the world of the tavern, Prince Hal can be the commentator on his own play. How very convenient when the cast is long.

Edgar's character as the chameleon agent in *King Lear* is naturally inscrutable; the Edgar who remains when Poor Tom and his successors have been set aside is all but nonexistent. He is the legitimate brother whom Edmund reviles, merely vulnerable and gullible — such negative attributes that he is scarcely more than the agent for Edmund's story also. His first soliloquy is primarily to prepare us for the ironic vision of the Bedlam beggar grimed with filth and stuck with pins (II. iii.); his second, carefully rhymed for impersonality, is pure choric commentary on Lear's suffering, necessary for our understanding (III. vi.); and his third, another chorus speech, points to the existence of hope at a time when the audience has been desolated by the madness of Lear and the blinding of Gloucester (IV. i.). Throughout the scene on the cliff he continues to lend the audience support, reinforcing our appropriate responses with his asides ("O thou side-piercing sight." "O matter, and impertinency mix'd,/ Reason in madness"). We do, of course, see him care for his father, work his ambiguous private miracles on the old blind man to restore his faith and play the part of the unknown knight, the last of his many roles, before he speaks (in the Folio) the final chorus lines over the dead king. But did Shakespeare intend a "character" for Edgar? If so, he has the weakest character and the strongest role in the play. It is the audience which has supplied any character there is in Edgar, not Shakespeare.

I have no wish to add to the arguments that surround Hal the so-called hero-hypocrite and the problems Shakespeare faced when he had to reconcile in one part the prodigal son and the popular king of legend. Structurally, Hal is called upon to be a good mixer, able to move easily in court circles and to live it up in low company, speaking verse or prose as the occasion demands. (Falstaff, for all his knighthood and his ingenuity, is never able to mix among the nobility, but remains the observer without, and can only disgrace himself when he gets involved with the politicians and the war.) But once or twice a realistic reading of *Henry IV, Part I* is brought up short when Hal the prodigal must meet Prince Henry the future hero of Shrewsbury in the same speech and in the same person.

The first time comes uncomfortably near the beginning of the play, very sensibly foreshadowing the unrealistic patterning of the action, but most awkwardly denying any realistic consistency of character. That annoying first soliloquy,

> I know you all, and will a while uphold
> The unyok'd humour of your idleness
>
> (I. ii. 183—184)

is so clearly set apart from the rest of the scene in tone and style, in its address to the audience and its choice of a richer verse, that it must speak far more for the play as a whole than for the character. How else might Shakespeare have done it? Imagine if some chorus figure in the person of Rumor, say, were instead to step quickly downstage and speak Hal's lines in the third person:

> He knows them all, and will a while uphold
> The unyok'd humour of their idleness

ending with

> He'll so offend, to make offense a skill,
> Redeeming time when men think least he will.

If that had happened, we should not now be so troubled by
having to devise excuses for Hal's hypocrisy and his priggish-
ness. All Shakespeare has done is to save the Lord Chamber-
lain's Men another salary and give his key chorus speech to the
most appropriate actor available on the stage — it would have
troubled even the Elizabethan audience if Shakespeare had chosen Falstaff or Poins to make the point of this speech.

With this in mind, it is perhaps easier to swallow Hal's other
mixed reponse, the electrifying line which Shakespeare gave
him to answer Falstaff's plea that he be not banished: "Banish
plump Jack, and banish all the world" (II. iv. 455). If Hal as the
pretended king says, "I do," it is Hal the chorus who says, "I
will." The change of voice which is required by the repetition is
perfectly possible to the actor who plays all the roles simultaneously: Hal, King, and chorus.[7] The critic arguing for realism
finds that Hal never hides his contempt for Falstaff; the audience
at a non-realistic presentation is content to applaud the actor who
can supply two or three perspectives for the price of one.

The result of such perspectives of character is that the audience can savor and enjoy a Hal who satisfies its need to witness
the legendary good fellow of Eastcheap tavern, so that it can
appraise for itself the wit of a man who can hold his own with
Falstaff in a duel of words. At the same time the audience has the
pleasure of knowing with Hal what is at stake in governing the
country and accepting the responsibility of kingship. Through
this device of divided character, *Henry IV* becomes a pertinent
political play which lacks none of the human dimension and
retains the personableness of an attractive central figure. We are
to enjoy Falstaff, but also to watch Hal trust him no further than
he would a rattlesnake, as J.B. Priestley once said. If Falstaff falls
away, it is only after he has served us well; and we are left in no
doubt that the play is about King Hal, and not about Falstaff the
merry agent of Hal's dramatic sovereignty.

If it is inappropriate to measure Prince Hal the heir to the
throne by the qualities required of a chorus, however, or Edgar

by the standards we might apply to real Bedlam beggars, how much more doubtful it is to use the same psychological yardstick on Lear's Fool as on Lear himself? It is even more questionable to set the same standards for the characters of comedy as for those of tragedy: should we ask the same questions of Rosalind as of Ophelia? It is as laughable to psychoanalyze Puck or Ariel. Shakespeare covered a whole range of conventions of character, each suited to the genre and style of a particular play. If we do not first ask the mode of the play, and what degree of freedom from actuality an audience must allow and be allowed, we could be shocked to find Rosalind caught up in the Silvius and Phebe burlesque, or Viola acting the fool in Andrew's farcical duel, or Titania demeaning herself in the wood with an ass. Come to that, how odd it was of Rosalind not to climb back into skirts as soon as she realized it was difficult to make love in breeches. Did she not know of the unwritten law which requires a character to stay in disguise until the fifth act? And if she is the clever Rosalind she is considered to be, would she have been in this impracticable situation in the first place?

The comic transvestites — boys as girls as boys, like Viola and Rosalind — are no doubt a special case in a theater of non-illusion. The full delight of their double act is just not accessible to an audience if they remain in character. Exquisite lines like Viola's to Olivia, "I am not that I play" (*Twelfth Night*, I. v. 176) and Rosalind's to Orlando, "By my life, she will do as I do" (*As You Like It*, IV. i. 145) should immediately remind us of the game of theater we are all playing, actor and audience alike. Our perception of the difference between the sexes is a central objective in these comedies, but the perception is only complete when the actor is ready to slip in and out of the part.

I offer as test lines these two of Rosalind's:

> men are April when they woo, December when they wed;
> maids are May when they are maids, but the sky changes when
> they are wives.

> (*As You Like It*, IV. i. 134–136)

This is from the delicious scene in which Rosalind, finding her darling Orlando in the same forest with herself, but unfortunately wearing the wrong clothes at the time, has to take very unfeminine steps to make him declare his love. Already a boy/

girl in boy's clothing, she agrees to play the part of Orlando's Rosalind in a scene of mock courtship. If we remember that the audience sees only two males offering each other their hands in marriage, and that Orlando sees only a boy offering to have him as husband, it is not hard to imagine that Orlando is not taking the business very seriously: any confession of love he might make to this mock-Rosalind is likely to be suspect. In other words, Rosalind's clever ruse is bound to fail. Yet she tries again, this time suggesting that she play the future Mrs. Orlando to see whether his love has any staying-power. So it must be a girl Rosalind who speaks the first line,

> Men are April when they woo, December when they wed.

This sentiment reflects some of the brazen mock-Rosalind, with a touch of the true, fluttering girl who first fell in love with Orlando when he overthrew Charles the wrestler. Then suddenly this temporary illusion is shattered by the male-chauvinist line,

> Maids are May when they *are* maids, but the sky changes when they are *wives*.

Who else can say this but Ganymede in doublet and hose or the boy actor speaking for all disillusioned Orlandos on the morning after the night before? Yet to the joy of the audience, it is the same actor who speaks both lines, which is not the same thing at all as if Shakespeare had given the first line to Rosalind and the second to Orlando. By speaking both lines, the actor/character Rosalind prompts another glimpse of reality — in the realistic argument, merely revealing perhaps another side of Rosalind, but suggesting a whole new angle on the battle of the sexes when the boy actor steps out of character and drops into a male voice for a sensational aside to the house. Certainly Rosalind is a refreshing, charming girl character, my favorite in the plays, but I wonder how much of her fascination in this unique scene actually stems from the business of the player performing her many functions.

Proof lies in performance, which only can test whether Shakespeare's incongruities of character are intrinsic to the full working of the play. A particular look is worth taking at our attempts to apply the verdicts of psychological realism to such intractable ladies as Cressida and Helena, characters who tie us in critical knots. I have for some time suspected that one reason why we call their plays "problem comedies" is that we find them such a terrible problem.

It is alarming to observe the division of opinion about Cressida's loyalty to Troylus. Many take the obvious line and repeat Ulysses' clearly biased judgment that she is a daughter of the game, even if this belies the scene of her reluctance to part from Troylus and ignores Ulysses' irritation at being outwitted by the girl after he himself had set up the kissing game; in this way critics can justify the uncertain tradition that labelled her "the lazar kite of Cressid kind" — forgetting that this too is not Shakespeare speaking, but Pistol's unsophisticated quip about Doll Tearsheet in *Henry V*. When it comes down to it, the verdict against Cressida to be presumed from the play itself starts with that infamous sonnet of couplets given to her early in the play:

> Yet hold I off. Women are angels wooing,
> Things won are done, joy's soul lies in the doing.
> (*Troylus and Cressida*, I. ii. 272–273)

For Alice Walker, this speech indicated that she is "a Daphne who enjoys the chase."[8]

Now the strange thing is that she had been speaking a perfectly lucid prose dialogue with Pandarus the moment before she broke into couplets. Why should she speak in rhyming couplets when she is alone with the audience? But we should recognize the warning: it is not the character who switches from prose to verse, but the actor—and a boy actor dressed as a woman to boot. The boy actor seems to speak for all the Cressidas in the house with an age-old truth which every lonely-hearts columnist of today will confirm:

> That she belov'd knows nought, that knows not this:
> Men prize the thing ungain'd, more than it is.
> (I. ii. 274-275)

Was this actually Cressida speaking? Certainly the speech supplies a reason why she did not jump at Pandarus' attempt to throw Troylus at her. However, when it comes to it, she does not hold off — she falls in love, and is into bed with Troylus before she can say "Robert Henryson." The lesson to learn from this is that if one should not be too ready to believe what any character says about another, neither should one necessarily take at face value what any character says about himself when speaking impersonally, and especially not when speaking in rhyming couplets to an audience in soliloquy. At such a time, the actor could be speaking chorically, his function being that of a tool of the stagecraft, an agent for the business of communicating the play.

We need not pursue Cressida's role-playing through to the end. If she is not an opportunist, deceiving Troylus and us unmercifully, kissing army generals with relish whenever they are gathered together to go into battle, then part of her is a realist, adapting to her environment, a girl in a man's world, unlucky in being taken as hostage, unlucky in looking for help from a Diomedes who prefers horses to women. The other part of her belongs to the actor who must account for the actions of a girl who must live by her wits. But it is one thing to seem knowingly to know what you are doing, and quite another to have someone else speak for you. It is awkward for modern production that a drama of non-illusion allows both functions to be performed by the same person.

What then is the "character" of Cressida? It is not that of the "opportunist", the "born wanton" of the commentators who read her choric lines as her own. Nor is Shakespeare showing us Cressida as the helpless victim of her circumstances. Through her we receive, I think, striking insights into the reality of being female, of the challenge presented to a woman in a hostile environment, and the practical expedients to which she must resort in order to survive. In the representation, Cressida is as real and universal as any of Shakespeare's creatures.

Of the role of Helena in *All's Well*, it has been said that no single view is possible.[9] Even more than Cressida, Helena is constantly commenting on her part in the inner play and reflecting the wider implications of the action. Time and again she seems to extend the audience an invitation to share in the business of running the show; and, as if Shakespeare were fully aware of the unfortunate situation his plot has placed her in, he prompts our insights into her problems objectively. Certainly, for a modest young lady she seems to do some most immodest things which call for explanation. As a result, one critic (Coleridge) finds here the loveliest of Shakespeare's characters and another the most egotistical; one finds her modest while another considers her to be a woman of sexual appetite. If the issue for the audience is whether a woman should be the aggressor, this is a matter with deeply realistic implications. Indeed, one would have thought that those speeches and scenes which touch on the issue would have been treated as realistically as possible. But Shakespeare is not Ibsen, and such is not the case. In terms of theatrical communication, Shakespeare's Helena is almost a dialectical role, passing in and out of character to invite opposite judgments upon herself.

The crucial moments in *All's Well* are again strangely marked by couplets, which have the automatic effect of distancing the characters, insisting upon their function as role-players, emphasizing the folktale qualities in the play, and lightening the tone for comedy. We remember the sonnet of couplets with which Helena closes her first scene:

> Our remedies oft in ourselves do lie,
>
> (I. i. 208)

so reminiscent in manner of Cressida's own first sonnet soliloquy. Helena's too follows a bantering scene in which an obnoxious fool, this time Parolles, challenges feminine modesty with his ideas on virginity as a "withered pear," and it too in the privacy of soliloquy appears to contradict the established character of the public scene. By concluding with

> Who ever strove
> To show her merit, that did miss her love?
>
> (I. i. 218-219)

and declaring that her "intents are fix'd," Helena like Cressida seems to betray her modesty and leave herself open to criticism.

We remember also the Countess of Rossillion's rhyming mixture of soliloquy and aside,

> Even so it was with me when I was young,
>
> (I. iii. 121)

as she observes Helena's long slow entrance in the throes of love for Bertram. The Countess speaks for age and experience in a choric way before she begins to probe for a confession from Helena. The level of impersonality and abstraction in such speeches is such that they might actually be sung. And Helena's lines in this scene are mixed with ambiguous couplets like:

O then give pity
To her whose state is such, that cannot choose
But lend and give where she is sure to lose;
That seeks not to find that her search implies,
But riddle-like lives sweetly where she dies.

(I. iii. 206–210)

It is a beautiful and moving scene, demanding our compassion for Helena in her embarrassment, that of a woman who feels desire for a man she cannot have. It would be strongly enhanced by having her speak her gnomic lines in behalf of a world of women, looking, let us say, at us at such moments instead of at the Countess, freely breaking the realistic illusion of the scene, and lending her voice within the flow of the poetry to emphasize the general statement of a woman's pain — all this without in some realistic fashion pretending to whisper what she should not say aloud.

The major sensational scenes of the healing of the King (II. i.), the choosing of a husband (II. iii.), and Bertram's reconciliation with Helena (V. iii.), are even more incantatory. In Tyrone Guthrie's signal open stage production of *All's Well* at Stratford, Ontario, in 1953, later transmuted to Stratford, England, in 1959, these scenes were done to music and dance, thereby asserting an appropriate degree of visual and aural ritual in the performance. The magic took effect when Helena (Irene Worth) began to soothe the brows of the King of France (Alec Guinness) to the rhythm of her rhyming lines in II. i.:

Ere twice the horses of the sun shall bring
Their fiery torcher his diurnal ring,
Ere twice in murk and occidental damp
Moist Hesperus hath quench'd his sleepy lamp:
Or four and twenty times the pilot's glass
Hath told the thievish minutes, how they pass:
What is infirm, from your sound parts shall fly,
Health shall live free, and sickness freely die.

(ll. 161-168)

Helena moved slowly behind the King's wheelchair and laid her hands gently on his forehead. He closed his eyes and sighed.

Methinks in thee some blessed spirit doth speak
His powerful sound, within an organ weak.

(ll. 175-176)

He touched her hand, looked at it, then slowly drew her round to face him. On her knees she made her pledge to him:

> If I break time, or flinch in property
> Of what I spoke, unpitied let me die.

(ll. 187-188)

And she kissed his hand and wheeled him offstage.

Such incantatory lines gave way to the new impulsion of dance in the "recantation scene" at court in the Guthrie production. Brooks Atkinson of *The New York Times* thought that the performance flowed "without effort across the apron stage up and down the stairs, through the forest of columns and out of the ports in the pit"[10] with the elegance of ballet. First, the arena suddenly filled with courtiers from all entrances, all discussing the recovery of the King. Then the court orchestra suddenly galloped into a waltz and the King entered dancing with Helena. On the cue

> Make choice and see,
> Who shuns thy love, shuns all his love in me,

(II. iii. 71-72)

she reviewed the eligible young officers and gentlemen to the rhythm of an elaborate dance suited to the stylized speech. Finally she concluded the dance with Bertram, and to general applause led him to the King:

> *Helena.*
>   This is the man.
>   *King.*
>   Why then young Bertram take her she's thy wife.[11]

(ll. 103-104)

All in a breath the choice was made and granted. But at this Bertram broke away, the music stopped, and all on stage were transfixed. When Shakespeare's rhyming ceased, it was as if reality had returned to supersede the magic.

Helena had now to face the tough problem of holding the man she had won by unconventional and dangerously romantic means, especially since the reality was that Bertram had not chosen her. She could have resumed her passive ways of the first act; but, happily for the play if not for her, Shakespeare decided to see what a realistic lady in love might do with the aid of a little theatrical license.

All of this had the effect of removing the desire of the audience to bring the pathological intensity of a Masters and Johnson case-history to Helena's motives. Instead, Guthrie's audience readily submitted to the controlling filigree style of the play. Coleridge's lovely lady of modesty and virtue, and the free spirit who steps over into the brilliant fantasy of the lightest of musical comedies, were both present: Guthrie and Shakespeare arranged that they need not conflict. It could have been Helena's dream enacted, with herself playing her own fairy godmother.

"How shall we find the concord of this discord?" asks Theseus towards the end of *A Midsummer Night's Dream*. One answer is, let performance be the judge.

Notes

1. Moody E. Prior, "Character in Relation to Action in *Othello*," *Modern Philology*, XLIV (1947), p. 225.
2. *How to Read Shakespeare*, (New York: McGraw-Hill, 1971), p. 86.
3. "Shakespeare's Games with his Audience" in *The Rape of Cinderella; Essays in Literary Continuity*, (Bloomington; Indiana University Press, 1970), p. 102.
4. *The Wheel of Fire*, (London: Methuen & Co. Ltd., 1930), p. 11.
5. L.L. Schücking, *Character Problems in Shakespeare's Plays* (London: Harrap, 1922; from the German, first printed in 1919). The reference is a general one to his whole line of argument.
6. *The Empty Space*, (London: MacGibbon & Kee Ltd., 1968), p. 60.
7. See my *Drama, Stage and Audience*, (Cambridge: Cambridge University Press, 1975), pp. 177-178, for further discussion of this role-playing.
8. *Troylus and Cressida*, The New Shakespeare, (Cambridge: At the University Press, 1957), p. 149.
9. G.K. Hunter, ed., *All's Well That Ends Well*, The Arden Shakespeare, (London: Methuen & Co. Ltd., 1959), p. xxxii.
10. July 16, 1953.
11. As punctuated in the Folio of 1623.

Shakespeare's Visual Stagecraft: The Seduction of Cressida

DOUGLAS C. SPRIGG

The extraordinary literary value of Shakespeare's plays too often has distracted critics from a thorough examination of the theatrical value of their enactment. Only comparatively recently have the plays been studied as the impetus and residue of a theatrical experience, a record of how Shakespeare used his actors on his stage to communicate with his audience. Inasmuch as Shakespeare creates many of his most powerful dramatic effects by means of visual and aural impressions that elude linguistic analysis, such studies of the relationship between text and performance can provide an important supplement to purely literary judgments.

Granted, the process of deducing visual and aural impressions from the written text is a precarious activity at best. There are an infinite number of ways in which a line may be read or a play staged, and each actor and director must discover the result that best fits the unique demands of the production being mounted. To argue that there is a "right" way for a play to be done is to deny theater the variations that give life to the art form. It would be equally foolhardy to assert that the text provides incontrovertible evidence as to how Shakespeare's plays were in fact staged in the Globe Theatre. The text may suggest the original staging, but, obviously, we can never be certain as to how a play was first performed.

Nevertheless, the suggestions in the text are important. The language can be explicit: "She strokes his cheek." More often, the language implicitly suggests a staging. "Come hither once again," implies that the person has "come hither" once before and subsequently gone away. And, of course, the dramatic situation itself, in conjunction with the language, contains many suggestions as to how the actors are to behave onstage. In these and in more subtle ways, the text reveals the potential for various kinds of nonverbal communication. It is possible to analyze the impact of such communication when realized on the stage.

Some sense of the range and complexity of Shakespeare's visual stagecraft may be obtained from a close analysis of the assignation scene in *Troilus and Cressida*. As the scene opens, Diomedes enters the empty stage with his flaming torch. An isolated figure on the expansive platform of the Elizabethan playhouse, he replaces the isolated figure of Thersites who has just exited through another door. The visual juxtaposition is significant. With his grotesque physical presence as well as his final words, Thersites has prepared for Diomedes's entrance. "They say he keeps a Trojan drab and uses the traitor Calchas's tent. I'll after. Nothing but lechery! All incontinent varlets!" (V. i. 104-106).[1] The torch reminds the audience that it is night, and, even in the actual daylight on the Globe stage, the flame would add the suggestion of a lambent texture to the fluctuations in Cressida's responses and the resulting fluctuations in the other characters around the stage. Whether or not he holds the torch throughout the scene, Diomedes initially is associated with its fire. He is visually attractive, and he is dangerous. The visual image of the man and the torch is striking. Cressida, moving toward him and away, will become the fluttering moth.

When he wants to draw the maximum amount of attention to the message of the language, Shakespeare keeps the physical movement to a minimum. Often, he will isolate a solitary, stationary actor center stage and allow the actor's voice to communicate; the ear savors the sounds and images undistracted by a darting eye; the eye settles quietly on a single visual source of interest so the ear may hear better. But, similarly, Shakespeare can reduce language to gestic monosyllables when he wants the visual impact of physical behavior to transmit the bulk of his communication.

(Enter Diomedes.)
Diomedes.
What, are you up here, ho? Speak.

Calchas.
   (Within) Who calls?
Diomedes.
   Diomed. Calchas, I think, Where's your daughter?
Calchas.
   (Within) She comes to you.
   (Enter Troilus and Ulysses, at a distance: after them, Thersites.)
Ulysses.
   Stand where the torch may not discover us.
   (Enter Cressida.)
Troilus.
   Cressid comes forth to him.

                                                 (V. ii. 1-6)

Notice that the words are perhaps less important for their linguistic meaning than for the physical and vocal behavior they
stimulate in the actor. The blunt, shouted, monosyllabic in-
quiries of Diomedes contrast with the muted responses from
within. While the seducer waits impatiently, perhaps pacing
back and forth upstage with his flaming torch, Troilus and Ulysses enter and, unnoticed, move with conspiratorial swiftness
downstage to a position "where the torch may not discover"
them. They are followed onstage by Thersites, who also sneaks
away from the flame to establish, unnoticed by the other two
groups, yet a third position onstage. Cressida enters and, in the
provocative manner suggested by her first line ("Now, my sweet
guardian!"), approaches Diomedes. During the first six lines of
the scene, the stage is alive with physical activity. It is this
behavior, more than the meanings of the words, that creates the
initial impact of the scene.

   At the same time that he establishes the mood of secrecy and
anticipation necessary for scenes of eavesdropping, Shakespeare
positions his characters onstage. With Cressida and Diomedes
upstage near the separate doors through which they alternately
threaten to retreat, it is reasonable to imagine that, on the
Elizabethan platform, Troilus and Ulysses would observe from
one downstage corner, while Thersites looks on from the other.[2]
Shakespeare has set his stage so as to magnify the implications of
the action that is to follow.

   By positioning a series of observers, each perceiving the
situation with degrees of greater awareness, Shakespeare creates

a complex scene of multiple eavesdropping. Cressida and Diomedes interact upstage aware only of each other's responses. Troilus registers the responses of the upstage couple, but perceives this interaction within an entirely different frame of reference. Thersites' perspective is broader still. He views the upstage interaction in juxtaposition to the reactions of Troilus. The audience provides the fourth group in the chain of observers zigzagging in toward the upstage scene. By creating such a system of observed observers, Shakespeare insures that the slightest response from the upstage couple will be magnified by a chain reaction of responses from the series of eavesdroppers. In a sense, Shakespeare has created a series of mutually informing plays within plays, each with its own frame of reference, receding in depth away from the audience toward Cressida.

> (Enter Cressida.)
> *Troilus.*
>   Cressid comes forth to him.
> *Diomedes.*
>   How now, my charge!
> *Cressida.*
>   Now, my sweet guardian! Hark, a word with you.
>   (Whispers.)
> *Troilus.*
>   Yea, so familiar!
> *Ulysses.*
>   She will sing any man at first sight.
> *Thersites.*
>   And any man may sing her, if he can take her cliff.
>   She's noted.
>
>   (V. ii. 6-11)

Cressida appears, and in the seductive tones suggested by the diction, she and Diomedes greet one another. But for Shakespeare's purposes, a seductive inflection is not a sufficient provocation; visible behavior is also necessary. The scene is centrally concerned with the potential for contradictory perceptions of human behavior, and, thus, Shakespeare is at pains to create physical actions between the upstage couple that may be perceived and reacted to differently by each of the downstage observers. Cressida's desire to whisper may be explained psychologically as either coyness or modesty, but Shakespeare uses the physical proximity implicit in this activity to create a chain reaction of responses. Troilus is aghast at the blatant physical familiarity; Ulysses, in response, interprets the familiarity as characteristic of her behavior; and Thersites reacts to Ulysses' reaction to Troilus's reaction to Cressida's behavior by emphasizing, for the benefit of the audience, the more indecent implications of such an interpretation. The characters simultaneously define themselves and present the audience with alternative interpretations of an action viewed by all. Shakespeare insures the impact of Thersites' jaundiced point of view by having him speak directly to the spectator, who completes the linkage in the chain of eavesdroppers. The viewer is treated as his partner in one of three duologues that comment upon each other in temporal juxtaposition. Thus, within the first eleven lines of the scene, Shakespeare positions his characters onstage and establishes the pattern of responses that will communicate multiple interpretations of the upstage action.

At the same time, the distinct visual groupings suggest emblems of abstract qualities. Thersites, at his down-left corner of the stage, functions as a Greek Pandarus, an emblem of the potentially repulsive aspects of sexual desire; and, as does Pandarus in earlier scenes, he provides the audience with an alternative to the point of view represented by Troilus. Like a priapic gargoyle, Thersites smiles his toothless smile out at the audience and then turns upstage to draw attention to the irony of Troilus watching Cressida betray him. As a sustained visual presence, Thersites, even when silent, functions throughout the scene much like a foul smell that taints the perception of all the other senses.

On the down-right side of the stage stands the naive, romantic Troilus. Even as Thersites suggests the sordid side of sexual relations, so Troilus suggests the idealization. The positioning of these two divides the stage into opposing camps of love and lechery, innocence and decadence, fidelity and venality. The stage begins to suggest the dialectics associated with the larger war of which this small skirmish is a part.

Between Troilus stage-right and Thersites stage-left, stand Cressida and Diomedes. She tends to remain near the stage-right exit into her tent, while he gravitates toward the stage-left exit back toward the center of camp. (See Figure 1.) Visually and

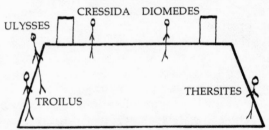

Figure 1. *Troilus and Cressida* (Act V, Scene ii).
Position of the characters on stage.

symbolically situated on a continuum between polar opposites,
Cressida is pulled stage-left by her lust for Diomedes (whose
pretty surface appearance makes palatable the dark desires less
attractively embodied in the syphilitic Thersites), and she is
pulled stage-right toward the exit by her memory of the undoubt-
ing devotion of Troilus. From the audience's vantage point,
every movement toward Diomedes sends her away visually from
the observing Troilus, and every movement away from
Diomedes brings her back visually toward Troilus. Equally important, a movement toward Diomedes is not only away from
Troilus; it is also a movement in the direction of Thersites. On
both a literal and symbolic level, the nature of her inner
psychological struggle is given an external physical manifestation. Cressida's movement, in relation to the positioning of the
other characters onstage, enacts her dilemma and creates a visual
emblem of the forces warring within.

The relationship between this conflict and its military
analogue is suggested by the situation and adumbrated by the
costuming. Diomedes, a surrogate Paris, is dressed in something
to suggest Greek attire, while Cressida, a surrogate Helen, is
dressed as a Trojan. Cressida's struggle between fidelity and
betrayal, the conflict between her desire to remain true to her
lover and her country versus her urge to betray both with the
enemy, mirrors the sexual decision over which the war ostensi-
bly is being fought. The implication is that lust, venality, and
betrayal extend beyond the boundaries of nationality. The
pairing of the Trojan Troilus with his cynical tutor, the Greek
Ulysses, further suggests the non-partisan nature of this conflict.
The scrofulous Thersites, dressed in the rags of a camp follower,

suggests allegiance to nothing beyond his own bile, which he
rains indiscriminately on Greek and Trojan alike.

Having used stage positioning and costumes to suggest an
emblematic polarity onstage, Shakespeare can allow information
to be transmitted as much by physical movement as by verbal
statement. The dialogue between Cressida and Diomedes is rich
in gestic suggestions; it draws them together to touch and
whisper, and then pulls them apart. They drift toward Thersites'
side of the stage and then back toward Troilus. Shakespeare uses
the language here as much to animate his actors as to inform his
audience. The dramatic impact is created by the sensual, fluctuating dance of the upstage couple, accentuated by the leers of
Thersites down-left and the convulsions of Troilus down-right.
The communication is largely visual.

Cressida.
   Sweet honey Greek, tempt me no more to folly.
Thersites.
   Roguery!
Diomedes.
   Nay, then —
Cressida.
   I'll tell you what —
Diomedes.
   Foh, foh! Come, tell a pin. You are foresworn.
Cressida.
   In faith, I cannot. What would you have me do?
Thersites.
   A juggling trick — to be secretly open.
Diomedes.
   What did you swear you would bestow on me?
Cressida.
   I prithee do not hold me to mine oath. Bid me do anything but
   that, sweet Greek.
Diomedes.
   Good night.
Troilus.
   Hold, patience!
Ulysses.
   How now, Trojan!
Cressida.
   Diomed —
Diomedes.
   No, no, good night. I'll be your fool no more.

Troilus.
  Thy better must.
Cressida.
  Hark, one word in your ear.
Troilus.
  Oh, plague and madness!

(V. ii. 18-35)

The words spill forth, suggesting a complex web of overlapping, interconnected physical actions occuring at all parts of the stage. The dialogue is not memorable, but the impact of the physical interaction sears a durable image in the mind of the spectator. Cressida's ambivalent movements and gestures — the eventual approach, the touch, and, for the second time in the scene, the lips delicately caressing a whisper — all have great power in the theater. To a large extent, the power is generated by the audience's experience of a young man cringing in agony as he watches the woman he loves touch another man. The scene could be acted in an unknown language without its impact seriously impaired.

Notice also the visual and mental alacrity demanded of the audience. Shakespeare forces the audience to participate in the swift alternation of conflicting responses by rapidly changing the center of visual focus on the stage. The eye must register the repeatedly oscillating responses of Cressida and Diomedes upstage-center, then sweep down to the left to catch the reaction of Troilus and Ulysses, and then immediately sweep down to the right to catch the response of Thersites to the actions of everyone else. Notice, especially during the more stichomythic interchanges, how swiftly the eye must move from one point to another across the estimated 1,200 square feet of the Elizabethan stage. As Gestalt psychologists would have it, this rapid change of focus creates a series of alternating configurations of a sharp figure against a dull background. As in a tennis match, the attention of the spectator must sweep back and forth to register the rich flow of information emanating from each new configuration of figure against ground. Such rapid changes of focus engage the spectator more actively in the alternation of conflicting viewpoints generated by the stage. At the same time, the incongruity of the viewpoints tends to provoke incongruous responses in the spectator, responses which he must reconcile with his personal view and evaluation of the situation. The spectator shares the confusion of a young woman trying to satisfy contradictory needs, the pain of a young man who actually witnesses his betrayal by the woman he loves, and the cynicism of a nihilist who revels in the agony of others. The frustration of Diomedes and the pragmatism of Ulysses also make some demand on the spectator's sympathies. The need to register and assimilate such incongruous and rapidly alternating views of the situation creates a vague sense of disorientation not unlike the sensation being experienced by both Troilus and Cressida. Shakespeare does not merely dramatize the anxiety of Troilus's attempt to reconcile conflicting views of Cressida, and Cressida's attempt to reconcile conflicting views of herself; he allows the audience to experience some part of it.

The dialogue, often, is purposely ambiguous. Cressida previously has sworn to "bestow" something upon Diomedes, but now demurs; yet every time he starts to leave, she moves after him and draws him back. A pattern of coitus interruptus is established, and Thersites and Troilus accentuate the visual seesaw with their disparate reactions. All the touching becomes an excitement to trembling rage and despair from Troilus on one side of the stage and an excitement to lecherous imaginings from Thersites on the other.

Ulysses.
    You shake, my lord, at something. Will you go?
    You will break out.
Troilus.
    She strokes his cheek!
. . . .
Thersites.
    How the devil luxury, with his fat rump and potato
    finger, tickles these together! Fry, lechery, fry!

                                              (V. ii. 49-57)

The entire stage becomes a physical manifestation of a moral tug-of-war. The bodies sway back and forth during each ascending cycle of approach and retreat as Cressida is forced to become increasingly physical to detain the increasingly frustrated Greek.

Shakespeare's use of "hand props" constitutes another important aspect of his visual communication. In this scene, the text indicates the presence onstage of only two physical objects: the torch and the "sleeve." On the bare Elizabethan platform, these props would have considerable prominence visually, and their isolation against a neutral background would lend them a strong metaphoric suggestiveness. The implications of the torch have been discussed. The other and more important property is the sleeve. In a previous scene, the audience has witnessed the sleeve used to pledge an oath of chastity and fidelity. Now it watches the sleeve used as a promise of fornication and betrayal.

Cressida.
    Here, Diomed, keep this sleeve.
Troilus.
    O beauty! Where is thy faith?
Ulysses.
    My lord—
Troilus.
    I will be patient, outwardly I will.
Cressida.
    You look upon that sleeve, behold it well.
    He loved me.—O false wench!—Give 't me again.
Diomedes.
    Whose was 't?
Cressida.
    It is no matter, now I have 't again.
    I will not meet with you tomorrow night.
    I prithee, Diomed, visit me no more.
Thersites.
    Now she sharpens. Well said, whetstone!
Diomedes.
    I shall have it.
Cressida.
    What, this?
Diomedes.
    Aye, that.
Cressida.
Oh, all you gods! O pretty, pretty pledge!
Thy master now lies thinking in his bed
Of thee and me, and sighs, and takes my glove,
And gives memorial dainty kisses to it,
As I kiss thee. Nay, do not snatch it from me.
He that takes that doth take my heart withal.
Diomedes.
    I had your heart before, this follows it.
Troilus.
    I did swear patience.

                           (V. ii. 66–84)

Cressida gives the sleeve, then snatches it back, kisses it, and finally has it taken from her. The object is used for all its many associations. As a visual icon, it emphasizes the irony of Troilus's presence onstage (he could, in fact, be holding the glove she mentions) and reminds the audience of the scene in which it first appeared. It reminds the audience of the phrase that recurs seven times within the seventeen lines surrounding the earlier exchange of tokens and vows: "Be thou true" (IV. iv. 59-76). A pledge of the highest ideals of romantic love has become a chit to assure sexual satisfaction. The audience previously has watched Troilus reverentially caress this object as the embodiment of his undying love; now it watches Troilus watch Diomedes finger the same object in a much more lascivious manner. The physical reality of the seduction is suggested by the physical treatment of the sleeve. Diomedes dangles the sleeve out of her reach, playing "keep-away" as with a child, while she struggles around him to retrieve it. The sleeve becomes the orchestration of a dance on tiptoe that mirrors the pattern of titillation and denial that structured the first half of the scene. But now it is Diomedes who demurs. By reversing the pattern of approach and avoidance, Shakespeare gives visual variety to the scene, while yet sustaining the overall structure of a cat and mouse game accelerating in urgency and intensity toward an eventually irrevocable decision. The visual image of Cressida dancing after the dangling sleeve creates an emblematic expression of the situation.

At the same time, Shakespeare prepares for the sleeve to function emblematically in a later scene. Diomedes will wear it on his helm during his fight with Troilus, an encounter for which Thersites again does the play-by-play commentary. "Hold thy whore, Grecian! Now for thy whore, Trojan! Now the sleeve, now the sleeve!" (V. iv. 25—26). Complex concepts and relationships are reified and made palpable by material objects and physical actions. The abstract is made visible.

The seesaw approach/avoidance conflict finally builds to a decision.

Cressida.
　　Well, well, 'tis done, 'tis past. And yet it is not.
　　I will not keep my word.

Diomedes.
    Why then, farewell.
    Thou never shalt mock Diomed again.
Cressida.
    You shall not go. One cannot speak a word
    But it straight starts you.
Diomedes.
    I do not like this fooling.
Thersites.
    Nor I, by Pluto. But that that likes not you pleases me best.
Diomedes.
    What, shall I come? The hour?
Cressida.
    Aye, come. O Jove! Do come. I shall be plagued.
Diomedes.
    Farewell till then.
Cressida.
    Good night. I prithee come.

                                        (V. ii. 97–106)

The familiar visual pattern is repeated one final time. Cressida decides to submit to Diomedes, and then, with an air of finality, decides against it and moves away toward her door. But the counter movement of Diomedes toward the opposite exit immediately motivates her to turn and run after him yet again. Finally, the bargain is made.

Before she leaves the stage for the last time in the play, Cressida turns toward the audience to apostrophize the absent Troilus. But, of course, Troilus is present, and on the neutral platform of the Elizabethan stage, a visual confrontation between the two occurs outside the framework of the dramatized locale. By means of a brilliant piece of staging, Shakespeare allows Cressida to create her final impression on the audience by speaking simultaneously, within different frames of reference, to herself, to Troilus, and to the audience itself.

Cressida.
    Troilus, farewell! One eye yet looks on thee,
    But with my heart the other eye doth see.
    Ah, poor our sex! This fault in us I find,
    The error of our eye directs our mind.
    What error leads must err. Oh, then conclude
    Minds swayed by eyes are full of turpitude. (Exit)

                                        (V. ii. 107–112)

Typically, Shakespeare balances this view of her behavior with Thersites' less considerate assessment of the situation: "A proof of strength she could not publish more/ Unless she said 'My mind is now turned whore'" (V. ii. 134–135). But in the process, the problems of perception experienced by Cressida are linked with the problems of perception experienced by those who observe her, including the audience. The ambiguous relationship between human behavior and the perception of human behavior is stressed throughout the scene. Cressida argues that her heart, through one eye, is drawn to the seductive surface appearance of Diomedes, while another eye still sees her obligation to Troilus. The ambivalence in her behavior has resulted from bifurcated vision. She has been unable to view her moral dilemma from a single point of view. Troilus has a similar problem. He also has been torn between conflicting views of the situation, and now tries to reconcile his previous image of Cressida with what he has just seen.

Troilus.
   Was Cressid here?
Ulysses.
   I cannot conjure, Trojan.
Troilus.
   She was not, sure.
Ulysses.
   Most sure she was.

   .   .   .   .   .

Thersites.
   Will a swagger himself out on's own eyes?
Troilus.
   This she? No, this is Diomed's Cressida.

                                        (V. ii. 124–137)

Troilus, after a fashion, is forced to accept the paradoxical dualities in human behavior and the related problems of perception. "This is, and is not, Cressida!" (V. ii. 146).

The genius of Shakespeare's staging allows the audience to participate in the characters' experience of such contradictory views. The stage picture communicates multiple views of physical love, and the audience, much like Cressida, is pulled in one direction by one view, and then jerked in a new direction by another. Like both Troilus and Cressida, as well as the various other onstage observers, the audience has had its mind swayed by its eyes. Having to embrace conflicting views of the situation, the audience is encouraged to experience something of Cressida's confusion in attempting to resolve the unsettling incompatibility between the needs of the body and the needs of the mind. At the same time, the audience, like Troilus, has experienced more than a single Cressida. It too has experienced the Cressida drawn toward Troilus struggle against the Cressida drawn toward Diomedes. But the audience has experienced many other images of Cressida as well: the idealized Cressida seen through the eyes of a naive Troilus, a sluttish Cressida seen through the eyes of a depraved Thersites, and a calculatingly coy and flirtatious Cressida seen through the eyes of an aroused Diomedes and a cynical Ulysses. The final image of Cressida becomes a composite view created and expressed in good part by a staging that reflects the contradictions within her personality and the multiple frames of reference within which those contradictions may be viewed. The labyrinthian complexities of human behavior are made to appear even more inaccessible to understanding by the inherent prejudice of any single point of view. The difficulties involved in distinguishing between appearances and whatever it is that constitutes reality result not only from contradictory impressions generated by the person perceived, but also from the subjective bias of the perceiver. Shakespeare does not merely have his characters talk about these problems of perception; he creates a situation in which the spectator experiences these problems with his own eyes.

The theater is concrete and specific. For concepts to be communicated from the stage, they must manifest themselves in something seen and something heard. As we all know, Shakespeare has an extraordinary genius for creating verbal images, but it is matched by a genius for creating visual images evolving through time in three-dimensional space. By embodying his ideas in physical objects, movements, gestures, and stage positioning, Shakespeare renders his communication immediately comprehensible on a fundamental level. The palpable sensory impact communicates "meaning" prior to intellectual understanding, while yet suggesting the most complex and expansive of abstract concepts. When we, the audience, watch Troilus watch Cressida stroke Diomedes's cheek, we are exposed physically to the concept of betrayal. The staging involves the audience in a specific physical action, while simultaneously creating a visual emblem of the moral battlefield upon which war and lechery corrupt the most noble of human aspirations.

Visually, Shakespeare structures the scene to provide the spectators with an experience analogous to the one they watch. Experiencing the action in a theater encourages an assimilation of various contradictory points of view and discourages an identification with any single view. Thersites no less than Troilus is deceived in what he sees; each view is one-sided, thus incomplete, thus a distortion of the truth. The spectator, like Troilus, makes this discovery by experiencing it with his own eyes. The act of perception is part of the discovery. It is not something that can be underlined in the text.

Notes

1. All quotations are from William Shakespeare, *Shakespeare: The Complete Works*, ed. G.B. Harrison (New York: Harcourt, Brace, and World, 1948).
   [Speech heads have been spelled out and placed on a separate line for uniform presentation.—*Ed.*]
2. These stage positions are suggested by J.L. Styan in *Shakespeare's Stagecraft* (Cambridge: Cambridge University Press, 1967), pp. 129–130. His work has had considerable influence on the approach taken in this essay.

Henry IV: A World of Figures Here

JAMES BLACK

The two parts of *Henry IV* are alight with young men's visions and old men's dreams.[1] The latter are readily inventoried: King Henry's dream of the Holy Land where his guilt will be cleansed; Falstaff's wonderful pretensions to judgeship, earldom or dukedom, or at least to the lordship of misrule wherein the laws of England are at his commandment; Glendower's conviction that the phenomena accompanying his birth have marked him extraordinary; Shallow's pathetic strainings to hear again the chimes at midnight, and his recollections which pluck dishonour from the pale-faced moon.

Only the King—serendipitously—will arrive at his Jerusalem. Meantime his son, whose dogged plan of redeeming time keeps him obscured in cloud until he bursts forth gloriously at the end of *Part 2*, seems merely farsighted, not visionary. The young men's visions in *Henry IV* appear to emanate from Hotspur, who when awake "apprehends a world of figures" and is perpetually "carried away" (II. iii. 76). It is the quality of these visions and dreams which I wish to examine here. I believe that the play quite literally *shows* us—in the sense of physically setting before our eyes—a searching commentary upon the characters' aspirations: the "visuals" test and search the visions.

From the first in *Henry IV* the tangible is forcing itself through—expressed, for instance, in the tactile and material images of the land daubing her lips with her own children's blood (I. i. 5–6), of "the edge of war, like an ill-sheathed knife, [cutting] his master" (I. i. 17–18), or of Henry's Jerusalem longings focussing in the vivid and cruel physicality of

> holy fields
> Over whose acres walk'd those blessed feet
> Which fourteen hundred years ago were nail'd
> For our advantage on the bitter cross.
>
> (I. i. 24—27)

Used at first to describe only the state of haste and confusion in which a nameless messenger left the Holmedon battlefield, the line "Uncertain of the issue any way" (I. i. 60) seems only an innocuous bit of narrative when it is delivered. But it springs to vivid life only a few minutes later when we realise how accurately and painfully it names and probes a center of the King's pain; for Henry is uncertain about *his* issue, the Prince of Wales:

> O that it could be prov'd
> That some night-tripping fairy had exchang'd
> In cradle-clothes our children where they lay,
> And call'd mine Percy, his Plantagenet!
>
> (I. i. 85—88)

For Falstaff, playing the King, any such doubts about "issue" are cleared by the outward, visible and comical evidence as Prince Hal stands before him:

> That thou art my son, I have partly thy mother's
> word, partly my own opinion, but chiefly a
> villainous trick of thine eye, and a foolish hanging
> of thy nether lip, that doth warrant me.
>
> (II. iv. 397—400)

As with "issue" and "issue," the play everywhere tends to make the abstract concrete. Often this is done in obvious visual jokes: Falstaff's paunch, Bardolph's nose, Pistol swaggering as a captain, the vaudeville contrast between thin Hal and fat Falstaff as they cross-talk (see especially II. iv. 237—244)—a contrast which carries over into *Part II* where, although Hal is less Falstaff's foil, the cheeky small boy is put into Falstaff's service "to set [him] off" (*Part II*, I. ii. 11—13). The "visual-metaphor" jokes are not always obvious, either: who has noticed, for instance, that Doll Tearsheet is seen for the very first time in a near-apoplexy from drinking too much "canaries," "sick of a

[qualm]" and "as red as any rose" *(Part II,* II. iv. 22—36) — seen as
quite literally a scarlet woman? The tavern's very name, "The
Boar's Head," calls up a festive picture—and threatens at every
moment to turn itself around into a wonderful spoonerism, "The
Whore's Bed": "this house," says Falstaff, "is *turned* bawdy-
house" (III. iii. 96—97, my italics). And everywhere in both plays
there are skits, routines, turns: the play extempore in *Part One;*
Pistol's cyclonic appearance at the Boar's Head in *Part Two;* the
"battles" which are acted out, such as Falstaff's, "Thou knowest
my old ward—here I lay, and thus I bore my point" (II. iv. 190f.),
and Shallow's, "A would manage you his piece thus, and a
would about, and about, and come you in, and come you in . . ."
(Part II, III. ii. 273f.). When in *Part One* Francis the Drawer is
called simultaneously by Poins and Hal from opposite sides of
the tavern and "stands amazed, not knowing which way to go"
(II. iv. 77 S.D.), he could be Hal caught in the philosophical
tug-of-war between the Court and Eastcheap. Hal knows which
summons he will answer, but Shakespeare wants us to *see* the
agony of choosing (it will be Hamlet's dilemma) when "business
and desire"[2] call with equal insistence.

Of course, what we see usually undercuts what we hear.
Falstaff's belief that he plays the king "so gravely, so majesti-
cally, both in word and matter" (II. iv. 429—430) is at odds with
the visual evidence that his "state is . . . a joint-stool, [his]
golden sceptre a leaden dagger, and [his] precious rich crown
. . . a pitiful bald crown" (II. iv. 375—377). Derided and deposed
as "King," he recognizes the ridiculousness of his appearance in
the role of Prince (see II. iv. 437—438). When we remember his
great ability to "devise matter" out of people's idiosyncracies for
the entertainment of others,[3] it is easy to visualise him tickling
(his word, 1. 437) the Boar's Head audience by aping that villain-
ous trick of the eye and foolish hanging of the nether lip which he
had just professed to see in Hal.

Falstaff is easy game for the exposure of pretensions, and
everywhere in the play there are clear signals that appearances
can be deceptive. Sack may look fresh but have lime in it; velvet
may appear to be of good quality when it is only gummed (II. ii.
2); cracked crowns may be passed current (II. iii. 94—95);
Falstaff's seal-ring, which he alleges is worth forty marks, may
only be copper; the battlefield at Shrewsbury is full of pretend-

kings. In *Part One* the great theme of appearance and reality
surfaces everywhere: were the shirts which Mistress Quickly
bought Falstaff really, as she says, holland of eight shillings an ell
or, as he says, "Dowlas, filthy dowlas," fit only for bakers' wives
to use as bolters (III. iii. 65–70)? Is Bardolph's red face repulsive
or coinable (III. iii. 76)? Is Glendower a magus or a fraud? Is
Mistress Quickly fish or flesh, or neither? Is not Falstaff's epic of
eleven buckram men and the knaves in Kendal green a far better
story than Hal's plain and statistical tale of "we two . . . you four
. . . We two . . . you four"? (II. iv. 249–254). Was Richard II a
sham king when he "carded his state,/ [and] Mingled his royalty
with cap'ring fools"—for to "card" is to adulterate—; or was
Henry a greater sham when in Richard's reign he "stole all
courtesy from heaven,/And dress'd [himself] in such humility/
That [he] did pluck allegiance from men's hearts"? (III. ii. 250-
263). Within *Part One*, especially, words alone seem inadequate
to pierce through the subterfuges, the more so as the characters
are rarely able to communicate with one another. Mortimer cannot talk with his Welsh-speaking wife, but neither can Hotspur
quite talk to *his* wife, nor to Glendower, nor indeed really to
anyone, even though Worcester tries to explain to him (III. i.
171-183) that discretion with one's tongue is the better part of
valour; Hal and his father are only momentarily on terms of
understanding; any kind of rational exchange with Mistress
Quickly is hilariously impossible (see III. iii.); and important
messages get twisted. Hal "can drink with any tinker in his own
language" (II. iv. 18–19) and join with Falstaff in wonderful
duets of insult chiefly because he enjoys a lie well elaborated:
"Prithee, let him alone," he tells Poins when the latter seems to
insist too much upon facts in the middle of Falstaff's buckram
story. Lies and truth run so close together in the play that even in
his planned reversion to his "real" self Hal intends to "falsify
men's hopes" (I. ii. 206).

"False stuff" is everywhere, and while the "issues" (the
matters in question, the true or false coin, offspring) are King
Henry's, it is Hotspur who brings the play's world of figures to a
focus in which spoken visions turn to seen reality. Hotspur, as I
have already said, "apprehends a world of figures . . . ,/ But not
the form of what he should attend" (I. iii. 207–208). We shall see
how, in this play, *figure* turns to *form*. Figure, as in Hotspur's

"world of figures," is the fantasy of plucking bright honour from the pale-faced moon and all the visions of personal splendor which go to make up that fantasy. Form is the reality to which Hotspur will not attend; in the play reality is eventually bitter, concrete, and visible.

What A.R. Humphreys rightly calls the theme of horseman-ship is everywhere in *Part One,* but most of all in Hotspur's visions and speech: "Horsemanship is a symbol of chivalric prowess, which is a main subject of the play."[4] Oddly enough, although Hal will be described as rising "from the ground like feather'd Mercury/ And [vaulting] with such ease into his seat/ As if an angel dropp'd down from the clouds/ To turn and wind a fiery Pegasus" (IV. i. 106—109), he talks in his own voice only once of horsemanship. This is at Gad's Hill, when he hides Falstaff's mount, and leaves the fat man doubly floundering by assuring him that "thou are not colted [that is, tricked], thou art uncolted" (II. ii. 38). Hotspur scarcely can talk of anything else but horses. His wife hears him in his sleep "Speak terms of manage to [his] bounding steed;" and to her deeply-felt plea that he confide in her, Hotspur's first response is to bellow for a servant and ask,

> Hath Butler brought those horses from the sheriff?
> *Servant.*
> One horse, my lord, he brought even now.
> *Hotspur.*
> What horse? A roan, a crop-ear is it not?
> *Servant.*
> It is, my lord.
> *Hotspur.*
> That roan shall be my throne.
> Well, I will back him straight: O Esperance!
> Bid Butler lead him forth into the park.
> *Lady Hotspur.*
> But hear me, my lord.
> *Hotspur.*
> What say'st thou, my lady?
> *Lady Hotspur.*
> What is it carries you away?
> *Hotspur.*
> Why, my horse, my love, my horse.

(II. iii. 68—77)

Carried away he is, and with, as well as by, his horse: "God's me! my horse!" he will shout after he has repulsed—possibly quite violently—her assault on his little finger, and

> Come, wilt thou see me ride?
> And when I am a-horseback I will swear
> I love thee infinitely.
>
> (II. iii. 101–103)

Even if there is a trace of bawdy here, the fact remains that all of Hotspur's fantasies are of the one kind. So also are his irritations: Glendower is as tedious to him as "A tired horse, a railing wife" (III. i. 154). Poetry, he says, is "like the forc'd gait of a shuffling nag" (III. i. 129). If Richard III would have given his kingdom for a horse, Hotspur's steed *is* his kingdom, that roan his throne. Mimicking him, Hal will shout that his roan horse is to be given a drench (II. iv. 104–105).

It is no sin, says Falstaff, for a man to labour in his vocation (I. ii. 101), and Hotspur's vocation undoubtedly is chivalry. Though it is Hal who eventually is apotheosized in chivalric terms by Vernon at Shrewsbury, we may be sure that Hotspur is equally glittering and equally agile. He and his followers will be, like their opponents,

> All furnish'd, all in arms;
> All plum'd, like estridges that with the wind
> Bated, like eagles having lately bath'd,
> Glittering in golden coats like images,
> As full of spirit as the month of May,
> And gorgeous as the sun at midsummer;
> Wanton as youthful goats, wild as young bulls. . . .
>
> (IV. i. 97–103)

What cannot be shown on Shakespeare's stage—the horses and the accoutrements—is turned into heraldry and heraldic terms for the audience's mental eye, into "arms" and "golden coats," and "images" of heraldic beasts unreeled in a verbal pageant: estridges, eagles, youthful goats, young bulls. "Gorgeous as the sun at midsummer" glances at the well-known heraldic device of the sun in splendor (as well as reminiscing on Hal's intention to "imitate the sun"), while Mercury and Pegasus in the descrip-

tion of Hal himself also have heraldic weight. Vernon's account
(IV. i. 111—124), with every phrase and image sharply struck as
from a mint, has the quality of Gerard Manley Hopkins' "Brute
beauty and valour and act, oh, air, pride, plume, here/ Buckle!"[5]
The iconography in Hotspur's response to the description of Hal
is equally strong: he sees his opponents coming "like sacrifices
in their trim," and calls up images of Mars and Bellona. Equally
accoutered, he will match Hal in every point:

> Harry to Harry shall, hot horse to horse. . . .

All of this, however iconically rich, is *heard*. But there now
occurs a seen antithesis, as Falstaff's ragged troop parades before
the audience. Obviously there would be no difficulty in showing
this aspect of the army on-stage, for raggedness, sickness, and
deprivation need few tiring-house furnishings, and any audience would be glad enough to settle for the appearance of only a
representative few of the hundred and fifty wretches whom
Falstaff says he has recruited. His description of his recruits,
then, is keyed to the state of those who appear. It also has its own
verbal icons—indeed, a whole animal farm of them—to stand
over against the heraldic beasts associated with Hal, Hotspur
and the officers:

> If I be not ashamed of my soldiers, I am a soused gurnet. . . .
> I press me none but . . . such as fear the report of a caliver worse
> than a struck fowl or a hurt wild duck. . . . And now my whole
> charge consists of . . . slaves as ragged as Lazarus in the painted
> cloth, where the glutton's dogs licked his sores. . . . You would
> think that I had a hundred and fifty tattered prodigals lately come
> from swine keeping . . . . A mad fellow met me on the way and told
> me I had unloaded all the gibbets and pressed the dead bodies. No
> eye hath seen such scarecrows.
>
> (IV. ii. 11—48)

In the ears and minds' eyes of the audience, what joins the
vigorous heraldry of suns in splendour, eagles, youthful goats
and young bulls with the plebeian iconography of soused gur-
nets, struck fowl, hurt wild ducks and glutton's dogs is of course
Falstaff's insistence upon "painted cloth," upon the

dishonourable-raggedness of an "old fazed ancient" (l. 31, that is, a tattered old flag), and

> There's not a shirt and a half in all my company, and the half shirt is two napkins tacked together and thrown over the shoulders like a herald's coat without sleeves.

That half-shirt clinches the point, and can do so visually. The "heraldry" of Falstaff's company poses the question "What is honour?" and more than suggests the possibility that it may be only "painted cloth."

These two scenes represent a movement which frequently occurs in Shakespeare—spoken thesis, seen antithesis. In *As You Like It*, no sooner has Jaques' dismissive summary of man's last scene, "Sans teeth, sans eyes, sans taste, sans every thing," been spoken than Orlando enters, tenderly bearing Old Adam, who is not a vegetable but "venerable" (*As You Like It*, II. vii. 163–167.) In *King Lear*, Edgar's brave certainty that the worst is over is abruptly contradicted by the appearance of Gloucester, blinded and poorly led (*Lear*, IV. i. 1–12); and as that play reverberates with the marvellous deliverance of Gloucester at Dover and Gloucester is told and agrees to "Bear free and patient thoughts," Lear comes in as mad as the vexed sea and fantastically dressed, completely unable to bear any such thoughts.

The pendulum of spoken thesis and seen antithesis— assertion and denial—in *Henry IV, Part One* takes its most wicked swings in the second last scene, V. iv., where Shakespeare gets down in earnest to visual business. The encounter between the royal and rebel forces at Shrewsbury is one of Shakespeare's most visually-detailed battles, and one which for that very reason keeps the audience guessing.

First Douglas meets, fights with and kills Sir Walter Blunt, who is disguised as the King. Nowhere during their encounter is there any indication that Douglas' adversary is not really King Henry, and Blunt actually says as he lays on, "Thou shalt find a king that will revenge Lord Strafford's death" (V. iii. 12–13). After killing Blunt, Douglas exultantly tells Hotspur, "Here breathless lies the King," only to be disillusioned: "The King hath many marching in his coats." (Predictably, although he looks straight into Sir Walter's face and identifies him, Hotspur the pursuer of honor as far as the pale-faced moon does not see what Falstaff sees in that face a few moments later—"such grinning honour as Sir Walter hath.") Hal and Falstaff now come together briefly. Hal seems to have broken or lost his sword, tries to borrow one from Falstaff, is offered a pistol which turns out to be a bottle of sack, and throws this angrily back at Falstaff. In this battle, nothing seems to be as it appears. But Hal really is wounded (V.iv. 1), saves his father from Douglas, and then is left alone (1.57)—

Enter Hotspur.

This moment has been promised to the audience in each of the four preceding acts: in the King's comparison of the young men in I. i.; in Hal's "I am not yet of Percy's mind . . ." in II. iv.; in Hotspur's vision of their chivalric encounter, "hot horse to horse . . ."; and especially in Hal's promise to the King in III. ii. 132f.:

> I will redeem all this on Percy's head,
> And in the closing of some glorious day
> Be bold to tell you that I am your son. . . .
> . . . I will tear the reckoning from his heart.

The *alikeness* of the two young men is stressed when they meet here. They might well have been exchanged in cradle clothes; and Hotspur's alliterative stress on their equality is borne out in the first words which pass: ". . . Thou art Harry Monmouth." "My name is Harry Percy." This is a recognizably Shakespearean fifth-act moment; for instance, *The Comedy of Errors*:

> *Duke.*
>   One of these men is genius to the other;
>   And so, of these, which is the natural man,
>   And which the spirit? Who deciphers them?
> *Dromio of Syracuse.*
>   I, sir, am Dromio. Command him away.
> *Dromio of Ephesus.*
>   I, sir, am Dromio. Pray let me stay.
>
> (V. i. 333–337)

"An apple cleft in two is not more twin/ Than these two creatures"—this is said in *Twelfth Night*, (V. i. 223–224) of Sebas-

tian and Viola/Cesario. So might it be of these two Harrys, who
now stand before one another or circle one another, each no
doubt in some variation of the golden coats mentioned in Vernon's description, two stars who for a moment keep their motion in one sphere. They are twinned as well in the play's quizzi-
cal emphasis upon deception, one of them is Heir-*Apparent*, the
other champions a *Pretender*. Hal also has alliteration to stress
their alikeness: "I am the Prince of Wales, and think not Percy
. . .: Harry Percy and the Prince of Wales." The doubly-
emphasized "Prince of Wales" is, however, also Hal's claim to
uniqueness—his assertion that he is *not* a changeling or a sham:
"I am the Prince of Wales" is the full equivalent of "I, Hamlet the
Dane."

But this is a play where proof is demanded, and the young
men begin to fight when, surprisingly,

> *Enter* Falstaff

He comes on a not inappropriate cue, for Hotspur has just said to
Hal, "I can no longer brook thy vanities." (The ventriloquism
works both ways between these two, and just as Hal talks like
Hotspur talking to his wife so Hotspur talks like Hal talking to
Falstaff.) But at this moment of the solemn testing of who is the
better man between Hotspur and Hal, Falstaff's presence seems
intrusive. Yet even if the audience is distracted for a moment, its
eyes are urged back to the young men through Falstaff's own
concentration upon them and by his words: "Well said, Hal! To
it, Hal!" Then Falstaff himself is forced to fight:

> *Enter* Douglas, *he fights with* Falstaff, *who falls down as if he were dead.*
> The Prince *killeth* Percy.

It might seem a mistake on Shakespeare's part to divide the
audience's attention here, of all moments. We have waited for
this for more than four acts; we do not need and do not want a
supporting bout. So I think that the audience's attention is fixed
upon the main contest; they may register the fact that Falstaff
exchanges passes with Douglas and "falls down as if he were
dead," but this surely is seen and meant to be seen only
peripherally. The struggle between the young men goes on after
Falstaff is down, and doubtless it was played so as to rivet the
attention. Shakespeare knows how to direct an audience's eyes:

in *Hamlet*, Bernardo's arm—and probably his guard's weapon as well—irresistibly directs everyone to look where he points to "Yond same star that's westward from the pole/ ...[illumining] that part of heaven/ Where now it burns," (I. i. 35—38) and the Ghost then enters from another direction. Likewise, when that Ghost enters for the second time in the first scene of *Hamlet* the audience has been wound into a rapt attentiveness to the seated Horatio as he goes through the exposition and the complicated analogy with the eve of Caesar's death (I. i. 79—125). And as the characters' and the audiences' eyes try to look everywhere in I. iv. when it is just midnight and time for the Ghost to re-appear—just as eyes are alert not to be deceived again the loud crash of a cannon roars into ears: "What does this mean?," and the answer unfolds in the "nature's livery or fortune's star" speech with its parentheses demanding fuller and fuller attention, until suddenly and surprisingly,

Enter Ghost.

It is quite likely that many members of Shakespeare's first audiences for *Hamlet* could not have said, after these three entrances, exactly from where the Ghost had emerged.

So also is the eye held or directed, in this scene in *Henry IV, Part One*, to the young men as they fight out the single combat towards which so much in the play has pressed. Then Hotspur is down and dying, with his visions turning into the materiality which has characterised the play: "the earthy and cold hand of death/Lies on my tongue." What Hal now does is both touching and visually telling. He first finishes Hotspur's last sentence: ". . . For worms, brave Percy." Then he takes his plumes or the ostrich-plume insignia[6] of the Prince of Wales and covers Hotspur's face:

> If thou wert sensible of courtesy
> I should not make so dear a show of zeal;
> But let my favours hide thy mangled face.

In a play where there have been so many "shows" this is one show which is spontaneously authentic. It goes against the grain of belligerence, for Hal had promised his father that he would take "every honour sitting on [Hotspur's] helm. Would they were multitudes," and again to Hotspur's face had said he would crop "all the budding honours on thy crest.../ To make a garland for my head." Honor and loyalty have up to now been won by the Lancastrians through "plucking" others—from "plume-pluck'd Richard," for instance (*Richard II*, IV. i. 108), in whose crowned presence Hal's father "dress'd [himself] in such humility/ That [he] did pluck allegiance from men's hearts" (*Henry IV, Part I*, III. ii. 50–54). Even Hotspur was determined "to pluck bright honour from the pale-fac'd moon,/ Or dive into the bottom of the deep.../ And pluck up drowned honour by the locks" (I. iii. 200–203). Among the play's chivalric icons, the plume is as important as the horse. But now Hal gives away his plumes—the ostrich feathers of the Prince of Wales; and in "doing these fair rites of tenderness" for Hotspur he seems to act out the motto of the princedom: *Ich dien*, "I serve." John Dover Wilson properly notes that "the epitaph on Hotspur contains not a word of triumph".[7] Hal *is*, as he said, the Prince of Wales, not in taking as Hotspur would have taken, but in magnanimous giving. He earlier laughingly reported that the Boar's-Head drawers had said of him "that though I be but Prince of Wales, yet I am the king of courtesy" (II. iv. 9–10). Now (as Juliet's nurse put it), to see how a jest shall come about:[8] Hal is king in courtesy. As for Hotspur, he now has all the honours that even he could have desired, for along with his own, unwrested from him, he has Hal's favours as well—though Falstaff's words may come to us as we look at the dead man lying in his honour: "Doth he feel it? No. Doth he hear it? No. 'Tis insensible, then? Yea, to the dead" (V. i. 137–139).

Now Hal *spieth* Falstaff *on the ground* (the Quarto stage-direction), and the epitaph he speaks over his old acquaintance emphasises how Falstaff somehow still remains *large*,[9] where the philosophical eulogy on Hotspur stressed that Percy seemed to have shrunk in death (we may recall that Antony also found Caesar smaller when dead than he had seemed to be when alive, *Julius Caesar*, III. i. 148–150). "Ill-weav'd ambition," says Hal of Hotspur, (and we are back to the play's web of references to spurious materials)

> how much art thou shrunk!
> When that this body did contain a spirit,
> A kingdom for it was too small a bound;

> But now two paces of the vilest earth
> Is room enough.

For Falstaff it is,

> Could not all this flesh
> Keep in a little life?
> Death hath not struck so fat a deer today.

Hal exits, and for a long moment—a great theatrical moment—we see the diminished Hotspur and the larger-than-life Falstaff lie together: the Prince may even drag them together, grimacing at and commenting on Falstaff's bulk as he does so, "So fat a deer," and leaving them close beside one another, "Till then in blood by noble Percy lie." Falstaff is almost sure to be behind Hotspur—else how could Percy even be seen?—and no doubt he is meant to lie in such a way as to emphasize his bulk, while the actor of Hotspur might lie in such a way as to de-emphasize *his* proportions. A Hotspur physically like Hal would be thin in any case; and the visual effect or sight-gag of fat and thin is still being achieved, for in this position Falstaff's mountain belly is bound to be much in evidence.

J.L. Styan has suggested that in presenting the two fights together Shakespeare was aiming at a "visual joke, [which] is capped by Hal's twin epitaphs upon the dying Hotspur and upon Falstaff shamming death nearby."[10] This assumes the audience would know that the fight between Douglas and Falstaff is not serious and know also that Falstaff is alive. But Shakespeare has given no hints: the audience has seen Douglas kill Blunt and very nearly overwhelm King Henry; it also has seen both Hotspur and Falstaff "fall down as if [they] were dead." In the situation up to this point, there are theatrical possibilities far richer than the jokes which Styan identifies; Shakespeare has created these possibilities, and he now is set to exploit them.

If we put ourselves in the shoes of naive spectators viewing the play for the first time without having read it, and seeing what Shakespeare has contrived that we see, what does this spectacle of the bodies offer? We have, as naive spectators, concentrated upon the primary and long-awaited combat between the two young men. We have seen Hal's total conviction that Falstaff is dead (and when has Falstaff ever before been so totally silent?

Short winded as he is, see III. iii. 158-159, he even in sleep fetches his breath hard and snorts like a horse, II. iv. 521-523; it is a remarkable feat for him to lie so quiet and so still). We have heard the eulogies and still hear them as we look at the bodies—it is possible after all, as Sonnet 23 says, "To hear with eyes." Now we see Hotspur and Falstaff lie together as if dead, both "in blood" (it is not the first time in the play that Falstaff has contrived to wear some blood for effect). As we watch and perhaps refect,

Falstaff *riseth up.*

This is a superb stroke of visual artistry. The gasp of surprise among first-time spectators of the play may still be heard in any theater where it is staged as Shakespeare wrote it to be staged. No one brought freshly through the experience of *Part One* up to this moment can know that Falstaff has been alive all along (Falstaffs who wink or mug on the ground as Hal speaks out his eulogy are not "[playing] out the play" as it should be done).

In his rising, Falstaff overturns the securities which Hal's battle has engendered. The audience has just been assured of "truth" and of the true prince. But now Falstaff, who a moment before was "the true and perfect image" of death, apologizes for his life and his deceit: "To counterfeit dying, when a man thereby liveth, is to be no counterfeit, but the true and perfect image of life indeed." Along with the faint hint of blasphemy on the theme of "losing" one's life to save it,[11] there also is a creepy logic to Falstaff's words; for if he is alive after his fall and his epitaph, may not Hotspur be alive as well? The nervous amusement in this moment quickly is stilled when we see what Falstaff proceeds to do to Hotspur's body. "Therefore, sirrah, with a new wound in your thigh," he says, suiting action to the words. The wound in the thigh has a quality not merely of "hitting below the belt": it ensures an appropriate amount of blood from the artery in the inside upper leg—Hal spoke of embowelling or embalming, and Falstaff has picked up the word; an embalmer would draw blood from a major artery. But as well as yielding blood to substantiate Falstaff's claim, attacking the corpse in this way makes visual and gives ghastly substance to an especial horror of war which supposedly was committed in Wales and reported

from there. We may recall that in I. i. the King relayed an account of

> A thousand of [Mortimer's] people butchered,
> Upon whose dead corpse there was such misuse,
> Such beastly shameless transformation,
> By those Welsh women done, as may not be
> Without much shame retold or spoken of.
>
> (ll. 41–45)

"Such beastly shameless transformation...as may not be...re-
told" minces the matter.But what could not formerly be spoken
of straightforwardly now is seen, as Falstaff the camp-follower so
explicitly violates the corpse and robs it of the honor just con-
ferred. There have been many robberies in the play,[12] some of
them actual and some figurative: Gad's Hill, the picking of
Falstaff's pocket while *he* lay helpless, the "theft" of the kingdom
("And then I stole all courtesy from heaven..." III. ii. 50) and of
Hotspur's life ("O Harry, thou hast robb'd me of my youth!" V.
iv. 76). But all of these had at least some element of daring, or of
fun. There is neither daring nor fun in the looting of Hotspur's
last honors and dignity; what Hall has given, Falstaff disgrace-
fully takes away.

Nor do the indignites perpetrated upon Hotspur end there.
Falstaff now *Takes Hotspur on his back* and carries him, either
off-stage to re-enter in a few moments, or about the rear stage as
Hal and Prince John make their entrance. They speak a line or
two, then see Falstaff come up to them. Their first reaction is
amazement, not at Falstaff's burden which being behind him is
mainly obscured by his bulk, but at his being alive (or a ghost).
Hal's surprise is the audience's of a few minutes before:

> I saw [Falstaff] dead,
> Breathless and bleeding on the ground. Art thou alive?
> Or is it fantasy that plays upon our eyesight?
> I prithee speak, we will not trust our eyes
> Without our ears: thou art not what thou seem'st.

Falstaff continues to treat the corpse with indignity, probably
throwing it down. At the end of his lying account of how they
"rose both at an instant, and fought a long hour by Shrewsbury
clock" (which echoes Hotspur's doubtless spurious tale of how

Mortimer "did confound the best part of an hour/ In changing hardiment with great Glendower," I. iii. 99–100), Hal tells him to take up the body more fittingly—"Come, bring your luggage nobly on your back"—and the scene ends with Falstaff, alone, hefting up and carrying out the undoubtedly now much-battered corpse of Hotspur.

Hal has just called that corpse "luggage," the luggage of an army, which usually was hauled about by pack-train. As we see Falstaff first get the dead man on his back and march about with him, then toss him down, and at last resume the burden, we surely are meant to be reminded in a pitying way of Hotspur's great and informing vision of himself—alive, crested, and mounted in chivalric splendour:

> That roan shall be my throne
> Well, I will back him straight.
>
> And when I am a-horseback I will swear. . . .
>
> Come let me taste my horse,
> Which is to bear me like a thunderbolt
> Against the bosom of the Prince of Wales.

Now all that chivalric vision has dwindled to this physical degradation. As I have said, Shakespeare's procedure in *Henry IV* is to set figure—the visions we hear about—against form—the actualities that we see. We actually see Hotspur "mounted" only upon the back of Falstaff, who has recruited the dead man into his last and most montrous lie in *Part One* and who already has said,

> Hal, if I tell thee a lie, spit in my face,
> call me horse.[13]

(II. iv. 189–190)

This is our last sight of Hotspur, and it is a terrible parody—a concrete parody—of the vision he has woven about himself, and a tragic final answer to the question asked of him earlier and answered so flippantly: "What is it carries you away?" And all this while it was supposed to have been Hal who was "violently carried away [by] an old fat man" (II. iv. 440–442).

Just as Hal gave honour to Hotspur, so also does he allow

Falstaff to take—to steal—the honour of having killed Hotspur. After his initial amazement at Falstaff's re-appearance, he seems to see through Falstaff's story. His use of the word "gild" in warranting that story indicates that he knows he is not guaranteeing true coin: "If a lie may do thee grace, I'll gild it with the happiest terms I have." The Chief Justice's suspicions in *Part Two* lead him to use just the same word to Falstaff's face: "Your day's service at Shrewsbury hath a little gilded over your night's exploit on Gad's Hill" (II. ii. 147–148). Even Hal's generosity in allowing Falstaff's claim diminishes Hotspur, who at the least would have asked for a worthy and certain conqueror—Samuel Johnson illustrates the vanity of human wishes with the military case of Charles XII, whose anticlimactic "fall was destined to...a dubious hand."[14]

So Falstaff will strut through *Henry IV, Part Two* as the conqueror of Hotspur, as in fact a kind of spurious Hotspur (we may now recall that on Gad's hill he bellowed Hotspur-like for *his* horse, *Part One*, II. ii. 28–40). In his posturing he will weave about himself his own kind of dream, one not necessarily of chivalry but certainly of power and wealth, of a state wherein "the laws of England are at [his] commandment" (*Henry IV, Part II*, V. iv. 132–133). As I have shown elsewhere, Hal, the only man who knows for sure what really happened at Shrewsbury, overcomes this counterfeit Hotspur as conclusively as he overcame the real one.[15] He does so in a scene which also is visually impressive. Falstaff, capering and sweating in his excitement, is dressed in his old and travel-stained clothes as he awaits the new King's entrance. His appearance is heavily stressed:

Falstaff.
　　O if I had had time to have made new liveries...But 'tis no matter, this poor show doth better, this doth infer the zeal I had to see him . . . It shows my earnestness of affection— . . . My devotion— . . . As it were, to ride day and night, and not to deliberate, not to remember, not to have patience to shift me—. . .But to stand stained with travel, and sweating with desire to see him, thinking of nothing else, putting all affairs else in oblivion, as if there were nothing else to be done but to see him.
Pistol.
　　'Tis *semper idem*...

　　　　　　　　　　　　　　　　　　　　　　　(*Part Two*, V. v. 10–29)

How very like Hotspur's is the impulsiveness that Falstaff would suggest—to ride day and night, not to deliberate, not to remember, not to have patience, thinking of nothing else, putting all affairs else into oblivion. But this is no fit counterpart to, or companion for, Henry V. Pistol's reassurance, *"Semper idem"* (ever the same), is ironic. Falstaff metaphorically, literally, visually, is unchanged. But the new King Henry's first words have been about the change which has come over him: "This new and gorgeous garment, majesty, Sits not so easy on me as you think" (V. ii. 44-45). And as the King now appears, wearing his coronation robes, the distance between what he has become and what this scruffy old man still is is pathetically visible; banishment is *seen* to be inevitable. Once he has been rejected, the only thing Falstaff has left in common with Hotspur is that his final exit is made in ignominious and painful silence: it is superfluous to note that he too is at the last "carried" away, to the Fleet (V. v. 91).

In *Henry IV*, the audience is, like Lear, being schooled to "see better": to *see* that war is horrible, that courtesy lies in doing and giving, that Hotspur's visions and Falstaff's dreams are unattainable and ultimately pathetic. From the beginning to the end of these two plays, and especially, as I have tried to show, in the overcoming of Hotspur, the visual artistry at work is so skilful that Shakespeare afterwards must have had his tongue in his cheek in giving a "deferential stance"[16] and a mouthful of apologies to the *Henry V* Chorus for the supposed inadequacies of that play's historical spectacles. The ideal performance prescribed within *Henry IV, Parts One and Two* sets the argument so clearly before our eyes that with these plays at any rate there scarcely is any need to ask an audience to

> be kind
> And eke out our performance with your mind.[17]

Notes

1. Cf. *Joel* 2:28; *Acts* 2:17.
2. *Hamlet* I. v. 129-130. Mark Rose also finds a parallel between Hal and Francis in this scene: "The prince's responsibilities are calling and his reply so far has been the same as Francis'" (*Shakespearean*

Design Cambridge, Mass.: Belknap/Harvard University Press, 1972, p. 51). Rose also says that "the principal thrust of the episode is emblematic."

3. Cf. Falstaff's intention to take off Shallow for Hal's enjoyment (*Part Two*, V. i. 75-77): "I will devise matter out of this Shallow to keep Prince Harry in continual laughter the wearing out of six fashions. . . ."

4. A.R. Humphreys, Introduction to the New Arden *King Henry IV, Part One* (London: Methuen, 1960), p. ix. Horsemanship also is treated by Hugh MacLean in "Time and Horsemanship in Shakespeare's Histories" (*University of Toronto Quarterly*, 35 (April, 1966), 229-245). MacLean's theme is "As each [of Shakespeare's historical protagonists] rides, so he manages his span of time." Hotspur rides and lives impetuously—"rushes at time", whereas Hal manages his time as he manages his steed. All references to *Henry IV, Part One* in this essay cite this edition, and references to *Part Two* cite Humphreys' New Arden text (London: Methuen, 1966).

5. G.M. Hopkins, "The Windhover," ll. 8-9.

6. Herbert Hartman's interpretation of the meaning of "favours" as the plumes of Hal's helmet seems to me to be the most persuasive: "Prince Hal's 'Shew of Zeale'," *PMLA*, 46(1931), 720-723. Hartman does not concern himself with the ironies inherent in Hal's gesture.

7. *The Fortunes of Falstaff* (Cambridge: Cambridge University Press, 1943), p. 67.

8. *Romeo and Juliet* I. iii. 45.

9. While Hal's words emphasize Falstaff's physical bulk, it might be that the tone in which he delivers them—a tone, say, of affectionate bemusement: "Could not *all* this flesh keep in a *little* life?"—tends to comically deflate Falstaff rather than enlarge him. This of course is the essence of Falstaff's comic mystery: "If I do grow great, I'll grow less..."(V. iv. 162-163).

10. J.L. Styan, *Shakespeare's Stagecraft* (Cambridge: Cambridge University Press, 1967), pp. 172-173.

11. Cf. *Matthew* 16:25 "...Whosoever will save his life shall lose it...." This thought is repeated in *Mark* 8:35, *Luke* 9:24, and *John* 12:25.

12. Cf. Derek Traversi, *Shakespeare from Richard II to Henry V* (Stanford: Stanford University Press, 1967), pp. 62-63 and Rose, *Shakespearean Design*, p. 79: "Here is Hal playing at highwayman while elsewhere his enemies are planning to rob him of his crown."

13. See also Falstaff at III. iii. 7-9: "And I have not forgotten what the inside of a church is made of, I am a...brewer's horse."

14. Samuel Johnson, *The Vanity of Human Wishes*, ll. 217-220.

15. See my article "Counterfeits of Soldiership in Henry IV," *Shakespeare Quarterly*, 24 (1973), 372-382.

16. Herschel Baker's phrase, in his Introduction to *Henry V*, *The Riverside Shakespeare*, ed. G. Blakemore Evans *et al*. (Boston: Houghton Mifflin Co., 1974), p. 934.

17. *Henry V*, III. Prol. 34-35.

Some Dramatic Techniques in *King Lear*

WILLIAM H. MATCHETT

When a playwright sets out to engage an audience, he has numerous options. He may aim at apparent artlessness, for example, writing dialogue and arranging situations for the sole purpose of advancing his story, trusting that playgoers following it will be moved by what they see and hear. He may work less directly, arranging mysteries in his plot or presenting seemingly unrelated or discordant events in order to challenge curiosity. He may attend closely to creating an atmosphere—through setting, costume, lighting or language—which will predispose his audience to a particular response, perhaps for its own sake or perhaps in preparation for an ironic reversal. He may seek to arouse an emotion in the spectator either by assuming a sympathetic response to an actor's portraying that emotion on stage or by manipulating a series of events calculated to create that emotion directly as a result of active participation in a developmental process. A fine playwright will modulate among many such options, combining them in various ways at varying moments in the same play.

Among its other supremacies, *King Lear* seems to me unrivalled in the way it gains major effects through the attention its author has paid to direct manipulation—the phrase is descriptive, not pejorative—to direct manipulation of his audience's responses. Shakespeare thrusts experience upon us not only as observers of the suffering of his characters but as participants in a succession of unstable emotions of our own, emotions aroused by the rhythms of suspense and hope through which he compels us to pass. His is a superlative art of controlling our responses through keeping us off balance.

Such an art is naturally aimed at new audiences and may be lost upon those who come to Shakespeare's play knowing as much about it as we now inevitably do. Of course *King Lear* repays close attention and repeated exposure—the way meanings continue to exfoliate is another of its glories—but there is something to be said for trying to recapture the structure of experience created for an audience approaching this telling of the story without knowledge of its outcome. Such is the audience Shakespeare presumably had in mind as he wrote, playgoers still capable of surprise. If we can no longer be naïve, we can attempt to adopt or exercise a kind of sophisticated naïveté in order to study the way Shakespeare goes about manipulating this innocent playgoer's responses. Though they will not give us any final insight into *King Lear*, the results are at least not reductive: they can only add to our appreciation of Shakespeare's theatrical skills.

I will place primary emphasis on two scenes—Gloucester's attempted suicide and the deaths of Cordelia and Lear—but I want to begin by suggesting how Shakespeare teases us from the very first lines of his play. The original audience is not likely to have been attending *The Tragedy of King Lear*, a title the play achieves only in the generic division of the 1623 Folio. Even the short version of the title on the 1608 Quarto— [*The*] *True Chronicle History of the life and death of King Lear and his three Daughters* – gives away more than that original audience was likely to have known in advance. Indeed, if they had seen the anonymous earlier version of the play, *The True Chronicle History of King Leir and his three daughters*, they would be expecting a happy ending. But let them derive their information from the play before them and what were they being prepared to expect?

Three well-dressed men come onto the empty stage, one old, one middle-aged and, hanging back from the other two, who are conversing, one young and handsome.[1] Who these men are, the audience can only learn as the lines identify them. The middle-aged man speaks first:

I thought the King had more affected the Duke of Albany than
Cornwall.

The old man answers:

It did always seem so to us; but now, in the division of the
kingdom, it appears not which of the Dukes he values most; for
equalities are so weigh'd that curiosity in neither can make choice
of either's moiety.

We hear of a kingdom being divided into equal halves in spite of
its king's presumed preference for one of the named recipients.
An audience exposed to earlier chronicle histories on this same
stage, or to any contemporary political theorizing, would know
immediately what to expect: when kingdoms are divided, civil
war follows. They are promised a kind of drama with which they
are already familiar.

Then the conversation shifts into jovial bawdiness as the old
man introduces the youth as his bastard son. Modern audiences,
hearing the pun on "conceive" (12), miss the scatologic pun in
"Do you smell a fault?" (16), which, given the silent "l" or "r" in
Elizabethan pronunciation of the noun, is also, as Herbert A.
Ellis has taught us, "Do you smell a fart?"[2] and leads to the
continuing double entendre of "the issue of it being so proper"
(17–18). Indeed, when this now obscured pun is called to the
attention of modern readers, they are apt either to deny its
presence as out of keeping with their sense of the seriousness of
the tragedy, or else to consider it an instance of Shakespeare's
weakness for bawdry whether or not it may be relevant. I would
suggest instead a calculatedly misleading tonal introduction.
The play will turn out to be no more a bawdy comedy than it is a
chronicle history of civil war. Both themes will reappear,
modulated into the play's own concerns with authority and
sexuality as aspects of the poor, bare, forked animal seeking to
define himself in relation to undefined gods, but either theme is
misleading for an auditor seeking a proper standpoint as the play
begins.

The point is that Shakespeare delights in deluding his audience, in creating misleading expectations. As *King Lear* unfolds,
Shakespeare returns at the beginning of both the second and
third acts to the idea of an impending clash between Albany and

Cornwall,[3] but Cornwall is killed by his own servant and their joint forces fight the invading French without the predicted dissension ever occurring. When their wives fall out over Edmund, it is lechery, not politics; and, though the probability has been kept tantalizingly before us, nothing ever comes of the plot we had thought—and were kept thinking—most likely to result from the dividing of the kingdom.

But the primary way in which Shakespeare misleads an innocent audience in this play is through his keeping before it the assumption—not merely the hope, but the expectation—that Lear and Cordelia will eventually win through to reconciliation and a happy ending. Precisely between the shutting of the doors on Lear at end of Act Two, for example, and his thundering re-entry in the storm at the beginning of III. ii., comes the short scene in which Kent tells us not only that Lear's tormentors are divided but that Cordelia has come with an army from France. In other words, the references to a schism between Albany and Cornwall is not just a blind alley but part of a specific pattern of misleading reassurance. Hanging over even the storm scenes is our knowledge that ultimate rescue has already been set in motion. This procedure might be compared to the way in which Portia's presence as judge assures us that everything is under control in the trial scene in *The Merchant of Venice*, or to the way in which Dogberry's having arrested Borachio and Conrade lets us know that, however the constable may stumble in trying to get his evidence delivered, everything will eventually come out all right in *Much Ado About Nothing*. Though Shakespeare may be making Lear suffer, his audience is given every reason to expect that the play is headed toward the happy ending of the earlier version.

The sufferings of Gloucester are, I would think, directly related to this false expectation. Critics have often commented on what Bradley called "the fact—in Shakespeare without a parallel—that the sub-plot simply repeats the theme of the main story."[4] I would call attention to the likelihood that this (as it turns out) unusual structure would also have the effect, on a first approach, of reassuring the audience as to the outcome of the main plot. Not knowing that the sub-plot repeats the theme, they would suppose that they were witnessing a contrast, that things would *not* go as badly for Lear as they were going for Gloucester.

I do not, of course, want to reduce the effect of the Gloucester plot to this single influence on audience expectation, but only to point out that such would be part of its original effect. There are naturally other considerations of more importance. However parallel the two plots may be, Shakespeare does also use the sub-plot to set up a number of contrasts with the main plot. The pretended madness of Edgar, for example, pulling out all the stops for a fully theatrical—indeed stagy—effect, functions in a way quite similar to one way in which the play-within-a play functions in *Hamlet*. The presence of this conventionally theatrical madness in a character who is, we know, pretending, helps inmeasurably to establish the "reality" of Lear's contrasted madness, not to mention the Fool's. As another example, the blinding of Gloucester vastly extends the range of cruelty and pain in the play, bringing in a physical suffering beyond any inflicted on Lear.

It takes little imagination to see both why Shakespeare would want so to extend the horror his play asks us to face, and how he would have harmed the outcome if he had decided to inflict the cruelty of the blinding on Lear himself. The *King Lear* universe involves suffering of all kinds, but if this physical pain were inflicted on Lear it might seem in itself a sufficient cause for his suffering and would only distract attention from the mental anguish we must see him undergo.

Even with Gloucester, we are constantly trapped into hope. The very blinding scene, as horrifying as it is, ends on an upswing. One servant has given his life (and, as we later discover, has killed the vicious Cornwall) in attempting to help the old man; the other two servants will bring him to "the Bedlam" (III. vii. 102) and will "fetch some flax and whites of eggs/ To apply to his bleeding face" (105–106). That is to say, these nameless servants will not only seek to soothe Gloucester's pain but will deliver him directly into the hands of his good son Edgar. It is a move toward comfort, revelation and reconciliation.

In returning to or remembering the play, we can see how such motions are frustrated time and again. Indeed, this becomes a basic rhythm in *King Lear*: "The Gods reward your kindness!" says Kent in thanking Gloucester (III. vi. 5), and the blinding is Gloucester's reward; "The worst returns to laughter," says Edgar (IV. i. 6), and his blinded father is led in, forcing

Edgar to realize (for this moment at least), "I am worse than e'er I was...And worse I may be yet; the worst is not/ So long as we can say 'This is the worst'" (26–28); "Bear free and patient thoughts," says Edgar, encouraging his father after the attempted suicide, "But who comes here?" (IV. vi. 80), and the mad king enters, "Crown'd," as Cordelia described him (IV. iv. 3), in weeds and flowers; "If ever I return to you again,/ I'll bring you comfort...Away, old man...King Lear hath lost, he and his daughter ta'en" (V. ii. 3–6); "The Gods defend her"—"*Enter Lear with Cordelia [dead] in his arms*" (V. iii. 255 and the stage direction immediately following). Every time Shakespeare raises our hopes, he pulls the rug out from under us. This is the rhythm of *King Lear*, and it remains consistently so to the end of the play; but the very repetitiveness of this rhythm would keep a new audience expecting it to break. *This*, we feel (over and over again), is the moment of change; *now* things have surely taken their turn for the better.

Consider the effect of the Dover cliff scene, Gloucester's attempted suicide. Edgar, we know, tricks his father; modern audiences are not aware of the extent to which Shakespeare tricks us. We know the results so well that we fail even to realize what we should have been experiencing along the way.

The first surprise is, of course, that Edgar maintains his role as Poor Tom even when he is left alone with his blinded father. We can invent motives for this—he doesn't yet know what his father now thinks or knows, or he is afraid to shock the old man further without preparing him properly—but no motives are stated, and so we must have at least a lingering uncertainty as to what his aims may be. Then, at the end of that scene, Gloucester asks to be led to the "very brim" of Dover cliff—"from that place/ I shall no leading need" (IV. i. 75–78)—and Edgar, making no comment to Gloucester or aside to us, agrees. We know, and we assume Edgar knows, that Gloucester intends suicide. We hope, indeed we probably assume, that Edgar intends to interfere with his father's intention—perhaps by making himself known, perhaps by staying away from the cliff—but we are left with the discomfort of not being sure just what is taking place.

When they next come on the stage, Edgar now dressed in the garments the old servant has presumably provided in accordance with his promise (IV. i. 49–50), Gloucester asks, "When shall I come to th' top of that same hill'' (IV. vi. 1); and we know that he still thinks himself headed for the edge of the cliff. What we see in Shakespeare's theater is the same bare stage we always see. We will only be where the actors tell us we are.

> *Edgar.*
>   You climb up it now; look how we labour.
> *Gloucester.*
>   Methinks the ground is even.
>
>   (2—3)

That is the giveaway, my students tell me—or, as they are more likely to call it, the "clue." That is where Shakespeare informs us what is really going on. But does he? He neither informs us nor even gives us a reliable clue; at best he teases us.

> *Gloucester.*
>   Methinks the ground is even.
> *Edgar.*
>   Horrible steep:
>   Hark! do you hear the sea?
> *Gloucester.*
>   No, truly.
> *Edgar.*
>   Why, then your other senses grow imperfect
>   By your eyes' anguish.
> *Gloucester.*
>   So may it be, indeed.
>   (3—6)

No one facing a bare stage and not knowing the story would be likely to feel that this exchange has firmly established that we are not headed for the cliff or that the sea is not there to be heard. At most, he might be left wondering; more likely he would take it as established that Gloucester, in his blindness and pain, is confused. He will still wonder what Edgar intends to do. Gloucester continues:

>   Methinks thy voice is alter'd, and thou speak'st
>   In better phrase and matter than thou didst.
> *Edgar.*
>   You are much deceiv'd; in nothing am I chang'd
>   But in my garments.

Gloucester.

Methinks you're better spoken.

(7—10)

Edgar is no longer acting the full role of Poor Tom. He is indeed
better spoken, as the next passage, his evocation of the view from
Dover cliff, will amply confirm. That Gloucester is right about his
altered voice might provide a logic allowing one to argue that he
is also right about the level ground and the sound of the sea, but
Shakespeare is not *telling* us any such thing; he is providing us
with a situation to raise doubts, a situation to make us wonder.
He building suspense.[5]

When Edgar describes the full view from the cliff, the birds
in the midway air, the sampire gatherer half way down, the
fishermen on the beach and the boats in the water, he sets the
scene exactly as scenes are always set on the empty stage. He fills
in the background in precisely the manner in which Horatio
brings morning to Elsinore or Duncan and Banquo evoke Macbeth's castle. This is the way scenes are always set in the
Elizabethan theater, and we have no reason now to believe we
are anywhere but where Edgar has placed us.[6] The very absence
of an audible sound of the sea becomes an additional confirma-
tion of the height of the cliff. "I'll look no more," Edgar concludes,

Lest my brain turn and the deficient sight
Topple down headlong.
Gloucester.

Set me where you stand.

Edgar.
Give me your hand; you are now within a foot
Of th' extreme verge: for all beneath the moon
Would I not leap upright.
Gloucester.

Let go my hand.

(22—27)

Whenever he may be on the stage, whether on some step or riser,
or near the front edge, or merely somewhere in the middle of the
empty space, Gloucester is, for the audience, on the edge of
Dover cliff. Edgar would not so much as jump up, much less

out—for fear presumably of the brink crumbling or of his merely losing his balance as he came down. It is a moment of maximal suspense. Surely Edgar will not let his father commit suicide. Or will he? Surely he will stop him from leaping. But even his potentially reassuring aside—"Why I do trifle thus with his despair/ Is done to cure it" (33–34)—allows the possibility that Edgar sees death as the best cure for his father's condition.

Gloucester falls, but only to his knees, and for us, tensing and then releasing (whether breath, muscles or concentration), there is as it were a syncopation or skipped beat in the suspense, which then builds the more strongly as the old man prays, renounces the world, blesses Edgar, and bids farewell to Poor Tom. Even his prayer has in it an element of audience teasing as the end of what turns out to be a run-on line gives, and then takes away, the literal action: "If I could bear it longer and not fall/ To quarrel with your great opposeless wills..." (37–38). There is, after his farewell, no stage direction in the Folio; the Quarto has merely "*He falls.*"[7] The actor is of course assisted by the fact that he is already on his knees, but there must for us be a moment of horror as Edgar says "Gone, sir: farewell" (41).

Only then does Shakespeare let us in on the trick: "Had he been where he thought/ By this had thought been past" (44–45). We were not on the cliff after all. In other words, Shakespeare makes us experience the suicide as we experienced the blinding, and only then lets us know with certainty what Edgar has been doing.[8] Taking on a new role, pretending to find Gloucester at the bottom of the cliff, Edgar continues to trick his father, but now, being in on the trick, we become observers of it and not, as we just were, direct participants.

Among the effects of this process are two to which I would call attention here. One is what happens to the rhythm of expectation, the struggle between hope and fear. The fact that we have been through the on-stage blinding has strengthened our fear that we may be headed for Gloucester's suicide. Not having been spared the one, we cannot be sure we will be spared the other. We still have hope, because it is Edgar, not Edmund or Cornwall, who is present; but our hope is kept uncertain by our not knowing how he perceives his father's situation. In relation to Lear, however, once Gloucester's suicide turns out to have been forestalled—once, having been through it, we discover that we have been tricked—we feel a new surge of hope. In spite of the blinding, the play is apparently not allowing its protagonists to die. Gloucester has been saved from death. And this, along with the death of Cornwall, Albany's growing revulsion against the evildoers—his vow, indeed, to revenge Gloucester's eyes (IV. ii. 94—96)—and, most particularly, the return of Cordelia, all serve to assure us that Lear will be saved. The tide has turned and the worst is now surely behind us.

The other effect is more complex. Edgar's cure for his father's despair is apparently to implant in the old man the conviction that "Thy life's a miracle" (IV. vi. 55). Since he has been preserved from suicide, a despairing project assisted by "some fiend" (72) which led him to the edge of the cliff, Gloucester is to recognize the divine nature of his preservation:

> therefore, thou happy father,[9]
> Think that the clearest Gods, who make them honours
> Of men's impossibilities, have preserved thee.
>
> (72—74)

We want this to be true. We recognize that faith is what Gloucester needs if he is to survive, and indeed we can assent to the general proposition that *all* life is essentially miraculous. We may be moved by what Edgar is doing for his father. But we are denied the very faith which Gloucester is being given, for we know that the miracle has been staged, that it is indeed a trick; and so we are left both relieved and dissatisfied—reassured that Gloucester will live, but cut off from sharing his basis for faith.[10]

And we are faced next with the entry of Lear, fully mad.

The ensuing scene remains a powerful one for a modern audience. For a Jacobean, the condition of Lear, still "every inch a king" (IV. vi. 110), would directly shake, would well nigh shatter, the philosophical foundations of society. Maynard Mack has spelled it out:

> here onstage, as during the scene on the heath, a familiar convention was again being turned upside down and made electric with meaning. A king of the realm—like their own king, guarantee of its coinage ("they cannot touch me for coining"), commander of its troops ("There's your press money"), chief object of its *paideia* ("They flattered me like a dog"), fountain of its justice ("O! let me kiss that hand")—was not only presented mad, crowned with

weeds, but in his madness registered for all to hear the bankruptcy of the very body politic (and body moral) of which he was the representative and head:

> Plate sin with gold
> And the strong lance of justice hurtless breaks;
> Arm it in rags, a pigmy's straw does pierce it.
> None does offend, none, I say none; I'll able 'em:
> Take that of me, my friend, who have the power
> To seal th' accuser's lips. Get thee glass eyes;
> And, like a scurvy politician, seem
> To see the things thou dost not.[11]

Like Gloucester, an audience faced here with the way the world goes, will "see it feelingly" (150). The mad king is an excruciating image presented as an inescapable fact: "I would not take this from report; it is, And my heart breaks at it" (142-143). This could not be imagined. It is.

Lear's madness is not uniformly high-pitched but, like the storm, has diversified rhythms which keep our responses active. After the two extravagant identifications of Gloucester, for example—"Goneril with a white beard" (97) and, most cruelly, "blind Cupid" (139)—the sudden quiet sanity of "I know thee well enough; thy name is Gloucester" (179) is nothing short of breathtaking. This unexpected moment of balance re-establishes a world of possible human relationships, and then Lear's moving sermon on patience veers off into his dream of revenge with its crescendo in inhumanity: "kill, kill, kill, kill, kill, kill!" (189).

Yet even this scene ends in hope. Though Lear mistakes his rescuers for enemies and runs from them, they have come, we know, from Cordelia and—after Edgar has again saved his father's life, killing Oswald and collecting the useful evidence of Goneril's plot against Albany—we can once more be assured that we are headed for restored harmony. Indeed, the convergence for which we have been longing occurs in the next affecting scene when, to the reinforcing accompaniment of off-stage music, Lear wakes in Cordelia's presence. Though she judges him still "far wide" (IV. vii. 50), we can follow the logic of his confusions and recognize that Lear is fumbling his way back to sanity, while their tearful reunion and her denial of any action requiring forgiveness—"No cause, no cause" (75)—would seem to insure most poignantly the joyous conclusion we have been led to expect, or, if not to expect, at least to desire with reasonable hope. Though the gentleman at the end of the scene anticipates "arbitrement...like to be bloody" (94), we know that both Edgar and Kent are at hand and not, as he thinks, "in Germany" (91), so that little seems to remain beyond rounding up the villains who are already at odds with each other.

Shakespeare is not yet done with holding us in suspense, however; and, following Edmund's capture of Lear and Cordelia, the Captain's exit with orders to kill them hangs over all subsequent action. "If it be man's work," says the Captain, accepting Edmund's written orders, "I'll do't" (V. iii. 40). That unresolved conditional clause raises directly what is also a central theme in *Macbeth*, the problem of what properly pertains to a human being. When, for example, Lady Macbeth accuses her husband of cowardice in hesitating to murder Duncan, Macbeth responds, "I dare do all that may become a man;/ Who dares do more is none" (I. vii. 46–47). Whether murdering his sovereign-benefactor-guest becomes a man is a question on which Macbeth allows himself to be misled. We have, then, a dual suspense with Edmund's Captain, the suspense of whether he will find it in his nature to carry out his orders, and the further suspense of whether, if he tries to do so, the act will be prevented.

The Captain no sooner departs than Albany enters and demands Edmund's prisoners. When Edmund palters, offering to yield them "Tomorrow, or at further space" (54), our suspense is keen, and we are pleased to have Albany assert himself:

> Sir, by your patience,
> I hold you but a subject of this war,
> Not as a brother.
>
> (60–62).

This firmness is thwarted, however, as Regan and Goneril scramble for the right to defend their paramour. Albany's demand for the prisoners is shunted aside and the rapid action centers on Edmund's future: Regan, announcing that she is ill, claims him as her "lord and master" (79); Goneril objects, and Albany denies her right to object; Edmund denies Albany's right to intervene, and Albany arrests him "On capital treason" (84), adding the bitter jests Goneril dismisses as "An interlude" (90);[12] Albany calls for a champion to fight Edmund, offering his own challenge should none appear; we learn from Goneril's aside that she has poisoned Regan; Edmund accepts Albany's challenge; Regan is assisted to her tent and then the pace slows to a ritual formality, the Herald's invocation of a challenger and the three soundings of the trumpet, answered three times by a trumpet off stage and the appearance of a knight with his visor down. Surely no one in the theater audience will be surprised to discover that this is Edgar in yet another of his many disguises, and yet Shakespeare has the scene played out at length as though we might be as unprepared for the news as are Edmund and the others on stage. It is possible that Shakespeare is engaged merely in providing the pleasure of watching others respond to a mystery we have already fathomed; I think it more likely that he has slowed the action to allow the suspense to build again. True, there is a fight before Edmund falls, and there is Albany's turning on Goneril and her defiant exit—the action is hardly static. Yet the twenty-five lines of Edgar's formal challenge and Edmund's answer, following on the Herald and the trumpets, give plenty of time for the audience to recall the overarching suspense of the Captain who set out with orders to kill Lear and Cordelia.

Edmund's defeat, his forgiving Edgar and the latter's insistence that "The gods are just" (170) all tend to confirm again that the play is moving toward a happy resolution; yet the suspense remains, and we may even be made uneasy by Edgar's glib explanation for Gloucester's blinding. And then the length of his narrative as he relates his care for his father, the old man's death and his own reunion with the dying Kent, will add further to our uneasiness, with the result that the sudden appearance of the *"Gentleman, with a bloody knife* (S.D. following 221) will swing us to expect the worst.

> *Edgar.*
>   What means this bloody knife?
> *Gentleman.*
>   'Tis hot, it smokes;
>   It came even from the heart of—

Lear? we want to know, or Cordelia? and he completes the interrupted syntax with "O! she's dead" (223—224), which to us

can only mean Cordelia. It comes as a complete surprise therefore
to discover that he is speaking of Goneril; and the relief swings
us back to expecting once more that Shakespeare, having tricked
us, is indeed going to save our heroine.

Everything moves once again toward a satisfactory resolution. Albany calls the deaths of the two sisters "This judgment of
the heavens" (231). Kent arrives and, finally, brings attention
back to Lear and Cordelia—"Great thing of us forgot!" (236), an
awkward line perhaps, but true to the fact of all the action and the
nearly two hundred lines of dialogue which have intervened
since Albany last demanded that Edmund give them up. Even
now there is further interruption as the bodies of Regan and
Goneril are brought onto the stage. Many have objected to this
"unnecessary" action, blaming it on an unfortunate Jacobean
taste for tragedies ending with corpse-laden stages. But consider
the implications of the tableau at this moment: Lear's opposition
has been completely destroyed. Here are the two wicked
daughters, both dead; Edmund is prone and dying; we may
recall that Cornwall and even Oswald have been killed. Only the
virtuous remain. True, Gloucester is dead and Kent is said to be
dying; but Kent, unlike Edmund, is still on his feet, while Edgar
is clearly victorious, and we can no longer doubt Albany's
worthy intentions. The well-meaning, however ineffective they
have been at times, have visibly outlasted the cruel and vicious.

Even Edmund is now moved to do "some good . . . Despite of
mine own nature" (243–244), and the messenger is at last des-
patched to countermand the Captain's orders. We may now be
sure it is a drama of last-minute rescue: 'Haste thee, for thy life"
(251).

The short interval while we await the news is filled with
Edmund's explanation ("He hath commission from thy wife and
me/ To hang Cordelia in the prison, and/ To lay the blame upon
her own despair,/ That she fordid herself" [252–255]), Albany's
horrified response ("The Gods defend her!" [255]), and the business of carrying Edmund from the stage.

"The Gods defend her": *"Enter Lear with Cordelia in his
arms."*[13] It is the supreme instance of the undercutting which I
have called the play's basic rhythm—but, even so, we cannot yet
be sure what we are seeing. We are not done with suspense.

Lear enters not merely calling upon others to howl, but

himself howling. The similarity to the tone and words of his first entry in the storm—"Blow, winds, and crack your cheeks! rage! blow!" (III. ii. 1)—floods this scene with all our memories of that earlier one. "O! you are men of stones:/ Had I your tongues and eyes, I'd use them so/ That heaven's vault should crack" (V. iii. 257–259): "Crack Nature's moulds, all germens spill at once/ That makes ingrateful man!" (III. ii. 8–9). Lear's massively destructive storm has come again.

Cordelia, he tells us, is dead:

> She's gone forever.
> I know when one is dead, and when one lives;
> She's dead as earth.
>
> (V. iii. 259–261)

But he no sooner gives us the information than he throws doubt upon it:

> Lend me a looking glass;
> If that her breath will mist or stain the stone,
> Why, then she lives.
>
> (261–263)

Is it wishful thinking or a dramatic possibility? May we still hope? We do not know. As we look upon the living actress—in Jacobean times, the living actor—playing Cordelia, we are likely to see what Lear yearns to see: facial movement, breathing, signs of life. May we trust them? We want Lear's hope to be justified. But the living actress may of course, by the usual stage convention, be representing a dead Cordelia. If so, we must deny the life we see as Lear struggles to deny the death he sees.[14]

The comments of the three virtuous remnants show that, unlike Lear, they accept Cordelia's death as the fact.

Kent.

Is this the promis'd end?

Edgar.
  Or image of that horror?

Albany.

Fall and cease.

(263–264)

Kent's question is personal and individual as well as universal. Given a slight additional emphasis on "this," he is asking whether, at his own death, this heartbreaking father-and-daughter Pietà is to be the only reward for his own loyal service, whether Cordelia's death is to be the only result of Lear's suffering, and, of course, whether this suffering piled upon suffering means that the end of the world has come. Edgar, less totally involved with Lear (though his own father has died, he has at least salvaged some sense of justice in his revenge upon Edmund), is unwilling to go so far. He hedges Kent's question with his alternative, softening fact into metaphor. To which Albany responds: if this is not the end itself, let it come.

Though none of them doubt Cordelia's death, Lear is not aware of their choral accompaniment. In the intensity of his longing, his imagination keeps providing him with signs of life—"This feather stirs" (265), "What is't thou sayest?" (272). There is no one point at which the innocent playgoer would finally decide that Cordelia will not revive; somewhere during this final tableau, however, he must lose his last hope. It is as though the pendulum swings in shorter and shorter arcs until it comes to rest on the fact. "This feather stirs; she lives!" is followed immediately by an "if it be so" (265) throwing doubt upon it. The idea that she has spoken follows immediately upon "now she's gone for ever!" (270), and we presumably realize by this time that Lear's inability to make out her words results not from the excellence of the "soft,/ Gentle and low" voice he remembers (272–273) but from its having been stilled altogether.

The impact is the greater for our not having been given what Shakespeare has constantly led us to expect. Though the ground has been cleared and all their foes are dead, our protagonists are not permitted their triumph. Cordelia is killed by bad timing and Lear by the death of Cordelia. Nor, having been deprived of a happy ending, are we even allowed the usual ordering of tragedy. Nothing is finally done to sort out the implications or to soften the impact. Kent, for his faithfulness, is lumped among the "murderers, traitors all!" (269), and then—in contrast with those habitual final scenes in which everything is explained—Lear, when he finally recognizes him, fails to make the connection between Kent and the Caius who served him during his wanderings.

Albany tries hard to restore order. He knows what is called for at the end of a tragedy. Brushing aside the news of Edmund's death—"That's but a trifle here" (295)—he begins a formal proclamation: "You lords and noble friends, know our intent..." (296). We cannot but be reminded of Lear announcing the arrangements which unleashed the original trouble: "Know that we have divided/ In three our kingdom; and 'tis our fast intent..." (I. i. 37—38). Again, though with disquieting overtones, the wheel would seem to be coming full circle. But Albany's disposition of the future (he will see that Lear receives all possible comfort and will restore his "absolute power" [300], rewarding Kent and Edgar and seeing that all receive the justice they deserve), his tidying up which would permit the play to end properly, breaks against the rock of actuality: "O! see, see!" (304). In his perceptive analysis of this final scene, John Shaw speaks of Albany's "interrupted cadence."[15] We never learn what precisely leads Albany to break off—whether some change in Lear or merely the growth of his own sense of incongruity (for, however suitable to ending a play, none of what Albany is saying is relevant to the circumstances)—but the effect is surely to force us to concentrate upon the event itself, abandoning such contingencies as might be used to protect ourselves from experiencing it.

There is much else here that we can never know; doubts, not assurances, are central to the experience. "And my poor fool is hanged," Lear says (305). Are we learning the actual fate of the Fool, who left the stage in the third act? or is this a term of endearment for Cordelia, who was, we know, hanged? or is Lear confusing the two?[16] Similarly, Kent's "Break, heart; I prithee, break!" (312) may be as meaningfully understood as addressed to either Lear's heart or his own. Nor can we be expected to give a satisfactory answer to Lear's question, "Why should a dog, a horse, a rat, have life,/ And thou no breath at all?" (306—307). Nor can we be sure, from Lear's final words—"Look on her, look, her lips,/ Look there, look there!" (310—311)—what he sees as he dies. Does he accept Cordelia's death? or does he die thinking her alive? Lear's peremptory "Look," like Albany's "See," provides no interpretation even while it insists upon direct personal involvement. Nor will Edgar's final words,[17] the last lines of the play, provide us with any formula for understanding or acceptance.

There is only the insistent fact of suffering and death—"No, no, no life!...Thou'lt come no more,/Never, never, never, never, never!" (305–308)—whether the repetitions beat like a metronome or rise and fall in a broken rhythm of corroboration. There is only the insistent fact, uninterpreted—but it is a fact set in a matrix, and this, though it does not provide interpretation, at least provides exfoliating perspectives. The whole of the play is of course this matrix, but I am now speaking of the surrounding lines here at the end of the play, lines which indeed keep evoking earlier moments.

There is no more breathtaking instance of this than the line which immediately follows the five "never's." In the midst of Lear's last agony, coming just after his excruciating question and his insistence on finality, and just before his own death, is the astonishing interruption: "Pray you, undo this button: thank you, Sir" (309). It is as multivalenced a line as occurs in the play, supreme poetry in the plainest of words.

There is, first, the realism of the commonplace physical necessity intruding upon the moment of greatest emotional force. Lear's difficulty in breathing stems from the suffocating mixture of his love and grief, anger and helplessness, but it presses upon him simultaneously the consciousness of the restriction at his throat, the button with which he is not able to cope.

Then there is the echo of that earlier moment—"Off, off, you lendings! Come; unbutton here" (III. iv. 111–112)—when he saw through to his own pitiful humanity and began tearing off his sophisticating garments to stand naked with Poor Tom. It needs but mention of the button to flood this final scene with the implications of all that Lear learned in the storm about his own common humanity and the sufferings of mankind. Shakespeare provides the button without further comment, allowing the poetic enrichment to occur without any debilitating insistence.[18]

Then, finally, there is "thank you, Sir." The words indicate that the service has been performed, but no stage direction tells us to whom they are addressed. Who, that is, should be the one to undo the button? The director's choice falls frequently upon Kent, which allows him to remain the faithful servant right up to the end. One can make a case for Edgar, who seems to be closest at hand, bending over Lear trying to revive him when he dies; or for Albany, who, as the highest ranking survivor, would be shown to be earnest and personal in his desire to be helpful. But, were I the director, I would bypass each of these possibilities for another, one which would make even more evident what is in any case implied: I would have the button undone by the lowliest anonymous servant or soldier within reach. For Lear's "thank you, Sir" shows the distance he has come. They are not the words of a despot accustomed only to giving orders and having his own way—"Come not between the Dragon and his wrath" (I. i. 122)—but the words of a man who has discovered human inter-dependence, a man who can now feel gratitude for the humblest service he would once have taken for granted.

Thus it would be possible on the basis of these three words, as common as any in the English language, to build a theory of Lear's ultimate self-realization as a tragic hero. The means are at hand. Yet Shakespeare once again veers away from insisting on a significance and declines to provide what might be expected at the close of a tragedy.

"Thank you, Sir" is followed immediately by "Do you see this?" (310), calling attention to Cordelia. Lear may possibly address all those standing around him, but it seems more likely that the "you" is the same individual addressed in the preceding line and that Lear, drawn to him by gratitude and fellow feeling, attending only to this one immediate relationship, seeks to explain the basis of his need. Except to point, however, he can find no further words. The meaning, for him, is in the object, the dead body of Cordelia, which represents—which is—simultaneously all that she has meant to him and the end of all that she has meant to him, just as, for us, the meaning of the play lies not in words but in what has been gathered into the implications of this final stage image.

As Lear dies, Edgar goes through the understandable human motion of trying to revive him, but Kent is in closer touch with the reality and knows that death is preferable: "he hates him/ That would upon the rack of this tough world/ Stretch him out longer" (313–315). Jacobeans, well acquainted with the rack, would feel more quickly that we, no doubt, the force of suffering in the pun of this terrifying metaphor. Even when Edgar announces that Lear "is gone, indeed" (315), Kent repeats the pun, as though mesmerized by this physical image of suffering: "The wonder is he hath endur'd so long" (316). And then he adds, "He but usurp'd his life" (317), with the new metaphor converting Lear's life into a kingdom improperly held. We may be reminded briefly of all the civil discord we had expected at the beginning of the play. Civil discord there has been, but it, like the storm, has existed less for its own sake than to build the total image of chaos.

And Albany, as though the political word had reminded him of a duty to find some political solution, tries once again to reward virtue and institute order by recognizing Kent and Edgar as Lear's successors: "Friends of my soul, you twain/ Rule in this realm and the gor'd state sustain" (319–320). He has provided a possible final couplet for the play, but those he addresses cannot accept it in silence. Any political solution or reward of virtue is irrelevant: Kent asserts that he is dying (as both Edgar and he had already told us [208–219, 234–235])—"My master calls me, I must not say no" (322)[19]—while Edgar brushes Albany's suggestions aside with the curiously vapid lines which conclude the play:

> The weight of this sad time we must obey;
> Speak what we feel, not what we ought to say.
> The oldest hath borne most: we that are young
> Shall never see so much, nor live so long.

After such emotions as the deaths of Cordelia and Lear have aroused, any summary must necessarily be anticlimactic, but these couplets, far from building to a peroration, are insistently understated, if that phrase is not too paradoxical. That Edgar should call for speaking "what we feel, not what we ought to say" is of course a quiet affirmation of Cordelia's original answer to her father's demands. "Nothing, my lord" was, under the circumstances and in spite of the consequences, the proper response. But, having called for speaking what we feel, Edgar expresses little feeling of his own. All he can assert of Lear is that none of the survivors may expect to experience as much.

This is disturbing. It is as though not only Edgar, but Shakespeare, had abandoned any attempt to round off the experience. The flat generalizations are completely inadequate as a summation of what we have been brought to feel.

I may seem here to have arrived at a contradiction: while arguing for Shakespeare's direct manipulation of audience response, I say of this conclusion that it gives the effect of his having abandoned any such control. But the contradiction is more apparent than real. Shakespeare's attention is still upon audience response; ending this play presents him with a particular problem.

The formal conclusion of a tragedy usually allows an audience to come to rest at last upon a sense that, whatever the losses, however harrowing the events, order has been restored. We have no doubt that things in Scotland will be better under Malcolm; and if we come to have such doubts about Denmark under Fortinbras, or the Roman empire under Octavius (in two plays), they tend to be afterthoughts, perhaps (though not necessarily) modern afterthoughts, and not the effect as the play is ending. Indeed, the very fact that the play *is* ending is in itself reassuring: the self-contained shapes of art imply fulfillment.

In the world of *King Lear*, however, such fulfillment turns out to be illusory. Our persistent hopes, stretched upon the rack of this tough world, finally expire. In spite of all our expectations—whether those arising from our general sense of the way form operates in art, or those carefully and repeatedly nurtured by Shakespeare in this play through the processes I have been tracing—the basic rhythm of *King Lear* does not break, not even to the extent of admitting a terminal Fortinbras. If we have abandoned such expectations even before we begin the play, we are insulated from responding to what Shakespeare has written.

To reject Albany's conclusion, as Shakespeare, through Kent and Edgar, does, is to sustain the *King Lear* rhythm at the expense of the very form of tragedy. Without that formal prop, and faced with the loss beyond loss, what could be said that would be adequate? The final couplet functions as Edgar's version of Albany's "O! see, see!" or of Lear's "Look there, look there!" It does not pretend to prescribe, or even to register, a sufficient response. It is open-ended, directing our attention away from encapsulation and back to the actual image, the staged image of life and death to which we have been responding and to which we now have no choice but to continue responding. After all the care with which Shakespeare in this play has manipulated our expectations in order to keep us susceptible, he leaves us at the end, as the greatest works of art always leave us, overwhelmed yet still responding on our own.

Notes

1. The play implies that Gloucester is old, though not as old as Lear. We learn his name at line 34 [all references in this chapter are to the Arden edition of *King Lear* ed. by Kenneth Muir (London: Methuen & Co., Ltd., 1957); however, speech heads have been spelled out and placed in a separate line for uniform presentation.—*Ed.*], when the kind (named at line 139) sends him offstage with "Attend the Lords of France and Burgundy, Gloucester." Edmund, named at line 25, is called "this young fellow" early in this first scene (13), and his attraction for Regan and Goneril follows most easily if he is handsome. That Kent, named in line 27, is middle-aged, I assume with less certainty. He could be as old as Gloucester. Some productions surround Lear with aging retainers: Gloucester, Kent, a group suggesting the "hundred knights," and the Fool. The later character is effective whether Lear's calling him "boy" (I. iv. 112 and *passim*) is taken literally (in which case the contrast in ages creates a particular pathos and tenderness in the storm scenes) or is taken as old habit, a customary way of addressing an aging Fool who has been long in the household (in which case the pathos and tenderness are modified, but no less present). It might be noted that the Fool at one point addresses Lear as "my boy" (I. iv. 143).
2. *Shakespeare's Lusty Punning in "Love's Labour's Lost"* (The Hague: Mouton, 1973), pp. 128–130.
3. II. i. 11–14, 26–27; III. i. 19–21.
4. *Shakespearean Tragedy*, 2nd ed. (London: Macmillan, 1905), p. 262.
5. I have traced comparable instances of audience teasing in "Some Dramatic Techniques in 'The Winter's Tale,'" *Shakespeare Survey 22*, ed. Kenneth Muir (Cambridge: Cambridge University Press, 1969), pp. 95–98 and 102–103.
6. Indeed, modern critics continue to call this the Dover cliff scene, though (in spite of the fact that Lear and Gloucester must be near Dover when they meet) the logic of the scene turns out to indicate that the cliff is precisely where Edgar has *not* taken his father. The poetic description is so convincing that, in naming the scene, we continue to be taken in by the trick.
7. Though Q's stage direction is sufficient, editors have felt that more was needed. "He leaps and falls along," adds Rowe; Peter Alexander, "Gloucester casts himself down"; Dover Wilson (New Cambridge),"Gloucester falls forward and swoons"; Muir (New Arden), "He throws himself forward and falls."
8. The trick on the audience will only work on a bare stage; it is

dependent upon the theater for which Shakespeare wrote. Whether or not this was his reason, Kozintsev was therefore right to omit the whole Dover cliff incident from his fine film based on *King Lear*.

9. Edgar's frequent addressing of Gloucester as "father" (Cf. also IV. vi. 220, 257, and 288, and V. ii. 1) is also a form of teasing the audience. It means no more than "old man," but we keep hoping it will turn out to mean that he has revealed his identity.

10. Only since writing this account have I discovered, in his *Shakespeare and the Revolution of the Times* (New York: Oxford University Press, 1976), a lecture given by Harry Levin at Stratford-upon-Avon in 1958 (and first published the next year in *More Talking About Shakespeare*, ed. John Garrett [London: Longmans, Green, 1959]). Levin refers to Edgar's staged miracle as "a pious fraud" (1976, p. 180), and also preempts my point about Shakespeare's manipulation of our response to the location: "we are just as blind as Gloucester. Theatrical convention prescribes that we accept whatever is said on the subject of immediate place as the setting" (p., 1976).

11. *"King Lear" In Our Time* (Berkeley: University of California Press, 1965), p. 107. He is quoting IV. vi. 83, 86–87, 97–98, 134, and 167–174.

12. Editors are apt to gloss "interlude" merely as "a play" (*e.g.*, Muir in the Arden, Fraser in the Signet), but it surely has the more specific meaning of "a comedy," and probably still carries the connotation of an entertainment between the acts of a serious drama. Goneril mocks Albany's mockery as interrupting attention to Edmund's fate; the whole action is interrupting attention to Lear's and Cordelia's.

13. Beginning with Rowe, editors have added *"dead"* to this stage direction: *"with Cordelia dead in his arms."* Such of course turns out to have been the fact, but this addition gives it away before the audience (in this case the reader) should be sure. True, Shakespeare was not writing for readers, and the authentic phrase "as if he were dead," when Falstaff falls at Shrewsbury (*1 Henry IV*, V. iv. sd. following line 75) similarly tells too much too soon, but the innocent theatergoer's suspense about Cordelia might as well be preserved for the reader by not tampering with the non-committal entry.

14. I owe much of this formulation to a letter from Philip McGuire, who theatergoer's suspense about Cordelia might as well be preserved for the reader by not tampering with the non-committal entry.

15. *"King Lear*: The Final Lines," *Essays in Criticism*, 16(1966), 265.

16. Which of course makes emotional sense. The Fool was linked specifically to Cordelia when he was first mentioned—"Since may young Lady's going into France, Sir, the Fool hath much pined away" (I. iv. 77–78)—to which may be added the affection Lear holds for each of them and, less convincingly, some subliminal link provided if a single actor doubled the parts.

17. Edgar's in the Folio, Albany's in the Quarto. There are two primary

reasons for accepting the Folio here. First, the dramatic logic: Albany has offered the kingdom to Kent and Edgar. Kent says that he is dying. Albany would not be likely to speak again, or the author to end the play, without some response from Edgar. Secondly, there would be a motive, however mistaken, for someone to change the speech heading, unable to believe that Shakespeare would so far abandon convention as to let anyone other than the highest ranking remnant have the last word.

18. A similar moment of poetic richness without fanfare occurs when, hearing of her father's madness, Cordelia orders "A century send forth" (IV. iv. 6), thus dispatching to Lear's assistance the very number of knights Goneril and Regan had denied. A lesser poet would be more explicit; Shakespeare plants the implications unobtrusively for his audience to discover.

19. Though "my master" refers directly to Lear, it is one of many Christian overtones mingling with the theological questions of Lear's pagan world. But this is a separate topic.

Past the Size of Dreaming

BERNARD BECKERMAN

What are the dimensions of *Antony and Cleopatra*? Is it truly "a vast canvas" depicting the clash of empires? Is it indeed "the most spacious" of Shakespeare's plays? Its epic stature is so generally conceded that only an eccentric would suggest that, far from being monumental, *Antony and Cleopatra* is delicate as porcelain, fragile as a lyric of elusive affection.[1] Yet so odd and mysterious has the play's history been, both in the library and on the stage, that even such eccentricity may be justified in order to examine its idiosyncratic nature anew.

At first glance *Antony and Cleopatra* seems to be a sprawling spectacle. Theatrically and imaginatively it overflows the customary bounds of the drama. Its forty-two scenes are the greatest number that Shakespeare ever crammed into one play. Leaping from Egypt to Rome and back to Egypt, they create an image of world-ranging events. The names "Antony," "Cleopatra," and "Caesar" ring out like a roster of the gods. An imperial atmosphere permeates the stage. And yet, these impressions belie the heart of the action. Though the play shows the fall of an empire, little time is devoted to how political and military events turn out. There is one scene of negotiation between Antony and Caesar, but that quickly focuses upon a marital issue. And crucial though battles are to the fortunes of Antony, Shakespeare does not dwell on the fighting itself. Instead, our attention is

This essay previously has appeared in *Antony and Cleopatra*, Mark Rose, ed., (Englewood Cliffs, New Jersey: Prentice-Hall, Inc., 1977), pp. 99–112. Reprinted with permission.

repeatedly directed to the subtle motions of thought and feeling passing between Antony and Cleopatra.

The play falls into two main parts. During the first part the prevailing impulse, to the extent there is one, comes from Antony. He endeavors to accommodate the demands of his political and military position to his desire for things Egyptian. The hinge of the narrative, at almost the exact center of the play, occurs early in the third act when he finally abandons Rome and gives himself to Egypt unreservedly. The second part of the narrative traces his attempt to accommodate his allegiance to Cleopatra with the need to defend himself politically and militarily.

For Shakespeare such bifurcated story-telling is not uncommon. What is uncommon is the way he has joined the two parts of *Antony and Cleopatra*. In all the major tragedies preceding this one, Shakespeare raised the final moments of part one to a high pitch. Invariably the third act unfolds in a series of explosions which are the hero's reactions to the dramatic imperatives facing him. Hamlet moves from the exultance of unmasking Claudius in the play-within-the-play scene to the painful restraint of not slaying the orant Claudius and finally to the frenzied harangue with which he assaults his mother. Macbeth is unmanned by the appearances of Banquo's ghost, an experience that cuts him loose, once and for all, from humane constraints. And in the play that best exemplifies the design in Shakespeare's art, *King Lear*, the middle of the play rises to a plateau of maddened passion in which the old king futilely endeavors to reconcile a world of order and degree with the unnatural rejection he has suffered at his daughters' hands. But in *Antony and Cleopatra* there is nothing of this high central plateau of passion. And its absence is all the more curious because in this play Shakespeare is dealing with the overwhelming power of love, a love so hot that neither the fans of reason nor the harsh necessities of fortune can cool it. Yet here, after mastering the art of binding the two-part structure of Elizabethan narrative drama with a knot of sustained trial and passion, he discards the form. And what does he supply in its stead? An approximation of a heightened scene does take the form of a bacchanalia on Pompey's galley (II. vii.), but the end of part one comes a little later. Beginning with Act III, Scene iii, Shakespeare introduces a rapid montage of accusations and reports which hurtle the antagonists against each other.

Cleopatra first adjusts to Antony's new marriage, Antony then separates from Octavia, Octavia reaches Caesar, and through the reports of Caesar and Eros we learn the time of open conflict has arrived. The shift in narrative is accomplished, however, not by a soul-shattering wrench on Antony's part, but by the reverse, by a vacuum of feeling, a mouthing of claims that indicate inevitability of circumstance rather than exercise of will or passion. That center of emptiness cannot be traced to Plutarch. The source offers considerable transitional material, in the story of Octavia's faithful defense of Antony's home, for instance, to have permitted Shakespeare to exploit the contradictory impulses in Antony's mind. Instead, Shakespeare shows Antony acting out a foreordained role, as though stressing that the barrenness at the heart of the narrative is the issue of the play.

The very first scene of *Antony and Cleopatra* is a clue to all the elements that follow. It is perhaps the most intricate and adroit of all openings by Shakespeare. Not only does it contain the motifs that are later developed, but the very way in which the motifs are dramatized establishes the frame of reference for the entire work. The scene is divided into three parts, the first and third parts serving as a frame for the centered action. The scene begins with a commentary by Philo to another Roman soldier, Demetrius. Philo is criticizing Antony for his infatuation with Cleopatra. As the monarchs enter, he repeatedly advises Demetrius, and through him, the audience to: "Look where they come:/ Take but good note . . ./ Behold and see" (10-13). After they (and with them the audience) watch the exchange between Antony and Cleopatra, the third part begins with Demetrius' astonishment at what he has seen. He expresses sorrow that Antony's behavior confirms what the "common liar" says of him in Rome. Through this arrangement of a three-part scene, Shakespeare produces the effect of making the first and last parts serve as a frame for the middle section. Philo's insistence that we observe what is about to happen and Demetrius' reaction to what he has seen thus give perspective to the central action, and moreover define Rome's relation to Egypt.

In critical literature on this play, much is made of the contrast between Rome and Egypt. These two cultures are often represented as having equal emphasis, and Antony is regarded as choosing between the luxuries of the East on one hand and the

spartan virtues of the West on the other. But the action of the
opening scene belies this interpretation. Instead, the first scene
indicates that the acting-out of Antony and Cleopatra's love will
occur within a Roman frame of reference. We the audience are
invited to see events with Roman eyes, eyes that rarely see
anything but the imperfections of Egypt. And though we cannot
help being influenced by the Roman view, we are still gods in
our own right, as all audiences are, and so we can judge the
quality of Rome's view of Antony as we share it. Thus, the
opening structure encourages a double vision: the Roman vision
and ours that includes yet transcends the Roman vision. That
these two views ultimately merge is suggested in the last lines of
the play when Caesar, by then the sole "sir" of the world, gives
judgment on the pair: "She shall be buried by her Antony./ No
grave upon the earth shall clip in it/ A pair so famous." Caesar's
words sanction the union of the lovers (they ignore Octavia's
rights as wife), and thus are the final expression of a Roman
scrutiny that opens the play and persists in scene after scene.
That scrutiny stimulates a dynamic state in which Egypt is being
judged—and envied—by Rome, not one in which Antony must
choose between the two.

In contrast to the framing function of the first and third
segments of the opening scene, the central section illustrates the
event to be judged. This section prefigures what is to come and
reflects in its structure the mode of action for the play as a whole.
It begins with four simple sentences:

Cleopatra.
  If it be love indeed, tell me how much.
Antony.
  There's beggary in the love that can be reckon'd.
Cleopatra.
  I'll set a bourn how far to be beloved.
Antony.
  Then must thou needs find out new heaven, new earth.

(14—17)

These four lines give the musical theme, the thread of
melody we shall hear varied throughout the play. The subject is
the measure or lack of measure in love. Yet the subject is only the
raw material. More important is the motion. We must see
through the static emblem of unbounded devotion which these

lines seem to promise and discern the conflict they contain. Cleopatra initiates the action by challenging Antony, not only demanding to know the extent of his love, but insinuating in the word "indeed," that what he claims to feel may not "indeed" be love. Antony replies extravagantly if somewhat conventionally, rendering a pat answer to an impossible request. Immediately and yet delicately the actress must convey Cleopatra's mercurial temperament, for her line, "I'll set a bourn how far to be beloved," reverses the challenge. Instead of applauding his dismissal of limited love, she will set bounds to his extravagance. He persists, and expands the dimensions of his affection by directing her to find a new universe to contain it.

This verbal duel is interrupted by a messenger who brings the concerns of Rome into their lives. The intrusion provokes Cleopatra's baiting of Antony and finally Antony's refusal to hear anything of Rome. Two features of this sequence are noteworthy: one, the structure of Cleopatra and Antony's duel, and two, the kind of activity introduced.

First, the structure of the duel. We saw in the first four lines how Cleopatra took the initiative, testing Antony's love. After the messenger is announced, she continues to exercise the initiative, urging Antony to hear the news from Rome, being all the more cutting as he refuses to do so. Gradually, however, as they wrangle, he moves from the defensive to the offensive. Against her mock insistence that he listen to the messengers, Antony exerts a counterforce, his image of their love which he calls "the nobleness of life." He pictures the fulfillment of that love as a form of sport. "Tonight," he says to her, "we'll wander through the streets and note/ The qualities of people" (53–54). Whether such restless sport is a satisfactory realization of their love remains to be seen. What is evident in this middle section, however, is that Antony, provoked by Cleopatra it is true, takes the initiative and, sweeping aside all other concerns, gives himself completely to the perfecting of their love.

This simple structure then, in which Cleopatra's teasing and testing yields to Antony's overriding image of rapture, serves as a paradigm—a schematic outline, as it were—for all the action of the play. In Shakespeare's hands, it is a particularly potent paradigm, for it is full of fruitful contradictions. Contradiction one: Idealized love can and cannot exclude the demands of

Rome. The opening shows that it does, though the rest of the play shows at what cost. Contradiction two: Cleopatra's detached and calculated mockery is a necessary yet finally unsatisfactory stimulant of Antony's rapture. In order to share that rapture, as Cleopatra does after Antony's death, Cleopatra must forego the mockery that provoked it. Contradiction three: The boundless love envisioned by Antony is expressed in the limited act of wandering the streets. Only with time and defeat do the lovers learn that they must lose the sensual delights of feast and flesh— the signs of love—before they can gain the transcendence marked out in the first lines. It is by subjecting these contradictions to the breaking point that Shakespeare refines the love so deliberately aroused by Cleopatra and so facilely rhapsodized by Antony. The play shows the irregular course of that refinement.

The second noteworthy feature is the kind of activity employed to stimulate the structure just described. As we have seen, the lovers are interrupted by one messenger announcing the arrival of another messenger from Rome. This double use of messenger is a foretaste of more to come. Messengers are not uncommon in Shakespeare, of course, and they have appeared in drama since the days of the Greeks. What is somewhat unusual, however, is the number of messengers Shakespeare brings on stage in this play. The double appearance in the first scene merely emphasizes their importance in *Antony and Cleopatra*. And yet we should not speak of messengers as generic types. Far more important is to direct our attention to the messenger sequences that abound. There are no less than thirty-five examples. In virtually every scene someone plays messenger, and so prevalent is the activity of delivering a message that this activity sets the rhythm for the manifold motions of the play.

In *Antony and Cleopatra* the messenger sequence is so constructed that a messenger or a minor character or even occasionally a major character delivers a report to another figure. Clearly, the report is crucial for the person who receives it. More important dramatically, however, is that only in a few instances does the message contain information that is wholly new for the audience.[2] In most sequences the audience is already aware of the news the messenger brings, as for instance in Act II, Scene i when one of Pompey's men, Varrius, tells Pompey that Antony is expected in Rome. Since the audience already has this information, its attention is being clearly directed to Pompey's response. Similar cases occur throughout the play. Sequences are structured not to reveal what happens off stage, as so often occurs in Greek tragedy, but to stimulate a response from one of the major characters.

The responses of these characters are of two types: I will call one active and the other reactive. An active response is one which is intended to achieve a specific objective, as in giving a command. When a soldier reports to Caesar that "Antony/ Is come into the field" (IV. vi. 7–8), Caesar immediately orders his troops into action. In this case his energy is directed towards a particular result. It is intended to affect others and thus is projected externally. The reactive response, on the other hand, lacks a specific goal. Instead, in responding to a messenger the character passes through a period of mental or emotional adjustment, as Antony does in Act I, Scene ii. Upon hearing the report of the death of his first wife, Fulvia, he sends the messenger away and then says,

> There's a great spirit gone! Thus did I desire it:
> What our contempts doth often hurl from us,
> We wish it ours again. The present pleasure,
> By revolution lowering, does become
> The opposite of itself: she's good, being gone,
> The hand could pluck her back that shov'd her on.
>
> (119–124)

This reactive response then yields to an impulse that will later become active:

> I must from this enchanting queen break off.   (125)

As we see here, Antony's energy is directed inward. It forces him to adjust to the report and work through his unsettled state. And as he passes through that unsettled state, we can perceive the subtle motions of thought and feeling which mark Antony and infuse the entire play.

These two types of responses: active and reactive, especially as they are sparked by the hordes of messengers, help to shape the rhythm of the play as well as define the characters. Caesar, for example, has a simple response to his messengers. It is usually active, but even when it is reactive, it is uniform. That is, the response is solely active or reactive in character. It does not alternate from one impulse to the other. Antony, on the other hand, often shifts from active to reactive impulse during the same sequence. On hearing of Enobarbus' desertion, he immediately commands Enobarbus' treasure to be sent to him. This is an active impulse. Then he laments, "O, my fortunes have/ Corrupted honest men!" This is reactive. The next word is, "Despatch," that is, quickly send the treasure to Enobarbus. This is clearly active. It is followed by another reactive lament of one word, "Enobarbus." Thus, the lines: "O, my fortunes have/ Corrupted honest men! Despatch.—Enobarbus" (IV. v. 16–17) contain alternate shifts of energy, first reactive, then active, then reactive. Such a rhythm communicates Antony's complexity and instability.

Naturally, the varying energies in the active and reactive patterns contribute to our sense of each character's personality. The contrast between energies is the main method by which Caesar's cool steadiness is set against Antony's irresolution and Cleopatra's famed variety. But these differing responses are even more central to the experience that the play produces. Together they embody the very forces that give shape to the action. Matched against the calculating sureness of Caesar, the impulsive shifting energies of Antony and Cleopatra follow an irregular course. It is *that course* upon which our attention becomes fixed. We are dazzled by its unpredictability and vitality. At the same time its waywardness prevents us—at first, anyway—from becoming emotionally engaged.

This course of fluctuating energies, however, does not unwind in a void. The messenger sequences and the responses to them provide a vibrant and crucial context, a context without example in Plutarch. By employing messengers so profusely, Shakespeare causes the major figures to deal with each other through intermediaries. This has the result of isolating them and thus makes overcoming the isolation a principal action in the play. In addition, the comings and goings of messengers emphasize the fundamental instability of the situations in which the characters find themselves. They can be disturbed at any moment. Isolation and interruption thus permeate the play; in essence, they are the obstacles Antony and Cleopatra must overcome. Isolation is not mere separation, however. There is a deep-seated division between the two major characters that needs to be bridged. Only as traces of an unwavering attachment to each other begin to appear do we feel moved by the lovers.

Until this point I have shown how Shakespeare introduces action patterns in the first scene that he varies and develops throughout the play. These patterns define the relationships to be explored, determine the scope of the events, and prefigure the modes of action. As a result, the first scene is actually a prologue that not only introduces the argument of the play but also summarizes how it will proceed. What I find of especial significance is how Shakespeare deliberately limits his use of materials. The messenger sequence is a case in point. Its frequency demonstrates the tremendous variety with which Shakespeare employs this activity, and at the same time its recurrence emphasizes with what a restricted palette Shakespeare paints his action. He does not rely on a wide range of activities, but is content to modulate the tension that he introduces early in the play. By dramatizing the essential issues in the first scene, he directs our attention both to the issues and their manner of development. These issues involve Cleopatra's effort to manipulate Antony and Antony's capacity to create a sustaining love. Related to these two motifs is another one raised by the Roman soldiers at the end of Scene i: what is Antony's true self? The issues are worked out in the context of isolation and interruption that the messengers establish. The backdrop of world-wide conflict and mythic figures lends a poignancy to the context, but the true centers of interest are not in the large motions of war and politics, but in the subtle jockeying that goes on between the main characters.

How subtly and economically Shakespeare develops his action can be seen in two later sequences involving Cleopatra. These occur while Antony is in Rome, the first in Act I, Scene v; the second in Act II, Scene v. Both are brief; both come immediately prior to the entrance of a messenger, in the first sequence just before the messenger comes to describe Antony's departure for Rome, in the second sequence just before the messenger arrives with word of Antony's marriage to Octavia. Both sequences have identical structures composed of three segments. Each begins as Cleopatra longs for a drug, either mandragora or music, in order to while away the days until Antony returns. This is followed by Cleopatra's banter with the

eunuch Mardian in which she mocks him for his sexual incapac-
ity. Finally, Cleopatra abruptly returns to thoughts of Antony. It
is here that a significant variation occurs, for in the first sequence
her thinking of Antony leads her to remember how she con-
quered Julius Caesar and Pompey before him, thus making Antony only the most recent victim of her charms. "Now I feed
myself/ With most delicious poison," she says:

> Think on me,
> That am with Phoebus' amorous pinches black,
> And wrinkled deep in time. Broad-fronted Caesar,
> When thou wast here above the ground, I was
> A morsel for a monarch: and great Pompey
> Would stand and make his eyes grow in my brow,
> There would he anchor his aspect, and die
> With looking on his life.
>
> (I. v. 26–34)

The time between the first and second sequence suggests an
historical progression as Cleopatra moves from remembrance of
old lovers to recollection of the new one. In the second sequence
she recalls amusing and teasing Antony, the climax of this memory coming when she delights in the power she exerted over him
by getting him to put on her dresses and mantles, "whilst," she
crows, "I wore his sword Philippan" (II. v. 22–23). In short, her
image of shared love is to recall her partner transformed into a
woman and herself possessed of the very sword of victory with
which Antony defeated Brutus and Cassius.

This image is a manifestation of the control that we saw
Cleopatra attempt to exercise over Antony in the first scene. It is
the fullest expression of one side of her love, that side which can
undermine Antony's true self. By utilizing these parallel sequences, Shakespeare shows the persistence of Cleopatra's way
of love at the same time he reveals her restlessness.

The persistence of Cleopatra's love image acts as a counter-
point to Antony's effort in Rome to assert his political position.
Yet even as he tries to do so, he knows that he can no longer look
at life through Roman eyes. Well before his marriage to Octavia,
he decides to return to Egypt (II. iii.). Even as he negotiates and
parleys with Caesar and Pompey, his activities and the effect they
have on the others only serve to remind everyone of Egypt and
make its attraction more palpable. For despite the supposed
contrast between Rome and Egypt, we find that the aura of the

East permeates the Roman scenes. In the first one(I. iv.) we hear Octavius calling out to Antony to return; in the second (II. i.) Pompey calling out to Cleopatra to "tie up the libertine in a field of feasts" (23); in the third, after the parley, we listen to Enobarbus praising Cleopatra (II.ii.); and near the end of the first half of the play we witness the re-creation of an Egyptian dance on Pompey's galley (II. vii.). This drunken and unloosed merriment is the ultimate point Antony reaches in juggling the things of Rome and the things of Egypt.

It is in the second half of the play, however, after Antony returns to Egypt, that the clash between Cleopatra's image of love and Antony's comes to a head. Until their defeat, their restless love lacks any sign of stability or continuity. For Antony it is a compulsion, for Cleopatra a challenge and necessity. Only after the naval disaster at Actium does the indication of a deeper relationship emerge. They are brought together by their attendants. Mournfully, Antony accuses Cleopatra of leading him to dishonor. "O'er my spirit/ Thy full supremacy thou knew'st, and that/ Thy beck might from the bidding of the gods/ Command me" (III. xi. 58-61). She does not argue. "O, my pardon!" she murmurs. He imagines the shame he is now forced to face, of submitting himself to Caesar, and then turns on Cleopatra again:

> You did know
> How much you were my conqueror, and that
> My sword, made weak by my affection, would
> Obey it on all cause.
>
> (65–68)

"Pardon, pardon!" she pleads. For the first time but one[3] Cleopatra appears divested of all calculation. For a moment, together they experience unaffected love. "Fall not a tear," Antony says, "one of them rates/ All that is won and lost: give me a kiss," and the kiss they exchange is one of reconciliation. "Even this repays me," Antony sighs.

But the mood lasts only an instant. Immediately, Antony calls for the messenger he had sent to Caesar.

> We sent our schoolmaster,
> Is 'a come back? Love, I am full of lead:
> Some wine within there, and our viands! Fortune knows,
> We scorn her most, when most she offers blows.
>
> (71–74)

This passage follows the patterns of shifting from active, to reactive, to active again, and so returns them to their restless state again.

The kiss they exchange in this scene is another echo of the first scene. It is a cousin to the one Antony gives Cleopatra when he tells her, "The nobleness of life/ Is to do thus" (I. i. 36—37). Although editors often add a stage direction to this line indicating that the lovers embrace, there is no authority for the gesture. The two may very well kiss, and a kiss, by comparison, is of far greater importance in the play, for kissing assumes dramatic significance in the second half.

In the scene following the naval disaster that I just cited, the kiss appears for the first time as a mark of tenderness, not lust. Later in Act III (xiii. 81ff.), it is the kiss Caesar's messenger Thidias places on Cleopatra's hand that enrages Antony because he regards it as a sign of disloyalty and lust. And in Act IV, Scene viii, Antony rewards one of his lieutenants with an identical kiss. There it is a sign of worthiness and loyalty. By the time Antony lies dying, the kiss has become a mark of spiritual union, as we shall see. I cite the various contexts of the kisses because their significance to the progression of the play outweighs their rarity. The kiss between Antony and Cleopatra after the naval disaster thus initiates those moments of unaffected tenderness in which each lover is at peace with the other. These moments grow in dramatic power during the fourth and fifth acts, and become the main counterweight to the impulses toward isolation and interruption. But unfortunately they are only moments. They are caught in the flurry of events. They run counter to the flamboyant love-making of Antony and Cleopatra. That is why they appear fleetingly and are so often overlooked, and that is why they often have a dream-like quality.

When after fantasizing that he will join her in Elysium, Antony is brought to Cleopatra's monument (IV. xv.), the dream might be expected to take on substance. The time seems ripe for the full expression of their love. But their close contact lasts only for the span of a kiss, for she lapses into railing against fortune and he gives her political advice. Thus their only genuine harmony is that last kiss, a long one taken to the chorus of "a heavy sight" (40). After he dies, her lament, "O withered is the garland of the war" (64), more eloquently expresses her union with him than anything she says as he lies dying. Moments like these, Cleopatra's "pardon, pardon," their rare kisses, and her brief elegy, convey a sense of spiritual union. These are rare instances when neither the active nor reactive energies are in motion, but instead an impression of absolute stillness is created.

Only in the last scene before her death does Cleopatra reach a complete state of spiritual identity with Antony. As prefigured in the first scene, his sense of love prevails. No longer does she need to emasculate him. She accepts him as he shaped himself during the last half of the play. Because their union was always so fragile, however, she experiences this union more as a dream than a reality, or a reality that has the substance of a dream, just as Antony did. "I dreamt there was an Emperor Antony," she says (V. ii. 76), and then conjures up an image of a demi-god. What she evokes is that still reality toward which their love moved, and even though she bargains with Caesar and thus exhibits her old habits, the image of Antony ultimately prevails.

But is her dream of Antony hollow? Is he the demi-god she imagines? After all his failures as a soldier, can we share her estimation of him? Again, it is through one of those subtle revelations that Shakespeare shows us an Antony redeemed. During the fourth act Antony mounts in stature, not as a soldier, but as a man in relationship to other men. This becomes evident in Act IV, Scene vii. Antony has just fought one of those minor scuffles by which he holds off defeat momentarily. He returns victorious, but shows none of his former excess of emotion or changeability. It is his follower Scarus who boasts of their success. Antony himself speaks only a few words. He is concerned about Scarus' wounds, he observes that Caesar's soldiers withdraw, he thinks of rewarding his men. It is right after this moment that he gives Scarus the unmatchable joy of kissing Cleopatra's hand. And indeed, the fourth act is filled with Antony's acts of generosity, not only to Scarus but also to his men at large. So, after scenes of self-pity and egotistical vaunting, Antony achieves a selflessness. It is for such a man that Eros slays himself and Enobarbus pines away, and it is such a man who justifies Cleopatra's dream.

As I see it then, the subtle motions of the play dramatize the growth of the still moments of communion in the teeth of the unstable shifts of will, passion, and calculation with which Antony and Cleopatra habitually meet the world. Because of this action, the scale of production must not be, as it invariably is, spectacular. The moments between Antony and Cleopatra, moments that hint at a transcendent devotion, are so fragile, so evanescent that they must be nurtured tenderly. Nor is the actor's task merely to make us cognizant of these moments. He must project them so that they affect us deeply, so that they assume such vivid life that they finally become the prevailing sense of the play. For what Shakespeare has created is not a symphony, but a chamber work. Great events occur. But they strike us by refraction. We are in the anteroom for the most part, not where great parleys are held but where private realization occurs. We receive the messengers who carry on the business of tying the world together, but we ourselves are left to ponder the messages. And therefore a certain intimacy, a certain nearness between the audience and characters is necessary. The spectacle of Antony's and Cleopatra's defeat as monarchs interests us but little. Their painful struggle to touch each other truly is what finally holds our attention.

Not that Antony and Cleopatra's positions as rulers can be ignored. Both exist in a world where they must use political power. They, however, want more than naked power. Sensual satisfaction, restless and fickle, appears to be the only alternative. In such a world, luxury and sexual fulfillment are often confused with politics on the one hand and love on the other. Against power and seduction, human contact of a spiritual nature is hard to sustain. Even when moments of a true intimacy occur, these quickly slip away. Shakespeare seems to indicate that Antony and Cleopatra—and perhaps we—can dream and occasionally touch this true intimacy, but perhaps can never live it fully.

Notes

1. A.C. Bradley uses the phrase "vast canvas" in his Oxford lecture on *Antony and Cleopatra* (1905) and Harley Granville-Barker begins his preface to the drama with the assertion: "Here is the most spacious of [Shakespeare's] plays" (1930). Maynard Mack, on the other hand, does point out the "delicacy" of the play in his perceptive essay,

"*Antony and Cleopatra:* The Stillness and the Dance," printed in *Shakespeare's Art,* ed. M. Crane (Chicago: University of Chicago Press, 1973), p. 80. Quotations from *Antony and Cleopatra* follow the text edited by M.R. Ridley as published in the Arden edition (1954). [Speech heads have been spelled out and placed on a separate line for uniform presentation—*Ed.*]

2. Such messages are delivered early in the play: I. ii. 115–118, on Fulvia's death; I. iv. 33–54, on the victories of Pompey and the sea pirates.

3. One may regard Cleopatra's forgetfulness while bidding Antony farewell ("O, my oblivion is a very Antony") as a symptom of genuine feeling (I. iii. 90).

Directions for *Twelfth Night*

JOHN RUSSELL BROWN

After the first dozen *Twelfth Night*s there are still surprises, new guises for the old masterpiece. Directors color it golden, russet, silver or white; blue for dreams, and sometimes pink; or they allow red and even purple to dominate. They can make it sound noisy as a carnival, or eager, or melodious, or quarrelsome like children; it can also be strained and nervous. In 1958, Peter Hall at Stratford-upon-Avon hung the stage with gauzes and contrived what *The Times* called a "Watteauesque light." And critics reported that a year previously, at Stratford, Ontario, Tyrone Guthrie contrasted Feste and Malvolio in "psychological terms," allowing the final song of the "wind and rain" to be "as plaintive and wonderful as a Jewish lament." Two years before that, at the English Stratford, Sir John Gielgud brought "a faint chill to the air" of his production; the comics were on their best behavior in deference to a pervasive "charm"; *The Observer* said that the polite word for this would be "formal," and the exact word "mechanical"; it seemed as if, during rehearsals of the last scene, Sir John had stopped the actors and commanded, "Be beautiful; be beautiful."

This play might have been designed for an age when each director must make his name and register his mark. Yet there is one difficulty: in most productions some part of the play resists

This article originally appeared as Chapter XIV in *Shakespeare's Plays in Performance*, (London: Edward Arnold, 1966), pp. 207–219. Reprinted with permission. Quotations from *Twelfth Night* follow Peter Alexander's edition of *The Complete Works* (London: Collins, 1951).

the director's control. In Sir John's elegant *Twelfth Night*, Malvolio yielded Sir Laurence Olivier a role in which to exploit his impudent and plebeian comedy, and in his last line — "I'll be revenged on the whole pack of you" — an opportunity for the cry of a man unmade. The grey and urban setting of the Old Vic's production in 1950 was enlivened by an untrained ballet of sailors and riffraff, but Peggy Ashcroft's clear, white voice was an unechoed reminder of other directions the comedy can be given. More commonly, without such trained stars to cross the director's intentions, robust comics usurp more attention than their part in the last act is allowed to satisfy, or an intelligent Sebastian will deny his own words, a too gentle Orsino devalue Viola's ardor. There is need for vigilance: Margaret Webster, who sees *Twelfth Night* as "filled with impermanence, fragile, imponderable"; has found that:

> The director will have to balance and combine his ingredients in carefully graded proportions, compensating for weaknesses, keeping a moderating hand on excessive strength. This play, above all, he must treat with a light touch and a flexible mind, keeping the final goal clearly in sight.[1]

What happened, one wonders, before there were directors to give directions?

For if we refer back, from the theater to the text of the play, we shall observe a similar lack of simplicity and uniformity. Malvolio can be a "turkey cock," a common "geck and gull" who is told to "shake his ears"; or a fantastic who asks what "an alphabetical position portends" and speaks repeatedly "out of his welkin." Yet Olivier's petty, ambitious vulgarian is also true to the text when he addresses his mistress with "Sweet lady, ho, ho!" and with tags from popular ballads. Even Michael Hordern's tortured Malvolio at the Old Vic in 1954, "dried up, emaciated, elongated . . . (as) an El Greco" — his hands, reaching out of the pit in the scene where Feste visits him as Sir Topas, the curate, suggested to one critic "the damned in the *Inferno*" — is authorized by Feste's disguise, by his own first words of "the pangs of death" and "infirmity," his account of how "imagination" jades him, and his physical and psychological isolation at the end. And yet again, Olivia's high regard for Malvolio — she "would not lose him for half her dowry" — justified Eric Porter's performance at Stratford-upon-Avon in 1960, as a solid, efficient steward waking with practical good sense to worlds unrealized.

Actors seeking to express their originality will find that "new" interpretations rise unbidden from a straightforward study of the text; Sir Toby is usually a domesticated Falstaff, but at the Old Vic in 1958 with tumultuous "gulps and shouts," he was seen as a plain "boor"; and for this there is plenty of support in his name, Belch, and in his talk of "boarding and assailing," making water and cutting "mutton." And the same year, at Stratford-upon-Avon, Patrick Wymark made him young and spry with a sense of style; for this, "she's a beagle, true-bred" was most appropriate language, and his easy confidence in "consanguinity" with Olivia and expertise in swordplay were natural accomplishments. One might imagine too, a melancholy Sir Toby, tried in true service and knowing from experience that "care's an enemy to life": his tricks upon Sir Andrew would then be a compensation for his own retirement, his wooing — offstage and presumably brief — of Maria, a just and difficult tribute to her service for him; lethargy comes with drunkenness and he "hates a drunken rogue"; he needs company, even that of a fool, an ass, and a servant.

Olivia is another role which can be seen to be of different ages — either mature years or extreme youth; and she can be melancholy or gay. Maxine Audley at Stratford-upon-Avon in 1955 presented a gracious lady, truly grieving for the death of her brother and strong enough to recognize an absolute passion for a boy; this Olivia had the "smooth, discreet and stable bearing," the majesty, to which Sebastian and Orsino testify. And three years later, at the same theater, Geraldine McEwen presented her as kittenish and cute, saved from triviality by fine timing of movement and verse-speaking, the dignity of "style." And yet another Olivia may be suggested by the text: a very young girl, at first afraid of meeting the world and therefore living in a fantasy capable of decreeing seven-years of mourning; then a girl solemnly repeating old saws with a new understanding of their truth:

> Even so quickly may one catch the plague. . . . I do I know not what, and fear to find Mine eye too great a flatterer for my mind. . . . What is decreed must be . . . how apt the poor are to be proud . . . youth is bought more oft than begg'd or borrowed,

and forgetting her "discreet" bearing in breathless eagerness:

> *How* does he love me? . . . *Why*, what would you? . . . not too *fast*:
> soft, soft! . . . Well, *let* it be, . . . That's a degree to love. . . . Yet
> *come* again. . . . I have sent after him: *he says* he'll come. . . . *What* do
> you say? . . . *Most wonderful!*

Feste, the fool, can be melancholy, or bitter, or professional, or amorous (and sometimes impressively silent), or self-contained and philosophical, or bawdy and impotent. Sir Andrew Aguecheek can be patient, sunny, feckless, gormless, animated or neurotic. (In 1958 Richard Johnson gave an assured performance of this knight as a "paranoid manic-depressive, strongly reminiscent at times of Lucky in *Waiting for Godot*.") Orsino can be mature or very young; poetic; or weak; or strong but deceived; or regal and distant. The text can suggest a Viola who is pert, sentimental, lyrical, practical, courageous or helpless. Shakespeare's words can support all these interpretations, and others; there are few plays which give comparable scope for enterprise and originality. The characters, the situations and the speeches are protean.

This is evident in a director's ability to alter the trend of his production, even in the very last moments, to achieve what Miss Webster has called his "balance," to arrive at his chosen "final goal." If sentiment needs reinforcing, Viola (as Cesario) can be given a down-stage position and a preparatory pause as the arrangements for her duel with Sir Andrew grow to a comic climax, and thus her "I do assure you, 'tis against my will" can be, not the usual laugh-line, but a reminder of her other full-hearted struggles of will and passion; this momentary seriousness, the more impressive for its incongruous setting, was managed with great grace by Dorothy Tutin at Stratford, in Peter Hall's productions of 1958 and 1960. Still later in the play, there is another opportunity for the strong re-emphasis of Viola's depth of feeling: Peggy Ashcroft mastered this in 1950, and J.C. Trewin has well described its effect in performance:

> At the end, as Sebastian faces his sister, he cries: "What country-man? What name? What parentage?" There is a long pause now before Viola, in almost a whisper (but one of infinite rapture and astonishment) answers: "Of Messaline." Practically for the first

time in my experience a Viola has forced me to believe in her past. . . .[2]

More simply and without affecting any established characterization, the balance of a production can be altered by the Priest's lines in the last scene, with their special idiom and assured syntax and timing:

> A contract of eternal bond of love,
> Confirm'd by mutual joinder of your hands,
> Attested by the holy close of lips,
> Strength'ned by interchangement of your rings
> And all the ceremony of this compact
> Seal'd in my function, by my testimony;
> Since when, my watch hath told me, toward my grave,
> I have travell'd but two hours.

If these lines are spoken in a weighty and measured way, they can restore a sense of awe, an awareness of general and timeless implications, to a dénouement which has become too headlong and hilarious for the director's taste. Or, at the last moment, Orsino can give "guts" to an over-pretty production: the sight of Antonio permits an evocation of the "smoke of war" and "scathful grapple," and can legitimately bring a harsh quality to his voice which has hitherto been tuned to softer themes. When he invites Olivia to live "the marble-breasted tyrant still" and turns to Cesario with:

> But this your minion, whom I know you love,
> And whom, by heaven I swear, I tender dearly,
> Him will I tear out of that cruel eye
> Where he sits crowned in his master's spite.
> Come, boy, with me; my thoughts are ripe in mischief:
> I'll sacrifice the lamb that I do love
> To spite a raven's heart within a dove

the director can call for physical as well as verbal violence towards Viola. The lines imply that Orsino cares more for his seeming boy than for the lady of his dreams and fancy, and thus they may be acted fully and strongly; the release of passion in a desire to kill Cesario shows the true object of that passion, and its power. (This reading of the subtext is authorized by Shakespeare, as by Freud and Stanislavski, for Orsino has just acknowledged that a "savage" jealousy "kills what it loves," not what it *thinks* it loves.) If the production is, at this stage of the play, too solemn rather than too sentimental or hilarious, there are opportunities in plenty for lightening the whole last act: Olivia's "Where goes Cesario?," after Orsino's outburst, can easily be spoken to invite laughter; and so can her "Most wonderful" as Viola and Sebastian confront each other. Nearly all Sebastian's lines can be tipped the same way, as "I do perceive it hath offended you" . . . "Fear'st thou that, Antonio" . . . and (about the mole on the brow of Viola's father) "And so had mine." Antonio's "An apple, cleft in two is not more twin" can be directed so that it implies laughter rather than rapt amazement, and Orsino's final "Cesario, come" can be a jest at the whole contrivance of the last act, or even at Viola's expense, rather than recognition of his own long, half-hidden affection for his bride-to-be.

The opportunities for swinging a production round into line with a chosen mood—to make it "what they will," to reverse roles as in a "Twelfth Night" revel—have encouraged directors to tackle *Twelfth Night* and to experiment widely in the search for original interpretations. But a second practical consequence of the freedom of interpretation is of greater importance: this play challenges us to provide a longer and deeper study than is normally given to a text in the theater. We may be assured that the diverse ways of playing the characters and controlling the mood are not finally irreconcilable. The experience of seeing many independent productions and reading about many more does not create a multitude of separate memories; each new revelation reflects on earlier ones and, in the mind, a single view of the play is continually growing in complexity and range, and in understanding. We may believe that a single production might, one day, represent to the full our single, developing awareness. Our knowledge of *Twelfth Night* and of human behavior may assure us that an Olivia is both mature and immature, according to which side of her personality is in view; a Sir Toby energetic *and* melancholic, vulgar *and* well-schooled; and a Viola lyrical *and* practical, *and* helpless. The world of the play is gay, quiet, strained, solemn, dignified, elegant, easy, complicated, precarious, hearty, homely; the conclusion close to laughter, song, awe *and* simplicity. And this is an understanding which begs not to be hid, but to be realized on the stage.

Of course, in the theater it is tempting to simplify too early, in order to be effective and make a "strong" impression. But with such a play as *Twelfth Night* we are drawn by another possibility, a more demanding course: five years' study, a repeated return to its problems in a succession of productions under different conditions and for different audiences, might make possible a production which would be original, not by one-sidedness, but by answering more fully than before to Shakespeare's text and combining the excitement of many interpretations. The time necessary to make this attempt would be an expensive investment; and it would be a risky one—for the speculator may not be capable of living up to the developing demands of his enterprise. Yet the business is a practical possibility, and must be considered. An exclusive pursuit of immediate effectiveness and originality leads to immature and insecure achievements, in theaters as in other fields of activity; a play like *Twelfth Night* offers, therefore, an opportunity and a challenge which it would be salutary merely to envisage, regenerative to attempt. Shakespeare's stage-cunning, human understanding and poetic imagination, which are all implicit in the text would be fine assets.

*   *   *

The necessary conditions for such an achievement would be a concern for, and skill in, all the arts of the theater—this is required for any sort of theatrical success—but, more peculiarly, a constant return to the details of Shakespeare's text. Here the popular misconception that close textual study is a dull and pedestrian activity, restricting originality and encouraging an exclusively verbal kind of drama—may inhibit the right kind of work, and must be denounced: a prolonged and careful study of Shakespeare's text, in association with other theater skills, can awaken and enrich a production in all elements of a play's life. If we trust Shakespeare's imagination, we know that *Twelfth Night* was conceived as a whole with each apparently discordant element reconciled to its opposite: and our only clue to that original resolution is the printed words. Every opportunity for visual realization or elaboration, for movement and variation of grouping, for temporal control, for subtlety of elocution or stage-business, for creation of character and mood, emotion and expression, that the text can suggest should be searched out, tested, practically evaluated and, finally, given its due place in the responsible and mature production which each successive, partial and conflicting production of such a play as *Twelfth Night* invites us to consider, and to hope that one day we may help to stage or witness.

The combination, or growing together, of elements from new interpretations of roles is, perhaps, the best charted part of a difficult task; it calls for a developing sympathy and understanding, and a grasp of the progressive and formal presentation of character, but it does not require, at the beginning of rehearsals a single limiting choice; moreover the actors are always in obvious contact with Shakespeare's words. Perhaps the problems of a textually responsible production will be most perplexing in choosing the stage setting, especially if the play is to be performed on a picture-frame stage with the full range of modern equipment.

Twelfth Night has received many visual interpretations: the elegant, controlled and overtly dramatic, as a Tiepolo fresco, is a common one; or domestic with dark shadows, like the Jacobean interiors in Joseph Nash's *Mansions of England in the Olden Times;* or Italianate, free and colorful in the fashion of the *commedia dell'arte.* Or the stage may be spacious and clean, like one modern notion of what an Elizabethan platform stage was like, or pillared, tiered and substantial, like another. Some designers have introduced the satins and laces of Restoration England, and others the boaters and billows of the theater of *Charley's Aunt.* The main difficulty is that all these, and others, are in some degree appropriate, usually in different parts of the play; and yet it would be distracting to a modern audience to move from one to another during a single performance, even if this were technically possible. If a mature production of *Twelfth Night* is to be considered, this problem will have to be solved in a single way — the more urgently because the proscenium arches and lighting devices of modern theaters have made the visual embodiment of a play, in setting, costumes and effects, a dominating — often *the* dominating — element of a production.

A resource to the text in the search for a comprehensive style and single stage setting does not involve the director in an antiquarian production which tries to reproduce original stage conditions; those are, in any case, irrecoverable, in their full complexity which involves specially trained actors and historically accurate audiences, as well as theaters which no longer exist. The study of the text can be of help in utilizing the modern technical devices of a picture-frame stage, and in answering the expectations of any particular audience. The verbal imagery can, for example, give valuable help towards deciding which setting is most appropriate; it can tell the director the kind of visual images which were associated with the action and characters in the author's mind and which he may usefully transmit to the audience in visual stage terms.

Illyria, the world of *Twelfth Night*, is obviously a land of love, music, leisure, servants, a Duke and a Countess; it must have dwellings, a garden, a seacoast and a "dark house" or temporary prison. Its institutions include a church and a chantry, a captain and officers of the law, an inn; and there must be doors or gates. Thus far the choice of a setting is not circumscribed; it might be English, Italian, French, Russian (before the revolution), or, with some adaptation, American or Utopian; medieval, renaissance or modern. But incidental details of speech and action at once limit the setting to something resembling, or representing, English countryside and domesticity. In the first scene there are mentioned a bank of violets, a hunt, sweet beds of flowers, and these are followed by wind and weather, a squash and a peascod, a willow, the hills, a beagle, roses, a yew, a cypress and box tree, and more flowers; familiar living creatures are a hart, a sheep-biter, a horse, a trout, a turkey-cock and a wood-cock, a raven, lamb and dove, and hounds; daylight, champaign (or open fields), harvest, ripeness, and oxen and wain-ropes easily come to mind; the songs of nightingales, daws and owls have been heard. The characters of the play do not talk of an elegant or fanciful scene, although the violets and beds of flowers might be interpreted in that way; their wain-ropes, sheep-biter and daws belong to a countryside that knows labor and inconvenience, as well as delights. Speaking of horrors and danger, they are neither sophisticated nor learned; they refer to tempests, the sea, fields, mountains, barbarous caves, and hunger. The domestic note is almost as persistent as that of the countryside: early in Act I, canary-wine, beef, a housewife and a buttery-bar are mentioned; even the Duke, Orsino, speaks of knitters in the sun; there is talk of pilchards and herrings (fresh and pickled) and of vinegar and pepper. If a director is to attempt a responsible production of the play, he should give substance to these references in his setting—not in an illustrative way which provides objects for the actors to point at, but in a manner which echoes, extends and, where appropriate, contrasts with the dialogue and stage business. This is the mental and emotional world of the *dramatis personae* as revealed by their language, and the stage picture can help to establish this, not insistently, but with subtlety.

It is the world of the play's action too, and its visual recreation will, therefore, aid the director towards an appropriate rhythm and acting style: an Italianate setting, which is often chosen, suggests the wrong tempo—the wrong temperature, even—and insists on distracting contrasts between dialogue and visual effect. An English summer takes three months to establish itself, through April, May, and June, and so does the action of this play—as Orsino states explicitly in the last scene. It would be convenient, therefore, to show this passage of time in modifications to the setting during the course of the play: the first acts green and youthful, the last colored with roses in bloom and strong lights; the same setting but at different times of the year. In the first scene Orsino would be seeking the earliest violets; later "beauty's a flower," "women are as roses," "youth's a stuff will not endure" would sound properly precarious in view of the visual reminder of the changing seasons; a "lenten answer" would seem more restrictive and "let summer bear it out" a fuller and more inevitable judgment. Orsino might stand in white, as the young lover in Nicholas Hillyarde's miniature (dated about 1590), over against frail, twining roses: this association represented for the painter his motto—"*Dat poenas laudata fides*," or "My praisèd faith procures my pain"—and it might serve in much the same way today. "Midsummer madness" and "matter for a May morning," which are spoken of in Act III, would be in key with the setting, and the talk of harvest, the grave and the immutable yewtree would sound in significant contrast.

The course in single days might also be suggested in the lighting of the stage picture. Talk of hunting in the first scene establishes the time as early morning. In the third, Maria's remonstrance to Sir Toby about returning late "a'nights" belongs to the first meeting of a new day, and then coming "early" by one's "lethargy" implies preprandial drinking. In II.iii., the chaffing about "being up late," Malvolio's chiding about "respect of ...time," and "tis too late to go to bed now" all suggest midnight; so one "day" is completed in due order. (Again Feste's song in this last mentioned scene, about "present mirth" and "what's to come" and "youth's a stuff will not endure," will be more poignant if it seems indeed to have been sung just before the "night owl," nature's reminder of death, is roused.) The following scene, II. iv., is clearly a new day with its first lines of "good morrow" and "we heard last night"; and the truth that "...women are as roses, whose fair flower/ Being once display'd doth fall that very hour" is more fully expressed if spoken in the transitory light of dawn. The next scene, II. v., beginning with "Come thy ways . . ." and with news that Malvolio has been "i' the sun practising behaviour to his own shadow this half hour," is still early morning. Act III, Scene i., which follows with Feste speaking of the sun shining everywhere, may be at noon, and later, when Malvolio supposes Olivia invites him to bed, his outrageous presumption would be more apparent if it were obviously not that "time of day." At the end of IV. ii., Feste visits Malvolio in prison and sings:

> I'll be with you again,
>   In a trice,
>   Like the old Vice,
> Your need to sustain;
> Who, with dagger of lath,
> In his rage and his wrath,
>   Cries, ah, ha! to the devil. . . .

—here stage lighting could simulate a sudden, passing storm, such as interrupts an easy summer's afternoon in England; it might culminate in thunder. This would be an elaboration impossible to stage in an Elizabethan theater, but it would be appropriate in a play which is continually concerned with the summer countryside of England, with "beauty that can endure wind and weather," and which ends with a song of the rain that "raineth every day." Sir Toby and Maria could take shelter from the storm, while the fool is left to bear it out and "pursue the sport." The sun would shine fully again for Sebastian's "This is the air; that is the glorious sun; This pearl she gave me . . .," and for the high afternoon of the ending of the comedy. Towards the close shadows might lengthen and, as the marriages are postponed till "golden time convents," the sky might become golden with a sunset's promise of another fair day. Then as the other characters leave, to enter perhaps a lighted house, Feste might be left in the grey-green light of early evening to sing alone of time and youth, and of the beginning of the world and the conclusion of a play.

(There is in fact a double time scheme in *Twelfth Night*: three months for the development and fulfilment of the action, and two consecutive days for the sequence of scenes. The representation of both schemes in the setting and in the lighting may help an audience to accept this double sense of time which suits, on the one hand, the rapid fairy-tale transitions and the "changeable" characterizations, and, on the other hand, the play's suggestion of the season's alterations and the endurance and maturing of affections.)

Such lighting effects require an outdoor setting for almost all the play. And this may be convenient for the action: Olivia's house might be shown to one side, with a terrace and garden before it, a main entrance and a way to the back door; and there might be a dovecote, small pavilion or gazebo on the other side of the stage to do duty as Malvolio's prison. There would be some inconvenience in staging the carousing scene between Feste, Sir Toby and Sir Andrew in a garden, but there is plenty of reference to outdoor affairs in its dialogue and the two knights could fall asleep around their table at the close of the scene and be discovered there next morning to be awakened by Fabian. The scenes at Orsino's court could also be in the open air, and could be set by bringing in tall cypress hedges to mask Olivia's house and garden, and to reveal part of the sky-cloth or cyclorama at the end of a long walk or vista in some spacious park. It would be appropriately affected for Orsino to seek the shade of such a walk in the early morning; there could be a stone seat on one side, and on the other a sculpture of Venus, or some such deity. For the brief scene outside Olivia's gate (II. ii.) and for the Sebastian scenes, "somewhere in Illyria" (II. i. and III. iii.), a "wall" could be let down from the flies, with a gate in its center: this would locate the action outside Olivia's estate and, if her house and the taller trees were visible over the top of the wall and through the gate, the audience would relish the physical proximity of Sebastian to his journey's end.

There remains one, apparently unrelated, scene (I. ii.) which begins "What country, friends, is this?" This might also be played "outside Olivia's garden," but Viola's mysterious entry into the play from the sea asks for a different visual presentation. It would be possible to play it in front of gauzes let down to hide the transition from Orsino's park of I. i., to Olivia's garden of I. iii.; these might be lightly painted and lit to suggest a seashore, touched, perhaps with fluorescent material low down, as if catching the surf of a strange sea. If Orsino had been contemplating a statue of Venus in the previous scene that figure might be caught by a higher light as the gauzes came down, and then, in a moment of darkness, Viola might take its place to rise from the sea as the stage is relit. If this were effected tactfully, this scene could easily take its place in the chiaroscuro: its sea-effects might be echoed later as Feste is also isolated in the "storm" of his "vice" song; and echoed differently at the end of the play, as he is isolated in the evening. Moreover the myth-like transition and transference would be in keeping with the "romantic" attraction of the lovers and the solution of their stories—the dream, or fantasy element, of the play.

The colors of setting and costumes could be those of an early English summer: clear, light blues, greens, yellows and pinks, and plenty of white. The buildings could be the honey-colored stone of the English Cotswolds, with marble ornaments for Orsino's park. Olivia would, of course, wear black while in mourning, and Malvolio always—the only character to take no color from the sun.

*   *   *

Such is one solution of the visual problems of *Twelfth Night*, and one which tries to answer the demands of the text in terms of the realism of the picture-frame stage—which is perhaps the furthest removed from Elizabethan practice. Other stages and other visual styles would call for different solutions. This way of staging the play is worth consideration chiefly as an example: for if any production is to be undertaken with a belief in the unity and imaginative quality of Shakespeare's text, its choice of setting must answer the same demands and others like them, as more are revealed through further study of the text and further experiments in eccentric productions.

The quest for a responsible direction for *Twelfth Night* will not lead to a series of stereotyped productions: changing stage-conditions, actors and audiences will prevent that. Nor will we rest content with our achievements, for the "idea" of the play, which grows in our minds as we meet it frequently in many guises, is most likely to remain several steps beyond our most truthful production. The desire for an authentic direction will not be satisfied easily, but those who try to respond to it will grow more aware of the wealth of Shakespeare's imagination and perhaps more expert in their attempts to give his masterpiece its theatrical life.

Notes

1. *Shakespeare Today* (New York: Dufour, 1957), p. 205.
2. *John O'London's Weekly*, 8 December 1950.

Hamlet and Our Problems

MICHAEL GOLDMAN

Henry V, by virtue of his public role, is forced to be something of an actor—hence his apprenticeship at roleplaying in *Henry IV*. But every private man is an actor too—for our acts are often performances, in the sense that they strive either to express or conceal something that we think of as inside us, our true self. We are all actors, then, to a degree. But in the ordinary, professional sense of the word, what is an actor? An actor is a man who wants to play Hamlet. Playing the role of the Prince proves you are truly an actor and not a clown, an entertainer, a personality, a "type," or a movie star. It is the ultimate validation of an actor's professional status—and yet, curiously enough, it is far from being the hardest of acting tasks. Most men of the theater would probably accept Sir John Gielgud's characterization of the play as "audience-proof"; and certainly Macready's observation remains true today: a total failure in the role is rare.[1] Many other parts are harder to make a success of, and some—like King Lear—demand skills which the successful actor of Hamlet may not possess. But Hamlet strikes us as somehow unique in requiring and displaying the actor's art.

Why should this be so? One answer lies in the variety that

This article originally appeared as Chapter VI in *Shakespeare and the Energies of Drama* (Princeton University Press, 1972), 74–93. Reprinted with permission. Citations from Shakespeare's works follow the New Cambridge edition, W. A. Neilson and C. J. Hill, eds. (Cambridge, Mass.: Houghton Mifflin, 1942). [Speech heads have been spelled out and placed on separate lines for uniform presentation.—*Ed.*]

Dr. Johnson recognized as a distinguishing excellence of the play. No other role offers so much action of so many different kinds. Hamlet is soldier, scholar, statesman, madman, fencer, critic, magnanimous prince, cunning revenger, aloof noble, witty ironist, man of the people, etc.; and he is regularly required to change from one role to another before our eyes or to maintain several—or a disarming mixture of several—at once. The play abounds in situations that require the principal actor to shift his mood or mode of action because of a change in audience. A number of examples result from Hamlet's having to deceive those around him, but there are many occasions when the shift does not come about as a result of the necessity for self-protection ("Horatio, or I do forget myself," the jokes with the gravedigger, his toying with Osric, the address to the players, the grand apology to Laertes). And there are intermediate stages where we cannot say with any precision whether Hamlet is "acting" or not. These are all occasions on which we are keenly aware of the actor's range and of the pleasures it can give us, of the different things the man on the stage is able to do and do well, and of his skill in making something coherent out of this variety.

The problems involved here are in an important sense exemplary of all acting. For as Hamlet suggests in his speech to the players, there is a critical technical and aesthetic difficulty inherent in the variety available to any professional actor. Great acting demands "temperance," "smoothness," moderation, control—and variety tests this control to the full. Lear is required to do just one kind of thing for most of his play, a very momentous and demanding kind of thing to be sure, but his problem as an actor is to find sufficient variety (and reserves of energy) to get through the evening. Hamlet's problem, assuming he is competent to execute the incredibly many separate "bits" the play allows him, is to control them, to focus them, to find an overall conception in which each has its place, and to give a meaningful smoothness to his transitions. Hamlet is not urging any principle of simple realism when he reminds the actors that their art consists in holding the mirror up to nature. The actor's task is to interpret life:

> to show virtue her own feature, scorn her own image, and the very age and body of the time his form and pressure.
>
> (III. ii. 25—27)

HAMLET AND OUR PROBLEMS

It is Prince Hamlet's task, too, and his problems are very similar to those of the actor who plays him.

Hamlet awakes in its audience a unique concern for the actor's art—and particularly for his interpretive skill, his ability to make satisfying sense out of all the actions he is called upon to perform. It is possible to ask of an actor who portrays King Lear, "How will he get through it?" and the "it"—what Lear undergoes—will be on our minds as much as Lear himself. But with Hamlet we ask as of no other play, "How will he act the part?"

We do not ask, "Will he make any sense of it?" In the theater at least *Hamlet* runs no risk of obscurity. Indeed one of the problems of Hamlet, and one reason why the role is both a supreme challenge and one in which it is very hard to fail utterly, is that even a crude, simplifying, singleminded interpretation—a making one kind of sense but not full sense of the role—can produce solid, effective theater.

Interpretation is one of the necessary questions of *Hamlet*; to an important extent it is something the play is "about." Like its chief character, *Hamlet* draws our attention to varieties of action and to the questions of interpretation they raise. Our experience of *Hamlet* in the theater is primarily an attempt to follow an action so various, intricate, and proliferating that it cries out for interpretation at every turn. The "problems" of the play point, finally, to the subtle means it employs for manipulating one of our most fundamental theatrical appetites: the desire for action that makes sense, especially for action that seems complete and resolved.

As an example, consider III. iii. where Hamlet comes upon the King at prayer. What does the audience see? Two great antagonists who have been maneuvering toward each other throughout the play are alone together at last. They do not look at each other. They do not act. In fact each is frozen in a posture that manifestly suggests an action he does not perform. We see a praying man and his armed opponent. Hamlet has brought his father's murderer to his knees. But the praying man is not praying and the man with the sword is not going to strike. The King, however, wants to pray, just as Hamlet wants to kill the King. The moment we have waited for so patiently arrives and it is not what we meant at all. It is a scene of extraordinary and peculiar tension. The frozen action allows us to register simultaneously an intense impulse to action, an incompleted action, and no action—action whose meaning may be the opposite of what we see. Criticism of this scene has focused on the reasons Hamlet gives for not killing Claudius, but clearly any doubts we may have as to the significance of what Hamlet says at this point are only part of our response to this powerfully engaging stage image, only one of many uncertainties as to action and its interpretation that are being deployed in us. But "doubt" and "uncertainty" tend to suggest speculative states, reflective categories that might be applied to the play in retrospect. Though they are not inaccurate to describe part of our feeling in the theater, they obscure the major source of that feeling and hence its precise quality, which springs from the maneuvering of bodies on the stage and the rhythm of our response to the action as it unfolds.

To understand this more fully, an important technical device must be discussed. III. iii. is one of a number of places in *Hamlet*—particularly toward the middle of the play—where what might be called a "stop-action" technique is used, that is, where one or more players is stopped in mid-gesture and the action frozen in a variety of ways. As, for instance, when the First Player describes Pyrrhus stopping in the very act of killing Priam:

> for, lo! his sword,
> Which was declining on the milky head
> Of reverend Priam, seem'd i' th' air to stick.
> So, as a painted tyrant, Pyrrhus stood
> And, like a neutral to his will and matter,
> Did nothing.
>
> (II. ii. 499—504)

It helps to visualize the Player performing in a style which marks him off as an "actor" from the other figures on stage, gesturing overemphatically, throwing himself into the part ("Look whe'er he has not turn'd his colour and has tears in's eyes"). We may expect that the player has suited the action to the word and frozen grandly.

The Player continues. Pyrrhus's gesture is started up again, but only after preparatory verbal fanfare that again draws attention to the stopped action:

> But, as we often see, against some storm,
> A silence in the heavens, the rack stand still,
> The bold winds speechless, and the orb below
> As hush as death, anon the dreadful thunder
> Doth rend the region; so, after Pyrrhus' pause,
> Aroused vengeance sets him new a-work;
> And never did the Cyclops' hammers fall
> On Mars his armour forg'd for proof eterne
> With less remorse than Pyrrhus' bleeding sword
> Now falls on Priam.
>
> (505—514)

A few lines later Polonius stops him; he starts up once again, and immediately Hamlet interrupts! (It might be noted that Hamlet in giving the first few lines of the speech interrupts himself twice. The pattern of interruption contributes to the stop-action configuration, though there is probably little gesture or physical action to interrupt.)

Hamlet's soliloquy after the players leave turns on a violent self-interruption, as the Prince catches himself in the full flight of some great melodramatic gesture:

> ...Bloody, bawdy villain!
> Remorseless, treacherous, lecherous, kindless villain!
> O, vengeance!
> Why, what an ass am I...
>
> (608—611)

Again the shortened line ("O, vengeance!") orchestrates a stopped action.[2] Here, as at so many points in the play, we are made conscious of the fine line between genuine intensity and pose. Indeed, there is no line—and this is what the stop-action reveals. Hamlet's response is genuine in the sense that it is strongly felt, irresistible, and grows naturally and persuasively out of the situation. There is nothing in the preparation that suggests pretense, nor need there be. Hamlet is throwing himself into the role of revenger. But by interrupting himself at the height of his outburst, by freezing the pose, Hamlet draws our attention to his theatricality of gesture and language. At this moment, sincerity and "acting" are hard to tell apart—and one is not necessarily to be preferred to the other. In fact, Hamlet now is prompted by revulsion at his own play-acting to use a much more elaborate piece of theatricality to catch the conscience of the

King—the play within the play. The sudden break has allowed action to be revealed as acting, and has also involved us more deeply in doubt as to the ultimate direction or interpretation of any action.[3]

The stop-action tableaus play upon a question that recurs in various forms throughout *Hamlet*: when is an action not an action? It is raised of course in the "To be or not to be" soliloquy, where Hamlet—who has a moment ago appeared ready to catch the conscience of the King—now analyzes the conditions under which action loses its name or falls into non-being. Hamlet sees his situation as paradoxical—action results in not being. To be is not to act. And the question *when is an action not an action?* reappears in a dozen guises, as, for example, when is revenge not revenge? when is a madman not a madman? when is a mother not a mother? when is a funeral not a funeral? when is a suicide not a suicide? when is play in earnest?[4] If there is a "question of Hamlet" it is this. As the role of Hamlet itself directs our attention to the problems of interpreting and making sense out of action, so the play is endlessly varying the motif of doubt as to the significance of action.

The famous problem of whether Hamlet is active or inactive may be understood as a misleading abstraction from this type of effect. The Prince may be described as either active or inactive because in *Hamlet* action is constantly losing its name. Though there is an endless variety of it, we are always aware—as in the stop-action sequences—of our appetite for a certain kind of completeness, a meaningfulness which we as members of the audience demand of action.

The critical approach that focuses on Hamlet's "inaction" typically concerns itself with his speculative capacities. But the familiar distinction that this interpretation turns on—between action and reason—is inappropriate to the play. Hamlet's Renaissance sense of human dignity unites reason and action in a single continuum. Man is a great piece of work because his capacity for both reason and action, for reason in action, is divine. Not only does reason exist to prompt us to action, it is only *used* when we act:

> Sure, He that made us with such large discourse,
> Looking before and after, gave us not

> That capability and god-like reason
> To fust in us unus'd.

(IV. iv. 36–39)

The actions that matter, of course, are the ones that make satisfying sense—full sense, not like Laertes' half-cocked rebellion, say, but like Hamlet's ultimate revenge. The importance of reason in action in *Hamlet*, of action that is meaningful in the face of difficult situations, may be seen if we compare three familiar speeches from the beginning, middle, and end of the play. The "To be or not to be" soliloquy where significant action is inhibited by the fear of death, is a paradoxical reversal of Hamlet's first soliloquy, in which he longs for death because he can no longer attribute significance to action ("How weary, stale, flat, and unprofitable,/ Seems to me all the uses of this world"). But by the end of the play he sees a unifying meaning to all his actions; his life is now a "story" ("And in this harsh world draw thy breath in pain/ To tell my story"). He is only afraid that death will keep it from being apparent to others.

Reason and action are not opposed in *Hamlet*, but for most of the play they fail to coalesce as either we or the characters would like them to. Without intelligible meaning, action is unsatisfying or disturbing, a fact exploited from the opening scene. We feel there not only doubt and interrogation but an immediate pressure to sort out the significances of a peculiarly tense and busy action. (Who's on duty here? Why does the wrong guard challenge? Why are they trying to get rid of Francisco? What does the ghost mean? Why are they on guard?) Our response is natural, as is that of the characters. Action and reason seek their meaning in each other, and nowhere more than in *Hamlet*. This may help to account for the special emphasis the play gives to the theme of speech (e.g. its concern with the way actors speak, the significant use of the word "discourse," the prominence of Osric, Hamlet's emphatic "say" at II. ii. 596, where one would ordinarily expect "do")—for speech is a kind of intermediary step between willing significance and establishing it. It is neither reason nor action, but a reaching out of one toward the other. And it is exactly this effort that the action of *Hamlet* repeatedly highlights and foils.

Most of the characters are engaged in a continuing struggle to find out—and interpret—what the others are doing or have done. Their efforts may be said to come to a head when Hamlet confronts the Queen. His address to the players has contained hints of the stress he will be under in this scene. In the very torrent, tempest, and whirlwind of his passion he will have to be careful, as the Ghost has warned him, not to o'erstep the modesty of nature. It is his toughest acting assignment so far, and when he comes to it he quite literally sets out to hold a mirror up to nature:

> Come, come, and sit you down. You shall not budge.
> You go not till I set you up a glass
> Where you may see the inmost part of you.
>
> (III. iv. 18–20)

Again the difficult relations between action, acting, and the self come to the fore. Gertrude is a striking example of divorce between action and meaning. She has allowed herself to sleep with Claudius and become his queen largely by refusing to think about what she has been doing. She has followed her senses and blocked out the meaning of her actions. "What have I done?" is her revealing cry, and Hamlet proceeds to interpret for her (the italics are, of course, mine):

> *Hamlet.*
>   Such an *act*
> That blurs the grace and blush of modesty
> . . . O, such a *deed*
> As from the body of contraction plucks
> The very soul . . .
> Yea, this solidity and compound mass,
> With tristful visage, as against the doom,
> Is thought-sick at the *act*.
> *Queen.*
>   Ay me, what *act*,
> That roars so loud and thunders in the index?
>
> (40–52)

The fierce and disturbing intensity of their dialogue derives from Hamlet's insistence on the physical actuality of his mother's crime. He wants to make her *see*, to put action and meaning together, just as he has wanted to say what is in his heart and to act on his cue for revenge. But at the very moment Hamlet is trying to make the Queen interpret her own actions, a great tangle of misinterpretation forms around them. Polonius thinks

Hamlet will kill the Queen. Hamlet thinks Polonius is the King. On two separate occasions and for different reasons, Gertrude thinks Hamlet is mad. To these we may add the Queen's "What have I done?" and our own curiosity as to why she doesn't see the Ghost. As so often in the play, an increasing pressure toward clarity has carried us into deeper uncertainty and doubt.

To act significantly in these circumstances it is necessary to be an actor—to play a part and hence to use disguise, to be and not to be. One's inmost part may be that which passeth show, and any action may be such as a man might play, but some kind of playacting seems necessary to reveal what ordinary action keeps hidden. After the play-within-the-play, Hamlet has announced, in rhetoric that reminds us of the theatricality of the revenger's occupation (" 'Tis now the very witching time of night . . . Now could I drink hot blood") that he is ready for violent action—but with his mother he intends only to act the part, "I will speak daggers to her, but use none." Though his appearance will perfectly suit the reality within him, it will be only a pretense. He will act and not act, but the acting will be so effective that it will cause Polonius to cry out from behind the arras and result in a violence Hamlet did not (and did) intend. Hamlet has now been seen twice to attack the King and not to attack him, and he concludes the scene with his mother by saying good-night five times before he leaves.

The play, then, is full of action, but the action is handled in such a way that our responses perform in effect an analysis of the feelings and appetites we attach to the very notion of action. We are regularly invited to complete an action—to consider what it means, to anticipate where it may lead—only to have our response blocked, distracted, or diverted, compromised in some way. The stop-action sequences; the early air of mystery; the multiple networks of doubt, deceit, and detection; the stress given to nuances and paradoxes of acting technique; the teasing verbal play with reason and action, saying and doing, being and not being, all contribute to this effect.[5]

Considered in this light, many matters which have provoked critical disagreement in the past may be recognized not as problems requiring solutions one way or the other, but as signs of the play's careful management of our response. The first act, for example, ends with Hamlet vowing vengeance and promising some secret course of action toward that end. In II. i. we learn that Hamlet has appeared to Ophelia in marvellous disarray, apparently mad. Is this part of his plan? The answer is that there are simply too many variables for us to be certain. When the Bristol Old Vic presented the play in New York, Hamlet actually appeared in this scene—out of Polonius's line of vision—and with a number of broad winks conveyed to Ophelia—and us— that he was just kidding; it was all part of the antic disposition. This is one way of clearing up the action, but it is not Shakespeare's way, which is not to clear it up. It is Hamlet's absence from the stage that gives the scene its significance. Shakespeare might have introduced him, could have rearranged existing material to do so. But without Hamlet we are forced to guess whether his charade was deliberately intended to mislead, or an expression of the anguish that is also developed in Act I. We only know for sure that Polonius's interpretation is wrong.

Shakespeare could also easily have allowed Hamlet to resolve another problem that has perplexed the critics: whether any significant delay occurs between Acts I and II. This is not simply a matter of the flexible time dimension of the Elizabethan stage. Shakespeare can be very explicit about linear time when it suits him. He can also deliberately follow an impossible sequence, as in *Othello*, and keep us from noticing—and he can simply be careless of time when it doesn't matter. But he does none of these things in this case. He does finally let us know that Hamlet has spent more time than he would have liked between I. v. and II. i., but he allows us this information only at the very end of Act II. Thus, here—and elsewhere—the question of whether Hamlet delays unnecessarily is deliberately left opaque. There are good reasons for him to delay, but they are fed to us at the wrong time dramatically and in the wrong way for us to be confident that they are the right ones, or even to be sure the delay has been so egregious as at moments he claims it is.[6] The play of course does not permit us to fall into careful examination of these questions; they exist only as part of the pattern of interrupted action and blocked significance.

The pattern (like the Oedipal pattern) is designed to excite both our deepest interest and our deepest resistance. Unfortunately, because it is so original (and perhaps because it is disturbing), it has often provoked stupid "improvements." Since the "To be or not to be" soliloquy breaks the arc of feeling between Hamlet's appearance in II. ii. and III. ii. many companies follow the mutilated First Quarto and place it in the midst of II. ii. It makes more "sense" that way, that is, it makes it easier to interpret Hamlet. For similar reasons, III. iii. which unexpectedly detours Hamlet into the King's closet, was for more than two centuries either omitted or substantially cut in most performances. But in both cases the break in our expectations, the resistance to interpretation, is vital.

Critics concerned with the problem of Hamlet's delay have long concentrated on the scene with Claudius and with reason. But the question to be asked here is not why does Hamlet delay, but why does the play delay—why are *we* delayed? There is more than a grain of truth in the facetious statement that Hamlet delays because there would be no play if he did not. Part of our response to the closet scene depends on our knowledge that the play cannot end here—and not merely because we have paid for an hour's more entertainment. As soon as Hamlet enters we know he will not kill the King. He cannot kill Claudius at prayer, not for theological reasons, sound as they may be, but for aesthetic ones. It is undramatic, too easy. The King's back is to him. There is no source of resistance. The play is going elsewhere. The action, we realize, would not satisfy us, though like Hamlet we have longed for it since the first act. If Shakespeare ever played with an audience, it is here: once again our desire for significant action is drawn upon in a way that also arouses our latent sense of how difficult this appetite is to satisfy.

When two such deeply opposed antagonists have been kept apart for so long by actions of such brilliance and complexity, we come to need an ending that will release all our pent-up energies. We need a spacious ending, a great clarifying release. And this is what we get in the splendid free-for-all that concludes the play, in which the King is hoist on both his petards, and Hamlet, after a display of athletic, military, and moral virtuosity, kills him in full possession of palpably damning evidence and is vindicated before a large audience. To the characters on stage the scene is confusion, an example of the futility of all efforts to force a significance on action, to grasp what Hamlet calls the invisible event. It is a tableau, finally, of "purposes mistook/ Fall'n on the inventors' heads," but for us it is nothing of the sort. If an

Elizabethan audience wanted to refer it to a theological principle, they might see it as an example of the workings of Providence; but their rhythm of response to the action would be much the same as ours. All through the play we have been reminded, both explicitly and by the imagery and movement of the verse, of the pleasure that attends any great release of energy in ample and unambiguous action:

> ...in grace whereof,
> No jocund health that Denmark drinks to-day,
> But the great cannon to the clouds shall tell,
> And the King's rouse the heavens shall bruit again,
> Re-speaking earthly thunder.
>
> (I. ii. 124—128)

> But I will delve one yard below their mines,
> And blow them at the moon. O, 'tis most sweet,
> When in one line two crafts directly meet.
>
> (III. iv. 208—210)

> And let the kettle to the trumpets speak,
> The trumpet to the cannoneer without,
> The cannons to the heavens, the heaven to earth.
>
> (V. ii. 286—288)

Even when Claudius uses the opposite figure of a missile missing its target, he does it by way of another beautiful evocation of a sudden, sweeping, clearly aimed discharge

> Whose whisper o'er the world's diameter,
> As level as the cannon to his blank,
> Transports his poisoned shot, may miss our name,
> And hit the woundless air.
>
> (IV. i. 41—44)

Now the final release comes in a scene which rarely fails to produce an overwhelming excitement and satisfaction.

Pressure toward a full physical clash onstage has begun at least as early as Hamlet's failure to kill the King at prayer, and progressed through his taunting of the King and escaping his guards, Laertes' abortive attack on Claudius, and Hamlet's inconclusive struggle with Laertes in the grave. We are also given the details of a wonderful fight at sea and the just deserts of Rosencrantz and Guildenstern (which is also the result of "a kind of fighting"). At last Hamlet is asked to "play" with Laertes, and the fencing match begins. It is an action whose significance keeps shifting: it means different things at different moments for the different players. And simultaneously we are aware of the gratifying opportunities it offers the actors. The court ceremony is elaborate. The fencing must be excellent. Nowhere is the Prince more various. The actors must show the difference between fencing in play and fighting in deadly earnest, with at least one intermediary stage between. But if the bystanders on the stage are confused by the results, we for once are not. All the significances are clear, and we watch them explode into action. Every piece of inner villainy leaves its tell-tale outer mark and is repaid in fully emblematic action. ("The point envenom'd too!/ Then, venom, to thy work!") The purpose of playing is achieved; acting and being are one. In form and moving all is express and admirable.

The play ends with a final unambiguous discharge of energy. Fortinbras, who has a soldier's simple sense of what is appropriate, orders a peal of ordnance shot off. The air has been cleared. We have experienced, in this long heightening and ultimate fulfillment of our basic theatrical desires, the equivalent of Hamlet's tangled meditations on action and human worth. Hamlet has been concerned from the first with the good actor's root problem—sincerity. Any gesture is, after all, such as a man might play; but if this is the case, how does one truthfully perform what is within him? In an earlier chapter I pointed out that Hamlet seems to be about eighteen at the play's beginning and thirty near its end. As a factual question the problem is of little importance, and there is nothing that absolutely contradicts the specific figure of thirty given by the gravedigger. But it is interesting that the two ages often mark a great change in a man's understanding of sincerity. At eighteen the imperative is not to live a lie. By thirty, one realizes how hard it is to be certain one isn't.

The problem of sincerity is of interest only in those for whom it is difficult. The obvious sincerity of Fortinbras, Laertes, and the First Player leave Hamlet irritated or envious. There is nothing within them that passes show. But to say "I have that within which passeth show," is really to challenge the whole enterprise of theater; it is to say I have a self which cannot be sounded in action, that any encounter I have with the world must merely be playacting in a derogatory sense. The crisis of young Hamlet's life comes when he is forced to act, forced by the Ghost to find a show that will be true to what is within him and to the world in which he finds himself. As with the actor who plays the role, the greatest strain falls on Hamlet's capacity for expressive coherence, for action that at each moment is true to the delicacy and difficulty of his entire situation. The tragic effect comes because we are made to feel that this achievement is possible for Hamlet only at the cost of great destruction.

A good way to see the nature of Prince Hamlet's difficulty in its relation to tragic emotion is to contrast his play with *Julius Caesar*, the tragedy immediately preceding it in composition. Prince Hamlet strikes us as an intellectual for much the same reasons Brutus does; we see them deliberating certain problems of action and attempting to formulate them in abstract terms. But Brutus' problem is that he would like to separate significance from the agents that produce significance. Though he cannot kill Caesar's spirit without killing Caesar, he tries to limit the significance of his act to the spiritual, to treat the "genius" as if it were independent of its "mortal instruments." Hamlet's problem, on the other hand, is to *attach* significance to action, to overcome his initial sense that all the uses of the world are flat and unprofitable, to fully unite action and reason, to find a revenge which is both internally and externally satisfying, an action that like all good acting holds the mirror up to nature.

But the achievement of clarity and full expressiveness in action is immensely difficult for Hamlet and immensely expensive. The destructive or demonic force that we are accustomed to encounter in tragedy seems in *Julius Caesar* to rise from the body of Caesar itself and is exemplified first in the blood that floods the stage and later in Caesar's ghost. The source of the energy that destroys Brutus, then, is the very element of the problem he has tried to overcome—Caesar's inescapable physicality, the mortal instruments that become genius only by virtue of their mortality. In the same way, Hamlet is finally destroyed and fulfilled by an action whose source is beyond his control. It is only when he has agreed not to force a significance upon his actions, not to look before and after but to let be, that he is swept to his revenge. The revenge kills him as it has also killed Gertrude, Ophelia, and Polonius. The destructive element turns out to be the very element in his situation which he has struggled in his mind to root out and overcome—whatever there is in the self that the mind cannot grasp and control in thought and adequately express in action.

We are thus brought back to the dubieties of the great central soliloquy. There are more things in heaven and earth than any man's philosophy can unravel. A taint of death lies not only in every action but in discourse of reason itself. Being and not being, play-acting and sincerity, action and letting be, the pressure to clarity and the proliferation of doubt are inextricably intertwined in mortal experience. Shakespeare's tragic heroes are men who insist on the self-destruction proper to their genius; sooner or later they seek out that death which allows their capacities most fully to illuminate the world for the audience that watches them die. The destruction Hamlet seeks allows him to take as far as possible and to test to the full an impulse we all to some extent share, and to which the art of the theater is dedicated—through action to make sense of life.

Notes

1. Rosamond Gilder, *John Gielgud's Hamlet* (London: Methuen, 1937), p. 50; *Macready's Reminiscences and Selections from His Diaries and Letters*, ed. Sir Frederick Pollock (London: Macmillan, 1875), p. 37.
2. The authenticity of this line has been questioned. But if Harold Jenkins is right, and it represents a playhouse interpolation, it still casts light on the way the speech was performed, and very likely on its intended effect. The actor felt the need or opportunity for marking the punctuation, for heightening the frozen posture with a posturing phrase. In any case, the stop-action is plain even without "O vengeance!" (See "Playhouse Interpolations in the Folio Text of *Hamlet*," *Studies in Bibliography*, XIII [1960], 31–47.)
3. Two or three other moments of stop-action deserve mention. The action of the play scene itself is stopped in a number of ways. The dumb show allows us to preview the murder of Gonzago in the slow-motion of pantomime, and later the performance is broken off sharply before the climax. The entrance of the Ghost in III. iv. provides yet another example. Hamlet breaks off in the midst of his attack on the Queen to bend his eye on vacancy, and they are fixed in this tableau for several lines.

Robert Hapgood discusses a number of "arrested actions" in

his "Hamlet Nearly Absurd: The Dramaturgy of Delay," *Tulane Drama Review* (Summer, 1965), 132–145; several of his examples strike me as contributing to the effects described above. I should add, however, that Hapgood's understanding of these moments (which he treats primarily as instances of delay) seems to be very different from mine.

4. Cf. Maynard Mack's superb essay, "The World of *Hamlet*," *Yale Review*, 41 (1952), 513–514. My concern is less with the authenticity of "acts," as Professor Mack's is, than with the problems posed by our appetite for significant "action."

5. There are a number of attractive minor examples of action losing its name. When the Ghost speaks up from the cellarage and Hamlet calls upon his friends to swear secrecy, the same action is repeated three or four times to the accompaniment of the Ghost's "Swear . . . Swear . . . Swear by his sword . . . Swear" [following Q2]. The repetition tends to leach the solemnity out of the action, to blur its clarity in the very act of insisting on it—to detach the significant gesture from the felt significance.

Similarly, when Horatio brings his great news to Hamlet in the first act, they are so incapable of interpreting each other correctly they are forced to repeat themselves:

Hamlet.
   My father!—methinks I see my father.
Horatio.
   Oh, where, my lord?
Hamlet.
   In my mind's eye, Horatio . . . .
Horatio.
   My lord, I think I saw him yesternight.
Hamlet.
   Saw? Who?
Horatio.
   My lord, the King your father.
Hamlet.
   The King my father!

(ii. 184–191)

Actions are frequently repeated, allowing us to note the effect of different interpretations. Hamlet and the First Player recite the same speech; Claudius's treason is narrated by the Ghost, acted in dumb show and then again with words. Osric plays the fop and Hamlet imitates him. And there is a very funny and intricate variation on the theme of sincerity when Hamlet insists on welcoming Rosencrantz and Guildenstern *a second time* before welcoming the players. He insists that he must overact this second reception, so that when he acts less sincerely (he claims) for the players it will not falsify the meaning of his welcome to his old school friends:

Guildenstern.

There are the players.

Hamlet.

Gentlemen, you are welcome to Elsinore. Your hands, come.
The appurtenance of welcome is fashion and ceremony. Let
me comply with you in the garb, lest my extent to the players,
which, I tell you, must show fairly outward, should more
appear like entertainment than yours. You are welcome.

(II. ii. 386—393)

He probably repeats his gestures of welcome two or three times
during the speech.

6. "How all occasions do inform against me" (IV. iv. 32ff) gives us our
strongest sense that Hamlet delays, and is the source for most critical
speculation as to his reasons. But it should be observed that the
soliloquy occurs at the only point in the play where Hamlet, under
guard and on his way to England, has absolutely no opportunity for
revenge.

Notes on Contributors

Bernard Beckerman, Brander Matthews Professor of Drama at Columbia University, is the author of *Shakespeare at the Globe: 1559-1609* and *Dynamics of Drama: Theory and Method of Analysis.*

James Black, the editor of *ARIEL* and Professor of English at the University of Calgary, has edited Tate's version of *King Lear* and written numerous articles on Shakespearean drama.

Stephen Booth is the author of *An Essay on Shakespeare's Sonnets* and Professor of English at the University of California, Berkeley.

John Russell Brown, Professor of English at the University of Sussex and an Associate Director of the National Theatre in London, includes among his works *Shakespeare's Plays in Performance* and *Free Shakespeare.*

Miriam Gilbert, Associate Professor of English at the University of Iowa, has written on and directed several Shakespearean plays.

Michael Goldman, a poet and dramatist who teaches at Princeton University, is the author of *Shakespeare and the Energies of Drama* and *The Actor's Freedom.*

Barbara Hodgdon, Assistant Professor of English at Drake University, has published essays on stage and film performances of Shakespeare.

William A. Matchett is the editor of *Modern Language Quarterly,* Professor of English at the University of Washington, and the author of numerous articles on Shakespeare.

Philip C. McGuire has published essays on Shakespeare and on the poetry of the English Renaissance and is Associate Professor of English at Michigan State University.

Edward Partridge, who has written a book on Ben Jonson (*The Broken Compass*) and edited two of his plays, is Professor of English at Newcomb College, Tulane University.

Marvin Rosenberg, a playwright and Professor of Dramatic Art at the University of California, Berkeley, is the author of *The Masks of Othello* and *The Masks of King Lear.*

David A. Samuelson is a Rochester, New York, consultant in communications. In his former academic career, he published articles on drama and popular fiction.

Douglas C. Sprigg has acted and directed professionally and is currently Chairman of the Drama Department at Middlebury College.

J.L. Styan, Professor of English at Northwestern University, has written several books on Shakespearean drama, the most recent of which is *The Shakespeare Revolution.*